SURVIVOR

S U R V I V O R

The authorized biography of
ERIC CLAPTON

Ray Coleman

SIDGWICK & JACKSON
LONDON

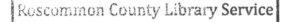

First published in Great Britain in 1985
by Sidgwick and Jackson Limited

Copyright © 1985 by Ray Coleman

ISBN 0 283 99141 0

Phototypeset by Falcon Graphic Art Ltd
Wallington, Surrey
Printed in Great Britain by
R. J. Acford, Industrial Estate, Chichester, Sussex
for Sidgwick and Jackson Limited
1 Tavistock Chambers, Bloomsbury Way
London WC1A 2SG

CONTENTS

Acknowledgements vii

Preface ix

PROLOGUE 1

1
THE PURIST 6

2
THE LONER 27

3
THE STAR 43

4
THE ADDICT 78

5
THE SURVIVOR 115

6
THE LOVER 155

7
THE INNER MAN 191

8
THE MUSICIAN 218

9
THE LAST CHORUS 260

ERIC CLAPTON DISCOGRAPHY 278

ACKNOWLEDGEMENTS

The author and publishers gratefully acknowledge permission to reproduce lyrics from songs as follows:
'Layla' © 1970, Throat Music Limited
'Wonderful Tonight' © 1977, Throat Music Limited
'Let It Grow' © 1974, Throat Music Limited
'Give Me Strength' © 1974, Throat Music Limited
'The Shape You're In' © 1983, E. C. Music Limited
'Ain't Going Down' © 1983, E. C. Music Limited
'Pretty Girl' © 1983, E. C. Music Limited
'Presence of the Lord' © 1969, Throat Music Limited
Words reproduced by permission of Chappell Music Limited, London, and Chappell & Co. Inc., New York.

Permission to quote parts of interviews with Eric Clapton in London's *Melody Maker* and *New Musical Express* is gratefully acknowledged; thanks also to the publisher Bruno Cassirer of Oxford for permission to reproduce extracts from the book *The Story of Layla and Majnun*, by Nizami.

SUITAR MAN (CLAPTON)

HE DRINKS LIKES A FISH
AND HE SMOKES LIKE A TRAIN
HE LOOKS LIKE A RAT, AND HE SMELLS LIKE
A DRAIN
HE KNOWS THAT HE'S CRAZY, HE KNOWS
HE'S INSANE
BUT HE DONT FEAR NOTHING EXCEPT
THE SOUND OF HIS NAME ~
    HE'S THE MAN, HE'S THE GUITAR MAN
YOU'D BETTER WATCH OUT WHEN HE
  MAKES HIS STAND
    HE'S THE MAN, HE'S THE GUITAR MAN, HE
CAN HOLD YOUR HEART, IN THE PALM OF
HIS HAND ~
SOMETIMES YOU MIGHT THINK HE'S GONNA
DROP IN HIS TRACKS
BUT DONT BE FOOLED, BY THE WAY THAT HE
ACTS
HE'S JUST PUTTING ON THE AGONY, PUTTING
ON THE STYLE
YOU CAN COUNT YOURSELF LUCKY IF
YOU SEE HIM SMILE
    (CHORUS)

PREFACE

'You've been described as the greatest rock and blues guitarist in the world, Eric . . .'

'*Really?*' he says. 'My God! Let me grab a fag, quickly!'

His modesty is beguiling but it has been essential in his survival. The road has been long, hard, dangerous and hugely successful for Eric Clapton. It is difficult to pinpoint any other figure from the 1960s era of popular music who has strengthened his gifts, kept an elusive aura of stardom around him, yet remained so accessible. Clapton has come through because of his steely determination, his magnificent artistry, and a will to live. Paradoxically, he is sometimes tearful, an emotional, often solitary man whose immaturity is both endearing and infuriating.

Above all, though, he's a musician. The romantic, lonely, almost swashbuckling life of a guitarist in the recording studio, writing songs and on the road suits him perfectly. Now, at forty, he will never hang up his guitar.

While there are many thousands of musicians, there is only one Eric Clapton. Fashions in popular music change very quickly. He has risen above them all and consolidated his position, because his natural art triumphs over his desire to entertain.

When Clapton plays guitar, he throws out something from deep within himself. True, he has been inspired by the great American blues masters of the past, but Clapton's greatness is demonstrated by his implanting his own multi-faceted personality into every tune he plays, every song he writes and sings. Soaring with joy, weeping with feeling, his playing captures the hearts of millions throughout the world; he is able to articulate the full range of human emotion.

The greatest player in the world? He reflected on it. 'No, I don't think I am, but I certainly aspire to be. Maybe we should all be careful what we want in life. Sometimes, we may get it. I had this *ideal* when I was young: to cross as many barriers as I could between the different types of music that existed. If I did that, and was good all the way, maybe I *could* become the greatest guitar player in the world. That seemed a good goal to set out for. What I learned along the road did me a lot of good, musically, but has also been blinding. But you know, that goal can only exist as an ideal. In reality, there isn't a greatest or a best guitarist. I hear lots of players I could mistake for myself occasionally. The most I could claim is that I am a good model . . .'

It's ironic that Eric, who pays full tribute to the blues giants, is now himself revered by young guitarists who want to 'play like Clapton'. As an honourable man, he finds that both flattering and wrong; he points out that they are getting their inspiration second or third hand. Better, he says, to go back to the roots that inspired *him* . . . but he enjoys the compliments.

There have been shattering changes in what the world has come to expect from guitar heroes. The players Eric grew up admiring, with such beautifully evocative names as Muddy Waters and Howlin' Wolf, lived with austerity but not the pressures of superstardom. They received scant recognition for their craft. Not until the 1960s were guitarists whose roots were in the blues sucked into the structure of rock 'n' roll. Clapton was in the vanguard of that movement and his voluntary move outside pop's front line in the Yardbirds to the periphery, with John Mayall and later Cream, was part of a renaissance. The emphasis of many players switched from making disposable hit singles to thoughtful, musicianly albums, with almost all the songs self-written. Some musicians of that period developed longevity, a career, as well as fame. Pop stars before them rarely achieved long-term success. Clapton's timing, for the role he would play, was immaculate. The rewards, in adulation and in money, were enormous. And Eric, who seems to have had an identity crisis of varying degrees all his life, fell victim to what he describes as 'the sins of the flesh'.

After the rarefied atmosphere of the late 1960s, he plunged into a three-year period as a hermit in his home, absorbed with heroin addiction, turning his back on the world, his family and his friends. When he cured himself of that, he lurched into seven years of excessive drinking. Between those periods, he had fallen in love with Pattie, then the wife of ex-Beatle George Harrison. Eric's story, his frequent returns from the brink of death and his obsession with a woman in one of popular music's most envied partnerships, evokes

Portrait of a musician

the ingredients of a novel rather than a biography. Against the backdrop of a true guitar virtuoso and a complicated man who inspires love, loyalty and incredulousness from all who know him, the fragility of the first forty years of Clapton's story becomes irresistible.

This book took root during an American tour by Clapton in 1980. I said to Eric that I'd like to prepare a thorough portrait of his life and his work. A little early, he said; his career had a long time to run. That seemed to me a positive outlook. I replied that there was quite enough to write about already. Nobody could have guessed that he would pack so much into the next five years, creatively and personally changing course, confounding his friends with such outlandish behaviour, that his story would twist and turn at incredible speed. The events of his life gathered momentum. By the autumn of 1984, nearly two years after I had begun to research his life, Eric and his wife Pattie – an integral part of the theme – temporarily split up. It speaks volumes for both of them that they continued to cooperate with me, showing great patience during the most delicate, difficult period of their lives. I thank them both warmly for their candour and patience, and Pattie for taking the striking cover photograph.

My wife Pamela and my sons Miles and Mark endured even more of my traditionally impossible behaviour during the preparation of the book, and deserve my gratitude for their support.

Roger Forrester, Eric's passionate, dedicated, protective manager, friend and partner in chauvinism, gave me unfailingly rich advice, practical help and penetrating observations. I thank him for making the project possible and authenticating many of the stories and anecdotes.

Eric's mother, Pat McDonald, and his grandmother, Rose Clapp, talked for hours about 'Rick', sometimes with an honesty that was painful. I thank them both for their illuminating recollections of his boyhood. Guy Pullen, Eric's longest-established mate, a friend since their years as toddlers in Ripley, Surrey, painted a no-holds-barred picture of the personality of the young Clapton and the adult boozer.

Many musicians, some of whose names are mentioned only fleetingly in the text, have been uniquely placed to put the working-and-playing Eric Clapton into proper perspective. My special thanks go to Pete Townshend, always our most articulate observer, for his valuable memories and views of the Clapton he has known and loved during two decades; to Jack Bruce, for an enriching night at his home in Germany; to Steve Winwood, for his reflections on Eric's difficult period with him in Blind Faith; to Micky Moody, whose admiration of Clapton's work helped to produce the chapter dissecting his career as a recording artist; to Phil Collins, a lifelong fan of Eric's who had the accolade of producing his 1985 album *Behind the Sun*; to Chris Stainton, the inspired keyboards player in the Clapton band, who applied his keen astrological mind to his boss's birth-chart to give some clues to Eric's personality; to Gary Brooker, ex-pianist with the band and an important motivating force in Eric's hobby of fishing; and to Paul Samwell-Smith for his honesty in describing the clashes between him and Eric that marred Clapton's days in the Yardbirds.

Meg and George Patterson, whose acupuncture treatment and 'open house' to Eric when he was at his lowest physical and psychological ebb from heroin, gave unstintingly of their memories, crucial to the portrayal of Eric at that time.

Ben Palmer in Wales, one of Eric's dearest friends since long before his fame, proved the most penetrating commentator on the subject's many complexities, and John Hurt, the great actor, showed a perceptiveness of the Clapton he admires as a friend and stylist. Thanks, also, to film maker Rex Pyke, who produced the largely unscreened gem *Eric Clapton's Rolling Hotel*, and to Toby Balding, Eric's racehorse trainer, for an enlightening day at the stables.

The Roger Forrester office works as an efficient, almost military machine: Nigel Carroll, Eric's personal assistant, has provided great insights into his boss and friend; Alphi O'Leary's love of Eric shines through; and I thank Diana Puplett for her help and patience in coordination.

In Paris, where she now lives, Alice Ormsby-Gore gave hours of crucially important recollections of the five years in which she and Eric lived together. I am grateful to her for describing, with her exceptional memory for detail, and her honesty, Eric's years with her as a heroin addict.

In Frankfurt, the veteran concert promoters Horst Lippmann and Fritz Rau gave me hours of amusing thoughts about Eric, from Yardbirds to present day; and in Miami, Tom Dowd's view on the man in the studio, from this experienced producer's standpoint, was important. Most of the picture research and the exhaustive discography was compiled by Mark Lewisohn. I thank Chrissie Masterman for transcribing hundreds of hours of taped interviews.

My editor, Susan Hill at Sidgwick & Jackson showed infectious enthusiasm for this project from its inception; her encouragement and advice has been much appreciated. David Grossman, my agent in London, and Merrilee Heifetz, at Writers House in New York, have been towering strengths, giving the project both wisdom and zeal when the idea was in its infancy and throughout its production.

When talking to so many sources during two years of planning, I was not surprised to find a universal affection for the man and, without exaggeration, sheer wonder for his art. When talking to Eric Clapton, it is impossible not to be touched by his honesty, modesty, naïveté and, sometimes, his crushingly perceptive self-analysis. He gave this book inestimable help: his time, his personal photographs, his support – 'Maybe I'll learn something about myself' – and his insightful private diary for the critical year of 1979. In it he ended most days' entries by writing the Hebrew word from the Psalms: SELAH. Loosely translated, it means 'pause'. This biography is intended as just that: an objective but none the less affectionate pause to glimpse into the life, work and pulse of a true giant of our music, whose *oeuvre* and popularity continues to grow.

Ray Coleman, London, February 1985

PROLOGUE

That night in Poland in the autumn of 1979, Eric Clapton wept. The strong-arm methods of the Polish police had viciously suppressed his audience's enthusiasm. Clapton's first visit to the Eastern bloc – planned, like so much of his life and career, as an essential diversion – went horribly wrong. The police, wary of such excitement among rock fans starved of live music from the West, manhandled dancing teenagers, dragging some away by the hair and hurling them over barriers out of the 8000-seater stadium in the bleak mining town of Katowice. From the stage, Clapton saw beneath him several police spray face-freezing Mace at young fans who refused to calm down. Eric's British stagehands clashed with Polish guards, and blazing exchanges between the band and the authorities followed.

The previous night, Clapton and his new all-British band had delighted 3400 people in Warsaw's Palace of Culture. His debut in Poland had mesmerized the stiff audience. And local critics, twelve years after Britain first deified Eric, were still writing: 'Clapton is God'.

But Katowice was an appalling experience. After the police brutality, a hopeless argument ensued, Clapton and his entourage versus the local authorities. The Poles insisted that what went on *off* the stage was their total responsibility. Clapton insisted that the crowd had come to see *him*, so he was entitled to proper communication with them.

'My work,' he said, 'is making music. Could *you* get on with *your* work if you saw right in front of you a crowd being beaten up?'

The second concert that night was cancelled by Eric. The police would not agree to cool down. Amid the general hostilities and confusion, Eric's public address system was smashed. He fled the

1

country on the first available plane next day – to Frankfurt and then on to Tel Aviv.

That incident, and particularly the memory of young Poles being knocked about because they were thrilled at the liberating atmosphere created by a British rock superstar, scarred Clapton. 'If I think they're getting too worked up, I usually play a blues to calm down an audience,' he said tearfully in his hotel after the debacle. 'But here in Poland, they seemed so repressed, *anything* excited them. And then – how could I play when I saw kids right in front of the stage, underneath me, being pushed about? The only sin of those kids was to show their enjoyment. The way they were treated was sickening.'

Tragically, this Polish debacle occurred at a glowing moment in the career of Eric Clapton. He was thirty-four at the time. 'As a musician, I'm just starting to feel the effects of middle age,' he told me in Warsaw. 'It's just hit me that I can't continue to do all the things I used to when I was twenty-one. Then, I'd easily do two shows a night and an all-night session as well. Now, that schedule would grind me to a halt. So I like to do unusual places, like Poland . . . It's time for guys like me to ease up a little bit. Rock's not like the routine of the old bands like Count Basie. They could grow old more easily, playing the same arrangements night after night. Rock's much more emotionally and physically draining because you're constantly trying to invent something new.'

Despite his blushing shyness, his uncertainty when in company with people he does not know, and despite a young life marked by death-defying triumph, Eric Clapton is acutely aware of his gifts. And, crucially, he springs to life at an audience's response.

'Nobody,' says Clapton's friend and pianist Chris Stainton, 'is quicker to realize whether an audience is with him or stone cold. And if it's a bad crowd, Eric can be very badly affected for a whole night and at least the next day.'

For many hardened professional rock musicians, the bad experience in Poland would have been written off, relatively easily, as a 'bad gig'. With Eric, the hurt ran deeply for years because he believes that music involves giving out feelings from within himself. 'The guitar,' he says, 'is simply the means to an end. My method of saying something to an audience. I like them to reciprocate.' When the Polish teenagers were prevented from making that contact, Clapton cried. On issues that matter deeply to him, Clapton is often tearful, but rarely maudlin.

Eric Clapton is an enigmatic and complex character, full of contradictions. He can be alternately soft and harsh, yet he is never brittle; self-centred and calculating but also warm and sensitive; shy and

In Poland. *Above:* Eric stands at the tomb of the unknown warrior in Warsaw. *Below:* Concert crowd enthusiasm is maladroitly handled by local police (*Camera Press*)

self-effacing as well as opinionated and stubborn. He's fundamentally insecure but he is aware of his importance in the rock Pantheon.
Yet while he outwardly demonstrates confidence, Eric continually
seeks reassurance from those around him that he has a worthwhile
role and career, and that the rapid rise and fall of other pop stars does
not affect his own validity.

He feels most comfortable in the company of musicians and artists
who share his lifestyle and temperament. It is surprising to find a
man so aesthetic, cerebral and elusive, striving so honestly to keep
his feet on the ground. Yet while he loves a roadside café fry-up, he
would not like to relinquish his Ferrari cars and his large wardrobe of
clothes. Infuriating though he can be, Clapton is finally endearing
because he always faces his own peccadilloes head-on. And he has
massive heart, as his music testifies. These chief characteristics shape
him as an extraordinary survivor who has defeated all the odds to
maintain his role as the world's foremost rock and blues guitar
virtuoso.

What underlines his stardom is his lonely vulnerability. For all his
confidence, for all his genius and for all his conviviality, the people
close to Eric Clapton worry about him . . .

1

THE
PURIST

'I always fancied myself as being part of an elite'

The eminent actor John Hurt remembers the event well. Eric Clapton had wrested Pattie away from her husband George Harrison, and the former Beatle decided it was time for a proper conversation to resolve the situation – maybe even a showdown. George Harrison invited Eric and Pattie to visit him at his mansion, Friar Park in Oxfordshire, for the evening.

'I thought this might be an awkward situation, because I was friendly with them both,' says John Hurt. 'When George told me Eric and Pattie were coming, I said: "Oh, you'll want me out of the way."'

'George replied: "Not at all, John."'

'He clearly needed a small audience. He then got down from upstairs two guitars and two small amplifiers and laid them in the hall.' For what seemed hours, Harrison paced up and down, awaiting the look on Clapton's face when he arrived to face a guitar duel, on George Harrison's chosen territory, as a kind of retribution. The woman they both loved would stand and watch.

'Finally, Eric did turn up, somewhat late, with Pattie and with a great deal of brandy inside him. George invited him to play. And it was literally like an eighteenth-century duel. But instead of playing with swords and foils, they had guitars. It was an extraordinary contest because George had quite clearly given him the inferior guitar and the inferior amplifier.'

The audience comprised about six people. The two men improvised for two hours in a historic guitar battle of superstars. Few words were spoken. 'To start with,' admits John Hurt, 'it might have been intended as a friendly gesture or a game by George. But it certainly wasn't when they were playing. It was an extraordinary duel to witness. The air was electric. Nobody dared say anything.'

we left poland (hold on to stomach to
keep from puking.) for frankfurt this
morning ~ it wasn't easy, the police had
a warrant for rogers arrest and we had
to give back the money that was made
from the first concert plus a thousand
pounds compensation for the one that
was cancelled, cheap at twice the price!
surprisingly enough the customs men
were no trouble at all... they didn't to
see our passports or look in our bags
they just wanted autographed photos
of the band ~ what a bunch of loonies.
never again ... my only really good
memory of poland was the party we had
at the american embassy in the marines
bar .... later ~ when we arrived in
frankfurt who do i run in to ? C.O.D!
i went "oh no, from warsaw to odle"
shes going out with mike shirley (well
known german promoter) and hes a
great bloke, so shes made a good choice
this time ~ anyway we had a few drinks
and talked about the outlaw dagsin
south .ken, when i used to meet nelly on
the quiet at the dominos' frat, and we
became good friends again, shes a nice
good, mean girl ~ then i had a nosh
with a couple of rudis, went to me
room, banged me head and went to bed.
its great to be back in the land of the
free, lads ~ hurray for democracy
and capitalism and free entreprise, at least
its honestly bent ~

seah ~

The general opinion was that Clapton won the musical scrap. 'Even though he was well pissed, he was unbeatable,' says John Hurt. George Harrison, a fine guitarist, and a friend of Eric's, had been weakened by his own annoyance and played 'too many notes, rather like John Mayall' (one of Clapton's earliest bandleaders). And Eric's triumph was as much a commentary on his personality as on his virtuoso technique; he did not allow himself to get rattled into making a sham of his art. He concentrated on playing a few meaningful notes in contrast to Harrison's instrumental gymnastics.

Eric's memory of the night is as much a commentary on himself as on the occasion: 'I know exactly how to play in a situation like that. If someone makes the mistake of exaggerating, or being a bit too flamboyant, you win by being simple. Let them overdo it.

'Every meeting I've had with George Harrison, on any level, has been competitive. He's the kind of person who puts you on the spot and insists on having the last word. In musical situations, he's the same. My rule is always: let your opponent make the first mistake.' Coolness, a refusal to be quickly irritated, and a determination to 'lie low' in the early stages of any confrontation, is an important factor in Clapton's make-up. He rarely forces confrontations, but everyone who knows him shudders at the prospect of Eric Clapton blowing his top. He operates on a long fuse, and although he sometimes lacks discernment by befriending people who exploit him or his generosity, his final decisiveness can be brutal.

Eric firmly believed then, as he does now, that, whatever the pressure, putting a gloss on anything was wrong. 'You have always to be true to yourself, even if sometimes that's the most painful route,' he says.

That simple philosophy has marked Eric Clapton's life. It began when, at exactly twenty, he quit the rising British group the Yardbirds because he felt uncomfortable with the blatantly commerical route their music was taking. For a scarcely known guitarist in a group that was gathering popularity and hit records, it was at first glance a foolish move, throwing away success, stardom and money. But Eric's resignation, that heady spring in 1965, when the British pop scene was bursting with vitality and innocent energy, proved the most crucial – and astute – decision of his career and perhaps his life.

The group, who were among the darlings of the burgeoning rhythm-and-blues circuit, enjoyed, early in their career, a small hit with 'Good Morning Little Schoolgirl'. After eighteen vital months with them, tearing around the British clubs and polishing his style, Clapton resigned in the middle of a recording session for their follow-up hit, 'For Your Love'. This was the year of the Beatles and the Rolling Stones, of British pop star supremacy, of adulation and compromise, exuberance and 'where's the next hit record coming from?'

Eric wanted none of that. His route in music, he told himself and anyone who would listen, was the pure blues.

Looking back today, Clapton's rationale for his lonely decision seems logical and clear, as it must have seemed to him at the time. 'I never did have my eye on fame as a pop star. When I listened to the radio at the age of about ten, the blues was the only kind of music that I called "non-company music". The pop sound of the period, Guy Mitchell, Kay Starr, Frankie Laine, was well produced and well rounded. That was on the radio every day. Maybe once a week I'd hear something stand out – something by Sonny Terry and Brownie McGhee, for example. And it was so incredibly *personal*. So was Big Bill Broonzy. I caught sight of him in a television film clip and I was . . . mesmerized. I was anti-big-business music and here was this sound that was not from a company, or a band, but from one or two people. It was raw, primitive, and that's what I always preferred, in art or anything . . .'

It is twenty years since Clapton made that remarkable decision to leave the Yardbirds and concentrate on becoming a musician instead of a 'hit-making machine', as he called it at the time. Paradoxically, he has earned more adulation, for a longer period, than he might have gained as a butterfly of the 1960s. He's mature enough now to enjoy it, but he still feels troubled by the thought that he gained stardom for interpreting blues music that was not rightly his but belonged to black America. 'How strange, it seemed to me, to be worshipped! To be called a god when all I was doing was presenting a case, as it were, for the music I loved. I was just its *representative*! The reason I left the Yardbirds was simple: compromise became the order of the day. It didn't matter about the musical policy, or recording a song by any well-known writer, as long as we got into the charts. That became the number one aim more than anything else. And that's when I finally gave up the ghost.' He regretted his departure only for a fleeting week or two – 'the money *would* have been useful. I was pretty broke!'

Paul Samwell-Smith remembers, with good reason, the idealism in the young Clapton. With singer and harmonica player Keith Relf, Paul Samwell-Smith ran a group called the Metropolis Blues Quartet.

By mid-1963, bass player Samwell-Smith and Relf had changed the name to the Yardbirds, identified themselves with the mushrooming rhythm-and-blues scene which had its roots in the music of American heroes like Chuck Berry, Little Walter and Bo Diddley. The r & b movement was finding an enthusiastic audience in a Britain polarized between the pure pop of the Beatles and the rhythm-and-blues trend nominally led by the Rolling Stones. The Yardbirds belonged, initially at least, firmly in the latter camp.

Looking for a lead guitarist, Samwell-Smith and Relf's eyes fell on the young man who was the most talked-about player in the pub where they gathered most Friday nights: the Crown at Kingston-upon-Thames, Surrey. The word was out, in this pub and at the parties in the area at which aspiring pop guitarists played: Eric Clapton was something special.

'Eric used to hang around the Crown and we saw him often before inviting him to join the band,' recalls Samwell-Smith. 'You couldn't miss him. He dressed so specially, with a sense of style that nobody else had. He always wore Ivy League jackets just before that style came into vogue. And he wore this extraordinary long college scarf all the time. Short hair, a very slightly suspicious look. But definitely *aware* of himself.'

Samwell-Smith had an early indication that Clapton was no ordinary eighteen-year-old hell-bent on pop fame and fortune. Just before the Metropolis Blues Quartet became the Yardbirds, the group played a pub session. Paul decided to take a rare solo as lead guitarist on a song called 'Papa Joe's Blues'.

Eric was in the audience, listening intently and unsmilingly to the group he would soon join. At the end of the session, he walked straight over to Samwell-Smith and said: 'Would you do me a favour?'

'Yes,' said Paul, anxious to keep Clapton happy at the prospect of joining the band.

'Don't play any more lead guitar solos,' said Eric.

Paul reflects with a smile: 'I clearly didn't have talent in that direction, and he spotted it.'

The jibe proved ominous. In the eighteen months he was in the Yardbirds, Eric's relationship with Paul plummeted. Theoretically, it should have been the perfect unit for Clapton, for the group grew up professionally in the footsteps of the Rolling Stones. When Mick Jagger and his band left their residency at Richmond's famous Crawdaddy Club, the Yardbirds stepped in. They built up attendances higher than those of their predecessors and achieved similar success at London's world-famous Marquee Club and in provincial cities. 'The most blueswailing Yardbirds', thus christened by their dream-weaving manager Giorgio Gomelsky, were, in the Britain of

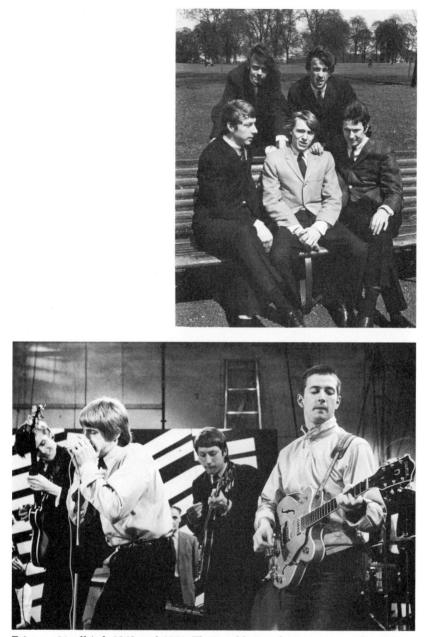

Eric as a Yardbird, 1963 and 1964. The mod hairstyle was soon replaced by a crew cut. In the bottom picture Paul Samwell-Smith is on the left, Keith Relf at the microphone (*Pictorial Press/Val Wilmer/Format*)

the mid-1960s, a cult with a rabid following. Still, Clapton was uncomfortable.

'How can we describe ourselves?' asked Eric at the time. 'Well, we're a *sort* of rhythm-and-blues group, I suppose, when you come down to it.' It was a reluctant, and prophetic, comment on the musical compromise he could not accept.

Paul Samwell-Smith might have been the target of Eric's musical frustration during that period, but there was a deep personal animosity between them that sealed Clapton's decision to quit. 'Had I known more about the music I was playing, had I known about the blues, he would have respected me more,' reflects Samwell-Smith today. 'But he just didn't like my attitude and we did not get on well, which makes things difficult when you are shoulder-to-shoulder in the van from London to Liverpool. Eric regarded me as a snob, a lower-middle-class Hampton Grammar School boy who was jumping on the blues bandwagon, and who had no right to lead the group *he* was in. And he hated the fact that I was not playing my instrument very well. I think that's what caused him to disrespect me. That, plus the fact that our manager told him, immediately he joined the group, that I was the leader and he must do exactly as I said. That didn't go down well at all. But I have no excuses – it's a shame we didn't get on!'

Clapton's memory of his aversion to Paul is cool and direct. 'I took an instant dislike to him because of several factors,' says Eric. 'He had such a very tweedy image. Then, he came from suburban *Twickenham* and he lived with his Mum and Dad and it was all so perfectly *normal* and *good*. He was such a good boy! I was much more into developing myself by hanging out with people who were more likely to be rebels, come from broken homes and were generally neurotic. Those kinds of people appealed to me more than Paul and his type. And on top of all that, he had a great love for folk music and white pop – Joan Baez and all that – and I was totally intolerant of that at the time. I came from the other end of the scale. It had to be black music in order to be valid. I mean – Paul liked the *Shadows*! I didn't.'

Yet Paul Samwell-Smith's distance from Eric enabled him to judge coolly the man's make-up. While other twenty-year-olds were in a hurry to achieve fame, Clapton's aspirations were very different. 'He was certainly the best musician in the band, the most fluid, with that muscular connection that happens with great natural players between their brains and their fingers. He seemed to have a sense of *knowing* about his guitar playing. Talent, when it's that big, is so strong that even the possessor of it sometimes has to look at his fingers and wonder how the hell he's doing *that*. I got that feeling with Eric – he'd move to the front of the stage and take a solo, and we'd all know it was something special.

'Despite my own attitude to music, which was mostly commercial,' says Paul, 'I registered that Eric's attitude to it all was also very strong. He had definite great likes – people like B. B. King – and tended to be very exclusive. He wouldn't even join in a band conversation about the commercial stuff. And it really became a bit uncomfortable. When you're on the road travelling, that attitude isn't easy. He was . . . rigid. He'd end any conversation on music he didn't like, or on compromise, with something like: "Oh, it's gotta be *right* or what's the point?" '

Both the musicians and the audience would remark on Clapton's sense of design and fashion. While the other Yardbirds wore jeans and denim jackets, Eric arrived for one memorable show at the Star, Croydon, just outside London, with a crewcut, smart shirt, neat, tight collar and Ivy League jacket. 'He never appeared ludicrous, just extraordinary,' recalls Paul Samwell-Smith. In those days when long hair was *de rigueur*, the audience gasped at the sight of the guitarist with neatly cropped hair.

Pete Townshend, then leading the Who to the top on the crest of the 'mod' look, remembers first seeing Clapton standing on a pavement in Ealing in 1964. 'He was waiting for a bus, like me, and he looked extremely smart and modish. He'd shaved all his hair off. We hardly spoke. Two weeks later I saw him at a clothes shop he went into regularly, Austins in Shaftesbury Avenue. They sold American clothes. We did have a short talk.'

But Clapton was aloof. 'Not many blues musicians in those days took the Who seriously,' explains Townshend. 'Although he was charming, he didn't treat me as if there was any substance to me. It was a bit of a one-sided affair. I'd never actually seen him play and I had no time for hybrid white blues anyway. I thought John Mayall's whole thing was stupid and Steve Winwood singing the blues was a waste of time. [Eric had jammed regularly with Winwood's group, the Spencer Davis Group, at the London Marquee.]

'To me,' says Townshend forcibly, 'a London white performer trying to play blues music was a joke. I felt that what the Who had at least done was turn it into slightly more of our own urban form of music that depended very much on the lyrics. It seemed to me the blues was a very simple music form and it's what they sang about that counted.' How could a young white boy from Surrey sing or play the blues?

'So there was little basis for communication, although I thought Eric Clapton in those years had a sense of appearance better than most of the people he was hanging around with. He had a style. But musically, *he* felt superior – and *I* certainly did.'

'I equated my fashion consciousness with the way modern jazz musicians looked,' recalls Eric. 'I always fancied myself as being part of an elite. That's why being a purist about my music was very convenient. Because being a blues guitar player was almost like being a jazz musician. In magazines like *Downbeat* there was always a page on blues, so I saw myself in that category. Not just an ordinary guitarist, a *blues* man! And I loved the idea that jazz musicians were very, very slick-looking guys. They were *always* clothes conscious. And I was always keen on clothes, even before I played guitar. So it all fitted in well.

'The jazz musician's look had developed perfectly, for me, from the art college beatnik thing. Even the way I shaved, or didn't sometimes, it all went into being an art student and then a blues player.'

All his money earned from the Yardbirds and Mayall went on clothes. 'Ivy League suits, white socks, loafers, Levi jeans, or straight slacks and sports jackets with shirt and tie and tab collar. It was all very conservative.' It contrasted, though, with the shabby, careless look of many other musicians.

With his instruments, too, Clapton was totally organized, unlike some of the others. Says Paul Samwell-Smith: 'He knew exactly what he was doing, where they were, and if he needed another guitar he said so and by the next gig he'd bought one. He was always on time – once, I failed to turn up for a show and I remember he thought that totally unprofessional, unacceptable. He made me feel very bad about it. And of course he was right. He knew precisely what he was about and did it beautifully, without any fuss or trouble, regarding it as his work. He had a set identity . . . which the girls found attractive.'

There was another aspect of Eric, contrasting vividly with his characteristics as a loner. He had a strong taste for traditional British custard-pie humour. He enjoyed the cut-and-thrust of chucking things at his mates, pulling horrific faces, bulging his eyes, wearing masks, spitting mouth rinse over the others. When it was time for work, though, or time to move on to an appointment, Clapton would be the one to look at his watch and apply self-discipline.

During his time with the Yardbirds Eric had acquired a firm reputation. 'My nickname of Slowhand came from Giorgio Gomelsky. He coined it as a good pun – he kept saying I was a fast player, so he put together the slow-handclap phrase into Slowhand as a play on words.' Eric, who loves words, enjoyed the tag. He also enjoyed the psychological boost it gave to his convictions in music.

The general memory of Eric Clapton within the Yardbirds, the band that shaped his future perhaps more than he realized, is of a dedicated, uncompromising, natural musician with a bit of a chip on his shoulder.

Their differences never reached a peak, but Paul vividly remembers the end of Clapton's eighteen months in the Yardbirds. 'It just seemed so inevitable. He realized he had to leave. He was so unhappy. We were making our new single, "For Your Love", which was not written by us but by Graham Gouldman. That alone wasn't good news for Eric. The Yardbirds played the twenty seconds in the middle, the rhythm-and-blues bit. It wasn't a record, it was a production!

'Giorgio had come to us and presented us with the song and said: "Come on, we need a hit, try this!" And since I was steering the band commercially I agreed. I produced the record. In the middle of the making of it, Giorgio got a phone call from Eric, very dignified, saying he was leaving. Nobody was surprised.'

Eric describes the atmosphere in the Yardbirds at that time as 'a political thrust towards the top of the charts'. And he says: 'I didn't have any goal in that direction. It didn't appeal to me at all to end up on television and do cabaret and package tours. I was really happy doing the clubs with the following we got, and I think those fans wanted us to stay doing that kind of thing. So the more ambitious they got for the gelt, the less happy I became. I wanted out.'

Fame and money were not on his horizon: 'That never occurred to me. I just wanted to play the guitar and play it all the time. I didn't want to be lazy and laid-back and I didn't want the things that money would have bought. In those days, if you had a nice pair of jeans you were laughing.'

Eric says it was a decision by Giorgio to confirm Samwell-Smith as the leader of the Yardbirds that made his decision easy. A memo from Giorgio to the whole band piled on the discipline. He saw the professionalism then needed to convert a scruffy band into a tight working unit. 'Time is money . . . if you're late for rehearsals you will be fined . . . and if you have any queries about this, report to Paul Samwell-Smith or come to my office immediately,' said the memo.

Clapton says that was the breaking point for him. 'I went to Giorgio's office next day and said I don't like it and I'm going to leave. Instead of being upset, Giorgio said: "Good. Okay, well, we're not really surprised. I can't say I'm happy about you going, but we wish you well." '

Eric had needed no persuasion to join the Yardbirds. It was when a music paper headline announced: 'Clapton Quits Yardbirds – Too Commercial' that his uncompromising attitude became publicly known. 'It's very sad – I suppose he likes the blues so much that he didn't like it being played badly by a white shower like us,' said Keith Relf at the time.

If Giorgio Gomelsky had not laid it down so forcefully that Samwell-Smith was the leader, a totally different route might have emerged for Eric. 'Keith Relf, the singer, was just as much a reprobate as anyone else, possibly more so,' recalls Eric. 'He and Jim McCarty were my soul-mates in the Yardbirds, if you like, and I used to enjoy going to parties and popping black bennies and drinking with them. As soon as I joined, I realized that Paul and Chris Dreja were too middle class for me. There was this two-way pull of people.'

He reflects on his seriousness as a musician. 'I took it all far too seriously. Perhaps if I'd been able to temper it, I might not have been so frustrated. I have regrets about my seriousness throughout my career. I still take it too seriously, in terms of relationships and being able to get on with other musicians. I'm far too judgemental, and in those days I was a complete purist. If it wasn't black music, it was rubbish.' The fact that 'precious' Paul Samwell-Smith was the boss was the final straw.

'Money never meant anything to me, because I've always been a bit of a scrounger. I've always managed to get by on other people's handouts. So when I quit the Yardbirds I fell on to the goodwill of my old friend Ben Palmer, who took me up to Oxford and gave me a roof over my head for a month.

'There's this big myth which says I locked myself up in practice there, but it wasn't true. I was simply trying to con Ben into making a blues record with me. I was just a purist, the music was all, but I certainly wasn't holed up in practice. I remember taking some money off a girl in Oxford who was very nice to me. I was broke. Oh, I was just a scoundrel. Being a bum, not even having a responsibility to a band, was far more attractive than security. I enjoyed having no ties for a while.'

Jeff Beck succeeded Eric in the Yardbirds. A dazzling guitarist, he was less committed to the blues and he integrated better into the band. The Yardbirds became, in fact, a breeding ground for several giant figures in rock, including Jimmy Page, who later achieved fame with Led Zeppelin. Ironically, Paul Samwell-Smith quit about a year after Eric, finding his niche as a record producer for such talents as Cat Stevens, Carly Simon, Simon and Garfunkel, Chris de Burgh and Murray Head. 'I began to appreciate Eric's guitar playing more when

Eric, aged 19, shortly after joining the Yardbirds (*Julian Hann*)

he left,' says Paul. 'From standing next to him on stage six nights a week, I suddenly saw him being hailed as a god. It was strange.'

*

Clapton had stepping-stoned his way into the Yardbirds from the periphery of blues and jazz groups which made the London pub scene so infectiously energetic in the early 1960s. While the Beatles and the Rolling Stones polarized the nation's youth, the semi-professional grassroots movement in the steaming clubs was stimulated by American-born traditional jazz and rhythm-and-blues. The jazz bands' instrumentation seemed cluttered and indirect to Eric; he found instant identification with the pure vocal and simple accompaniment, on guitar or piano, of the visiting blues singers like Roosevelt Sykes and Champion Jack Dupree. Pop stars did not impress him. Musically, his idols were Bo Diddley and Chuck Berry, and he greatly admired the style, the look, the individuality of Buddy Holly.

Forty miles west of London, in the Oxford area, a fanatical blues purist named Ben Palmer was itching to launch a band to interpret the raw sounds of Sonny Boy Williamson, Muddy Waters, Little Walter and Big Bill Broonzy. Two of his early colleagues were Brian Jones, eventually to become a star with the Rolling Stones, and Paul Jones, later to sing with the successful Manfred Mann band. No such dizzy ambition fired Ben Palmer, who was content to play piano and preach the blues gospel with kindred spirits more interested in the music than in fame. He was happy to play for free beer. Finally, with guitarist Tom McGuinness, Ben Palmer launched a group called the Roosters and moved to London.

The momentum of the Roosters was as erratic as that of literally hundreds of similar groups in Britain early in 1963. The crucial moment for the Roosters came through McGuinness's girlfriend who was studying at Kingston College of Art. Although Tom played guitar, she said, there was word around the Kingston area that another guitarist named Clapton was really good. 'She arranged for Eric to attend a Roosters rehearsal in a pub in Kingston,' recalls Ben Palmer. 'He joined the band there and then. He was so good, obviously a natural, we didn't even have to discuss it.'

The Roosters lasted six inglorious months, playing the Ricky-Tick Club circuit in Kingston, Windsor and West Wickham. Clapton, who had joined it when he was exactly eighteen, relished the baptism. With all its meagre pickings (a few pounds a night and sometimes free drinks for each player) the audiences, of about sixty people, were mostly discriminating. And for a teenager determined somehow to make his mark as a guitarist, the pace of life, the discipline of being collected by the band van at prescribed times, the promise of a faintly Bohemian lifestyle all looked good to Clapton. And the Roosters' music had integrity.

Most important, though, were the nights on which he could hone his guitar playing with critical colleagues in the band and audiences who were talking about Eric's exceptional verve.

'It was immediately obvious that he was something that none of the rest of us were,' says Ben Palmer. 'And he had a fluency and a command that seemed endless. The telling factor was that he didn't *mind* taking solos, which people of our standard often did because we weren't up to it. I noticed immediately with Eric . . . give him a solo and he didn't care how long you let him play. He'd go *on* and *on* . . . until sometimes you'd have to stop him, to bring the singer back in. I knew from the very first that he was quite different from the rest of us in the Roosters. Coherent, lucid, fresh, powerful – and always *building*. He had a sense of dynamics quite remarkable for someone of his age.' He was also intensely serious about his playing, negotiating the repertoire with Palmer and McGuinness, the nominal leaders.

The Roosters petered out when Ben confessed one night to most of the band that he did not enjoy playing in public too much. He preferred rehearsals. Anyway, his narrow horizons in music were too restricting and held back the more ambitious players like Clapton and McGuinness. 'I was quite happy for it to end and to stop playing,' says Palmer. 'I couldn't see us ramming the Chicago blues down people's throats successfully or fast enough for my temperament.' The split of the Roosters was amicable enough but a rock-solid friendship had formed between Clapton and Palmer. They were to become lifelong friends, partly perhaps because their paths diverged but mostly because their values and their uncompromising single-mindedness found an easy rapport. (Ben was to reunite with Eric three years later, as a road manager with Cream. Today, he is happy as a different kind of artist, wood carving at his home in Wales.)

As teenage friends, Clapton and Palmer had shared many days and nights living in a commune above a greengrocery warehouse at 74 Long Acre, in London's Covent Garden. Clapton was the only musician in a house which attracted a poet, a puppeteer, and occasional visits from John Hurt, then a student at the St Martin's School of Art. It was the time in Eric's life when he felt most free, drifting from band to band, and spending nights in Covent Garden drinking cheap Algerian red wine with Palmer, who had by then given up playing in favour of working for the embryonic jazz record label, Esquire, run by Carlo Kramer.

Eric and McGuinness's move, after the Roosters, lasted a mere month, into the Liverpool-based band Casey Jones and the Engineers. Led by a young hustler named Brian Cassar, who had ridden the Merseyside beat group boom by forming a band named Cass and the Cassanovas, Casey Jones and the Engineers was Eric's most improbable band. In July 1963, with the advent of the Liverpool beat group bonanza, Cassar had touted himself around the record companies. He picked up a one-record-only deal with Columbia. Casey Jones and the Engineers were an anonymous group of session musicians. But when his manager insisted that 'Casey Jones' should do some concerts, Cassar had to form a real band to back him. With deft persuasion, he recruited four musicians including guitarists Clapton and McGuinness. They played gigs in Macclesfield, Manchester and Reading with 'Casey', but quickly gave up. The band was musically bankrupt.

Clapton's next step after the Yardbirds was fired by his complete conviction that he 'needed to be true to myself . . . I am, and always will be, a blues musician'. In a move that at first seemed retrogressive, he joined John Mayall's Bluesbreakers in April 1965.

Clapton was in Oxford, trying to persuade Ben Palmer to return to action in London, when a phone call from John Mayall invited him to an audition. 'I was straight into his band without any problem. And as well as taking me into the band, he gave me a room at his house in Lee Green, a tiny room, just wide enough for its narrow single bed. That's where I did my practising. I stayed in there because I felt strange in the house: his family lived there and I didn't feel part of it, so I stayed in that room, practising and listening to John's vast collection of blues records.'

Mayall and Eric had a great rapport. 'He was very good in that he'd *listen* to me about music, one of the first people, apart from Ben, who did. We would listen to a lot of blues and pick songs that were right for the stage. He was easy company, and older than me, but keen to draw me out and find what I thought. It was most unusual, a very important band for me. I did flower a lot during my time with Mayall.' He also met Bob Dylan for the first time, starting a friendship that continues strongly: 'Bob came down to jam when Mayall had this record out, "Life is Like a Slow Train Going Up a Hill".' Clapton and Dylan got on well musically, although Eric was not at that time keen on Dylan's white-based folk music. He had been put off Dylan by the fact that Paul Samwell-Smith liked him. Later, Eric heard the *Blonde on Blonde* album and was totally converted to Dylan's music; today the two artists admire each others' work enormously.

'Inside Mayall's band, I was still a very moody character. In any situation, I've always found *something* that isn't right. In that band, it became John himself: my expectations of him began to rise. With a couple of the other members of the band, we started to gang up on John behind his back, muttering about him not being a good enough singer, being too flamboyant in his presentation. He went on stage bare to the waist.' In retrospect, though, the blues music, and the leadership qualities in Mayall, were a vital stepping-stone for Eric.

Twelve years older than Clapton, Mayall had a reputation not as a wizard keyboards player but as a gifted bandleader who acted as a catalyst for musicians who wanted to work vigorously. He ran his band almost along the disciplined lines of the jazz giants of yester-year, Duke Ellington and Count Basie. Mayall demanded, and received, total dedication to the business of making music . . . and he got it from such great talents, over the years, as Eric, bassists Jack Bruce and John McVie (later to help form Fleetwood Mac), and Hughie Flint on drums.

Joining Mayall, then, was for Eric as much a statement of intent as it was a move into the blues arena. Within a few months, he emerged strongly as a guitarist who had at last found his feet. Mayall recalls him as restless, evidently on his way to somewhere else. And one of the most remarkable periods of his life began as audiences recognized that he was indeed a special player.

Crowds began going to Mayall shows purely to see Clapton. They shouted 'Clapton is God!' 'Give God a solo!' 'We want more God!' And 'Clapton is God' slogans appeared on the walls of the London underground railway stations, as well as on advertising posters. For a twenty-one-year-old, even one who believed in his own ability, this was disturbingly heady stuff. Eric actually disliked the experience and that level of adulation. It came dangerously close to his being a pop star, and he preferred always to consider himself as a guitarist.

'My vanity was incredibly boosted by that "God" thing,' says Eric now. 'But it pushed me into myself a great deal. It made me very outspoken, because I got this false self-confidence, and then I realized I was talking so much rubbish to everyone around me. So I withdrew and became an introvert.

'I thought that if I was regarded as God then I had to be careful what I said. But I don't think I was mature enough in that period to reflect deeply on it, on the profound meaning of it all. I took it as a surface compliment and one that would probably fade. I became very cautious, I suddenly realized that people were very, very easy with their words. Then came a feeling of bitterness and

sensitivity about what people said about me; a lot of it could, after all, be nonsense. So then I became very full of judgement about other people's opinions of me and what I played.'

But he did have a super-confident belief in himself that stopped just short of arrogance. 'I didn't think there was anyone around at that time doing what I was doing, playing the blues as straight as me. I was trying to do it absolutely according to its rules. Oh yeah, I was very confident. I didn't think there was anybody as good. The only person I ever met who was trying to be as good as me was Mike Bloomfield and when he came to England he bowed down to me straightaway. So I thought, well, that's that.' His sense of euphoria was high, but modesty kept his ego in check.

'It was only when Cream came together that I began to bend the blues rules. During my time with John Mayall, I stuck to the letter of that music as much as I could without keeping my own creativity down.'

Yet that intoxicating year with Mayall sealed Eric's confidence. He voiced his disillusionment with Britain, his determination to settle in America where his music was born and thrived, and left us in no doubt that he saw himself separate from the mainstream of British rock 'n' roll or pop.

'I don't think there will be room for me here much longer,' he said at the time. 'None of my music is English, it's rooted in Chicago. I represent what's going on in Chicago at the moment – the best I can, anyway, because it's difficult to get all the records imported.

'The English are rooted in rock 'n' roll. What's coming out of England now makes me puke.' He then vociferously attacked one British singer of the day, Chris Farlowe. 'Everything you've heard him do has been done better, years before, in America by Negroes. He can't hope to simulate what the American Negroes do.

'The Miracles and Ray Charles make their records commercial for the American white public to buy. Therefore by the time Farlowe and the rest have got the numbers, they're about third hand.'

Eric said he was determined to get to Chicago, his 'spiritual home', as soon as possible. The Yardbirds had visited the city, and Jeff Beck, who replaced him as lead guitarist, had made a good impression. 'I gather it became Jeff Beck with the Yardbirds – the white Americans over there, who know what they're on about, dug Jeff a lot more than Keith Relf's half-hearted singing.'

He was certain, he said, that he would have to leave Britain. 'I deal in realism, nothing but realism, and the nastier the better. The buyers and sellers of records in England are not concerned with it. This is why I'm being driven out. Forming a blues band in England

Eric soon after he had joined the Bluesbreakers led by John Mayall, who is in the centre of the picture (*Melody Maker*). *Below:* Playing with the Bluesbreakers

is like banging your head against a brick wall. Nobody wants to do it and certainly nobody wants to record it.

'I'm not interested in guitar sound and technique but in people and what you can do to them via music. I'm very conceited and I think I have a power. My guitar is just a medium for expressing that power.

'This is the blues, this is true expression. I am contacting myself through the guitar and telling myself I have a power. I haven't a girlfriend or any other relationship, so I tell myself of this power through the guitar.

'And I don't need people to say how good I am. I've worked it out by myself. It's nothing to do with technique and rehearsing. It's to do with the person behind that guitar who is trying to find an outlet. My guitar is simply a medium through which I can make contact with myself. It's very, very lonely.'

Eric says now: 'I took it far too seriously. Perhaps if I'd been able to temper it, I'd have been happier as a person. I have regrets about that, and also about the fact that throughout my career I've taken everything too seriously. I still do. It's a strength, yeah, but it can also be a hell of a stumbling block in terms of relationships, like getting on with other musicians.' (Chapter 8 will elaborate on all aspects of Eric Clapton's musical career.)

Twenty years later, Clapton's view of himself and his music is easily accepted. His music and his often gritty personality have projected a positive portrait of the man. But in the mid-1960s, such self-analysis left him exposed to possible charges of pretentiousness. He was twenty-one at the time; it's possible that even Eric Clapton didn't realize how much his early years, before he became a musician, had shaped his determination and sense of isolation later.

Eric drew his musical inspiration from the black American artists, and he believes he is, and was, equally capable of the feelings his idols were so richly articulating.

'I think the blues is actually more of an emotional experience than one exclusive to black or white, or related to poverty,' he says. 'It comes from emotional poverty. The music I drew from came from an emotional deprivation. There could be poor white people and poor black people next to one another and they would make different music.' Eric's memory may be dim and his thoughts unfocussed, but the message is clear.

'Now I didn't feel I had any identity, and the first time I heard blues music, it was like a crying of the soul to me. I immediately identified with it. It was the first time I'd heard anything akin to how I was feeling, which was an inner poverty. It stirred me quite blindly.

Eric Clapton with his mother

I wasn't sure just why I wanted to play it, but I felt completely in tune.'

An emotional blight in his childhood definitely contributed to his being receptive to the blues. 'I must have been about six or seven, at primary school, and writing my name down as Eric Clapton, when I suddenly fully realized that my so-called parents were Mr and Mrs Clapp. So there was an inkling of something being wrong from the very first time I went to school. All the other kids bore the same names as their parents. My feeling of a lack of identity started to rear its head then. And it explains a lot of my behaviour throughout my life; it changed my outlook and my physical appearance so much. Because I *still* don't know who I am.'

2

THE
LONER

*'You're wasting your time on that guitar. It's a nice
hobby but not a* job'

'I knew from the moment Eric was born that there was no way I would have the opportunity to keep him, to bring him up,' says his mother. 'I shall never get over it, and never lose the guilt, but I suppose that's the penalty I have to live with for having an illegitimate child when I was only sixteen.'

Eric Patrick Clapton, born on 30 March 1945, was the son of unmarried Patricia Molly Clapton and a Canadian soldier stationed in England, Edward Fryer. Eric, born in the front room of his grandparents' two-up, two-down terraced house at 1, The Green, Ripley, Surrey, was raised there by his doting grandparents, Rose and Jack Clapp. Eric's surname came from Patricia Clapton's father, Reginald, who was Rose's first husband.

Eric's natural father used to play piano, veering towards the blues style, in various bands that visited the Surrey dance halls; that is how Pat met him. She was also attracted to him because he was a gifted artist, enjoying painting for a hobby. She is certain that both characteristics of the father who fled have flowered to perfection in Eric.

A striking, gregarious woman, Pat McDonald – as she became when she married – now lives back in the village that gave her so much agony. 'The locals were hard on me,' she says, 'but those were the days before the phrase "love child" had been heard of.' Edward Fryer was married when Pat became pregnant, and when he returned to his wife in Canada, Pat was left to decide on Eric's upbringing. Pat moved to Germany on her eventual marriage to Frank McDonald, a Canadian soldier by whom she had two daughters, Cheryl, born on 5 May 1953, and Heather, born on 27 September 1958, and a son, Brian.

Eric's half-brother died in 1974, aged twenty-six, the victim of a hit-and-run road accident while riding his motorcycle near his home in Canada. Eric was in the Bahamas when he heard the news and cancelled his concerts in order to be with Pat at the funeral in Canada. 'I was touched by that,' says Pat. 'I really knew then that he cared about me as his mother.' But she admits to having carried the scars of a lifelong problematical relationship with her famous first-born.

'Nobody wanted Rick to know he was illegitimate during his young days,' says Pat, who always uses this abbreviation for Eric. 'It would have been awful for him, going to school with what in those days had more shame attached to it than now. But as the years went by, Rick told me that, when he realized he was illegitimate, that was one of the reasons he *had* to make a name for himself – to overcome his background and strive for something.' His grandmother broke the news to him. Eric was nine years old when Pat returned from her new home in Canada to stay at her mother's house in Ripley and spend some time with Eric. She brought her six-year-old son Brian. It was then that she realized that Eric knew he was illegitimate. Eric said to his young half-brother: 'You see that lady over there in that bed? She's *my* mummy, too.' Pat wept when she heard him say it.

But by then, Eric's surrogate parents were firmly running his young life. Grandmother Rose's first husband, Reginald Cecil ('Rex') Clapton had died, and she had then married Jack Clapp, a plasterer and bricklayer. 'There's no doubt,' says Pat Clapton, 'that as a very young toddler he considered my mother and my stepfather to be his parents. It must have been confusing for him when I arrived ... because I left him after bringing him up from a baby until he was two years old. When I arrived back and he was nine, I found I'd been kept hush-hush from him, which was understandable. He had to be protected from the truth. But it hurt me like mad.

'I couldn't allow myself to love my own son fully because I knew I had virtually given him to my mother to bring up. And he probably deeply resented me for that while he was growing up. With good reason. Now he knows that I was in a hopeless position.' Pat's dilemma was complicated by the fact that her husband, Frank McDonald, came from a strict Roman Catholic family which would not tolerate the news that their son's wife had a child born out of wedlock.

Her memories of Eric as a child are limited but strong. 'At nine, I remember he seemed to me to be very deep, a bit of a loner.' Proper contact between mother and son came years later when his grand-parents took him to Germany to stay with his mother and stepfather

Above: Eric with his mother, Pat and *(below)* with his grandmother, Rose, outside her home in Ripley, Surrey

in the army barracks near Dortmund. Eric was a long-haired Yard-bird at the time. 'We still didn't – couldn't – talk about being mother and son,' says Pat. 'He looked at me, I looked at him; the knowledge was there but we both found it painful. My ex-husband [she was divorced in 1982] was a sergeant, and we told Rick that before he could come into the mess for a meal he would have to have his hair cut. Rick had an army haircut, a crewcut, under great protest, but when he returned to England he made it appear fashionable. He went from the sublime to the ridiculous.'

Because Eric's relationship with his mother was remote, he refer-red to her as his sister whenever they were in company. She agreed to the tactic. 'It saved us explaining the tangled web of relationships,' she says. But his adoption by, and of, his grandmother Rose was total.

Cheerful, protective and adoring, she has become a central part of 'Rick's' life. She is also one of his greatest fans. 'We brought him up as our own, but we had to be straight with him and tell him his real mother was away from England – and we told him when he was five, just before he went to school,' says Rose. 'He had to understand why I, or my husband, signed certain forms as his guardians and not parents.' To boost the household's income, Rose worked as a telephonist and later in a lemonade factory. Money was tight. 'It used to grieve me that we couldn't give Rick the same pocket money as some of his friends,' says Rose. 'Not that he had many . . . he was a lonely little boy really. He was so shy.' But Rose and Jack were determined that Eric should not feel neglected materially as well as emotionally, and did their best for him.

Baptized into the Church of England, Eric was known in the Ripley village as an exceptionally polite boy. 'We didn't take him to church a lot,' says Rose, 'but we drilled it into him that he must have manners and respect.' She was delighted when a very old villager expressed surprise to her that Eric, alone among the village schoolboys, doffed his cap to him regularly and said: 'Good morning.' No other children bothered, said the old man. In the tight-knit village community, a strong sense of friendship between each house was encouraged by the atmosphere of a pretty village in postwar Britain. In those years, long before its main A3 road carried heavy traffic to desecrate Ripley's charm, it was a calm, typically English haven of tranquillity – and gossip. Eric's manners would be as noticeable to the local people as the problems faced by his mother and grandmother.

When he was about eight, Rose asked him what he would like to be when he grew up. 'A doctor,' Eric answered. 'So that I'd stop people from going to heaven.' Then, as a quick afterthought: 'Well, no, I think I'll be a vicar. He helps people to get up there.'

Eric's childhood enthusiasms – a fondness for animals, particularly the black labrador Prince and his collection of snails, which littered Rose's small home and got on her nerves – were unremarkable except for one obsession probably inherited from his father. 'He wouldn't stop drawing,' says Rose. 'Leave him alone for a few minutes and he'd have a pencil or crayon in his hand and he'd be away, drawing cars or ships or animals.' He was only six years old when Rose persuaded him to enter one of his drawings in a local contest. He won first prize of a box of paints, but he was more pleased by the fact that he had triumphed over entries from fourteen-year-olds. Eric's winning entry was a drawing of horses with cowboys wearing hats; he was praised particularly for his attention to detail, having surrounded the prairie with cactus plants. 'Very observant little boy,' a judge told a beaming Rose.

He sauntered quietly through these years, and surprisingly he even joined the 1st Ripley troop of the Boy Scouts. He quite liked the team spirit and was a good cub and scout. The uniform, and particularly the need to wear a cap, reduced his enthusiasm.

As a toddler, Eric had been 'both an angel and a little devil, but even then, quite a perfectionist,' says Adrian Clapton, Rose's son from her first marriage. He was eighteen when Eric was born and came to live in the same house. Uncle Adrian was regarded by the young Rick as his brother; Adrian was a soldier in the Royal Signals for the first three years of Eric's life, but when he returned from service overseas they developed a good relationship.

'He was very pernickety and I remember being struck by his determination to do everything well, even at that young age,' recalls Adrian. Eric grew his fingernails 'literally half an inch long' and flatly refused to allow anyone to cut them for months. 'Rose wasn't allowed to go near them. He had a hatred of anyone cutting his nails.' Eventually Sylvia, Adrian's future wife, was allowed to shorten them occasionally.

Once, Guy Pullen and some of the other village boys shut Eric in the telephone box on a hot summer's day with the temperature in the eighties. The boys surrounded the box and seven-year-old Eric was ashen-faced and very shaky when he eventually emerged. It was a kids' game that went wrong, and it frightened Eric.

When Adrian returned from the army he began collecting big-band jazz records, and the young Eric was weaned on the sounds of Lionel Hampton and Stan Kenton. But once he discovered the raw blues sounds of the American Negro, Clapton was totally hooked. 'He was about sixteen when he persuaded Rose to get him that first guitar. Big Bill Broonzy was the big hero and I can see him now,' says Adrian. 'In his room he had a little Grundig Cub tape recorder with those three quarters of an inch reel-to-reel tapes. He swore and cursed till he could copy the sounds exactly, from as many records as he could get hold of. He ended up with seven or eight of those reels full of his practising, with the sound of the house's two budgerigars tweeting in the background.'

At five, Eric went to Ripley Church of England Primary School. He was an above average young pupil, excelling in English but not doing well in mathematics. His artwork was always a highspot, and the teachers told his grandparents there was no reason why he should not pass his examinations into grammar school when he was eleven.

But when he was nine, things went awry. Coinciding with the arrival home of his mother, and the trauma that caused Eric, Rose received a letter from the headmaster inviting her for a talk. 'What's happened to Eric?' asked the schoolteachers, all concerned about the boy who had been successful until then. 'This is a very important time in Eric's school life,' said the headmaster, 'and we think something is upsetting him emotionally – he should pass his exams easily, but he seems unsettled. I'm worried that all he is now is a borderline for passing his exams for grammar school.'

For the next nine months the teachers continued to report Eric's lack of concentration. He failed the eleven-plus and went to St Bede's Secondary Modern School at Send, near Woking, Surrey. The changed environment, the daily trip by bus, and the departure from Ripley of his real mother, who returned to Canada, probably accounted for a renewed enthusiasm for school. There were the normal boyhood fights with other pupils, but Eric did not enjoy them – 'I was a physical weakling, no good at games,' he says. Sport always seemed too rough, too knockabout, to him. But he enjoyed following its competitive aspects as a spectator.

At the age of twelve, Eric acquired a BSA air rifle and delighted in firing pellets at the door of the outside toilet. Uncle Adrian's method of chastizing him was to throw bricks on top of its corrugated iron roof whenever the young Clapton went into it. It irritated and scared his young nephew.

At home Rose, Jack and Adrian had to contend with a punctiliousness that was hard to accept in a young boy; nobody except Eric was allowed to pour the milk on his Weetabix, since it had to go into the dish at a certain angle. Even though he was good at making models of Spitfires and Hurricanes, he was less experienced and therefore less adept than his uncle, and his refusal to come to terms with this meant that he gradually tired of the craft, although he returned to it later in life.

'When he was fourteen,' says Adrian, 'I got married and moved to Woking, leaving my pride and joy, a BSA racing bike, temporarily at my mother's house in Ripley.' When he returned to collect it he was furious to find that Eric had stripped it, repainted it and changed the wheels. 'He said he was going to tour Britain by bike.'

Eric's two years at St Bede's passed uneventfully. Mr Swan, the art teacher, encouraged his natural talent. He told Rose that a big future could lie ahead for Eric in art. Responding to this news, Eric sketched things around the house and drew a picture to take to school on most mornings.

Two turning points occurred on Eric's thirteenth birthday. He and his few visiting schoolfriends had listened unfailingly to every week's 'Goon Show' on the radio. Now with the aid of Eric's small tape recorder, the first gadget bought for him by his grandparents, they started to learn to mimic the bizarre voices of Harry Secombe, Peter Sellers and Spike Milligan.

That year, 1958, was also a vintage year for rock 'n' roll. The swagger of Buddy Holly and Elvis Presley made a big impact on the young Clapton. One of his chief characteristics was that when he worked up an enthusiasm for something he had to saturate himself with the subject. This new sound of American pop music, he learned from the radio, had its origins in something called 'the blues'. He decided he would find out about this strangely named source. Even at that age, he did not like adopting something that was possibly 'secondhand'.

Secondly, he asked Rose and Jack to buy him a guitar for his birthday. They could scarcely afford it. But they went with him to Bell's instrument shop in Kingston. Eric chose a £14 acoustic model and his grandparents paid for it by monthly instalments. 'I can see, in my mind, his smile even now on the way home,' says Rose.

Almost, it seemed, as a repayment to them, Eric passed an art examination which gained him a place at Hollyfield Road School, Surbiton, which contained the junior art department of Kingston Art School, as the college was then called.

By now, in Ripley village, most of the locals regarded him as a 'weirdo'. He had always been known to have the best collection of toys during his childhood – 'Rose and Jack did their best to spoil him, probably to compensate for the fact that he didn't have a real Mum and Dad around,' says Guy Pullen, Eric's closest friend from those years. Now, he was the only one with a guitar. 'It was certainly no rags-to-riches story from childhood. But everyone remarked on him; he was the distant kid who was definitely a one-off, didn't join in. He wasn't a normal country boy. He had the tightest jeans, the longest hair, a dirty face, and eventually he sat alone on the village green playing this guitar to himself. Oh yeah, he was certainly the odd one out,' says Pullen.

Exactly the same age as Eric, Guy Pullen grew up six doors from Eric's grandparents' home. The two boys developed a solid boyhood friendship, both going to the same primary and secondary schools before Eric veered off into art college. They were in the same A-stream class together, both hopeless at gardening and woodwork. 'We got the boring jobs together because we were no good, like putting compost on the roses or digging over the compost heap every week.'

In lessons, Rick, as Clapton quickly became to Guy, showed an early independence: 'He never thought we should help each other out. He never participated in sport, and that marked him out as different because the village had always been very enthusiastic about it, with keen, talented footballers and cricketers. We'd rope him into coming to matches but he'd vanish, fade away, and we'd see him later sitting out on the green with the guitar.' One concession to 'knockabout sport' came through friendly boxing matches organized by Guy Pullen, in the back garden of his home. They set up matches with proper gloves and a ring made from rope around the trees.

'He was basically a loner. The artistic thing was strongly in him from the moment Rose got him that cheap guitar. All the boys in the village really envied him, and when he got the Grundig tape recorder that was just too much.' Other boys were bemused by his obsession with music. 'If another boy came up to him as he was sitting on the green, Rick would say "Hey, listen to this blues guitar." Then he'd try to emulate the sound and the notes, every day throughout the summer.'

The two boys would often go to the local cinema, which they called the Bug Hutch. 'We paid one and nine pence and always stood at the back, after sitting in the front or middle rows for the first few times and getting chewing-gum stuck in our hair from the kids behind.

'We used to sit in Rose's house – he had his first electric guitar in the early days of the Yardbirds first getting together. He'd sit there and sing . . . da . . . di . . . di . . . di. And then ask: "Is that all right?" Well, I wouldn't know, I knew nothing about music. I've never known anything about it, any more than he knows about sport. That's probably why our friendship has survived.'

He was known for his generosity. If Guy or other boys visited his house and admired a toy, Eric would give it to them to take away.

Eric aged eight and twelve. His childhood had been troubled

'He's always been totally loyal and overgenerous to certain people, particularly old mates,' says Pullen.

He wasn't a boy who chased girls, either. Pullen recalls Eric's first known date was with a local girl, Sandra Ploughman. 'But he wasn't exactly the local Romeo.' And although their friendship was solid, Clapton bore grudges. 'Once, we'd had a row. We were ten years old, it was his birthday party, but he didn't invite me. That's the sort of kid he was. He'd never forgive.

'He was cunning, a kid who manoeuvred himself into and out of situations. He'd stir up trouble, then walk away from it. Always avoided a fight.' The two sometimes clashed because Eric would not try his hand at games or support Guy Pullen's enthusiasm for football and cricket. 'But I realized when I saw him play why he never did it. He had no ball ability whatsoever. Same with tennis. He was static. No timing. The ball simply went by him.' Later, though, Eric became a staunch supporter of Ripley Cricket Club and went to many matches.

At Hollyfield Road School, Surbiton, he studied the basic design course for nearly two years before moving full-time to Kingston College of Art when he was sixteen. His natural flair convinced all his family and friends that he was on the way to a successful career in art. So great was Eric's enthusiasm that he even caught the bus into Kingston on Saturday mornings, theoretically to continue his studies.

Rose, however, noticed that on most days he was taking his guitar to Kingston with him. Strange, she thought. But by now, his fondness for art was matched by a consuming passion for the blues. Most nights, he would push his grandparents' patience to the limit by staying up until two or three in the morning, strumming his guitar, playing the blues records he had managed to get and struggling to learn chords with the aid of his tape recorder. 'Testing, testing . . . all night long,' recalls Rose. 'I can hear it now. I remember shouting down to him so many times: 'Rick, are you coming to bed? Your father's got to go to work in the morning!' Eric's practising was even keeping the two budgerigars awake.

Proud of his art college 'uniform' of maroon jacket and grey trousers, Eric seemed on course for a lively career. But at Kingston he was gaining notoriety for his lunchtime guitar playing in the cafeteria. And, increasingly, he went missing from lessons.

Rose received two letters in quick succession from the headmaster. One said that Eric's work was inadequate in quantity and, unless he improved his performance, he would have to consider seriously his position 'because he might be depriving someone else of a place here'. The second letter invited Rose and Jack to the school, to be told that, regrettably, Eric Clapton would have to leave. 'He had not been putting in enough time,' says Rose. She believed he had been playing truant. Within two years, a future in art or music was inevitable. Rose, Jack and Adrian grew suspicious that Eric was playing truant, and became convinced that he was 'up to something' when the time came to renew his quarterly Green Line bus pass. 'He said something about not having used the pass for the previous week, and that was the first inkling we had that he had not been going to school every day.'

'I had failed the eleven-plus miserably,' says Eric. 'Then I qualified to take the thirteen-plus, which was something new they'd intro-duced. I passed that in art and English, and because my marks were good in those two subjects I was sent to Hollyfield Road School, which had an art branch. We did ordinary lessons like English, mathematics, woodwork and physical training some days, then there would be three or four solid days of art alone. We worked with clay and paint and did still-lifes and figure drawing, and we also had the bonus of going to Kingston Art School night classes.

'When I was sixteen, at Hollyfield, I took my GCE O levels and got an A in art and an O in English. This didn't really qualify me for anything.' But he was building up an enthusiasm for a career in art.

'So I took a portfolio to Kingston. I didn't have enough certificates, but they liked what they saw. They did an interview to get me in and I got into the art school for one year on probation. Students go for four years, and in the first year they weigh you up. And at the end of the first year, simply because of my lack of interest and a lot of distractions (at that point I was sixteen, getting into the Bohemian, beatnik thing and listening to music and not really working very much), I didn't have a big enough portfolio for them to think it was worth keeping me on. The stuff I did was good. But there just wasn't enough – they were judging by quantity. So I didn't make it. They booted me out, along with another bloke – us two out of fifty, which wasn't too good.'

There had been an unfortunate start to his entry to art school. 'When they had asked which side of the college I wanted to go in, Fine Art or Graphics, I said Graphics. I'd been slightly brainwashed by Rose and Jack that if you wanted to make a living at art, you had to be a commercial artist. And I was nodding my head to that at the interview. They said, "What do you want to be?" I said, "Commer-cial artist." So they put me into Graphics. And after the first couple of weeks in Graphics, I realized that I was in the wrong department, because in the canteen I saw all the good blokes with paint all over them and long hair, and they were in the Fine Art department! And all our lot looked like chartered accountants! So I really thought I'd blown it from the word go. I just then started getting more interested in playing the guitar and listening to music.'

Still, there were no career opportunities in music. 'When they booted me out of college, I couldn't see an opening in sight. No band to walk into. I hung around the pubs and coffee bars in the Kingston area, playing, and I was quite serious in my interest and enthusiasm for it. But I couldn't have guessed it would be my next thing.

'In fact, I was very upset and shaken up at being thrown out of college. I couldn't face going home to break the news to Rose and Jack. They were upset for me, but they didn't give me a hard time.'

Rose still believes that Eric was banished from college because he had played truant in order to seek out friends and play guitar. 'Not true,' says Eric. 'Where would I go? The only times I can remember going out of college were spending the odd days in town going to galleries, which I felt was part of my work as an art student. I'd go to a gallery for a couple of hours and then go to one of those cartoon cinemas to kill a little bit of time. But I couldn't be classified as a truant.'

It had now sunk into Eric that he would never know who his father was, and that he had been handed over by his mother to his grandparents. It now hit again at his confidence and sense of identity. He was particularly aggrieved because 'I felt my work at art school was very promising compared with the other students. Most of them in that department were mathematicians more than artists. What I was doing was creative and imaginative. I was shocked.'

'I used to wonder why he was so late home for his meal in the evenings,' says Rose wistfully. He had been to the record shops or playing guitar. 'I often gave him a good telling off. My husband was not the sort to holler. But he made his point with Rick. He said: "You had your chance, now you've chucked it away." ' But a life in stained-glass designing, which was Eric's original choice, by now could not compete with the pull of music. Eric's grandfather said that to earn some cash and occupy himself during the day, Eric could go to Camberley with him as a bricklayer and help plasterers on the building sites. And that is what Eric sometimes did; his keen eye and flair soon showed in that work, too. 'Jack said he was an excellent worker – his perfectionism showed in the way he laid tiles,' says Rose.

There were signs of sentimentality in the teenager. When, at sixteen, he signed on as a postman to deliver the Christmas mail in the Ripley area, he returned from one round with £3 for Rose. It would help with the guitar payments, he said. Rose refused it, so Eric went out and bought her a bottle of perfume with the cash.

'I don't think he liked the work as a postman. He wasn't an energetic boy and the long round on the push-bike for the widespread area of Ripley wasn't much fun to him.' But he wanted that money! He bought her a vase for her birthday which she still cherishes.

And she remembers the days when she nearly went mad with the repetitiveness of his practising, once he had been booted out of art school and often stayed home all day. Her temper nearly snapped, but, as always, Eric was able to win her over with his quiet charm.

As the months passed, Clapton's dedication to music – nor merely the pop sounds of the day, but the primitive sounds of Broonzy, Jimmy Reed, Robert Johnson and anything with the pure touch of rhythm-and-blues as it was then called – dominated his life. Into the Roosters, then the Yardbirds he went . . . while at home, the same kind of scene was acted out throughout Britain. As American popular music – and particularly the guitar – strengthened its influence on youth, exchanges like those between Eric Clapton and Rose were occurring between thousands of teenagers and parents: 'You're wasting your time on a thing like that,' Rose said to the seventeen-year-old Eric. 'It's a nice hobby, but not really a *job*.'

'You won't say that when I'm earning £200 a week, Mum,' Eric answered.

'I remember laughing out loud at him, and he looked hurt,' Rose recalls. 'Of course, it was a difficult argument for him, at the time. He got about £20 a week in the Yardbirds.' Although this was fairly good money for a teenager in 1963, he was soon leaning on Rose and Jack to subsidize further his folly, part-exchanging his old acoustic guitar for a £100 electric model. Again, Rose committed herself to the hire-purchase payments. 'If that's what you want to do, okay, but don't blame us if things go wrong. Stained-glass designing would be safer, wouldn't it?'

In a prophetic assurance, Eric answered: 'It won't go wrong, Mum, don't worry.'

The momentum of Eric's life in music was unstoppable in his mind. He even persuaded Rose to go, on one memorable night, to the Station Hotel, Richmond, where the Yardbirds had succeeded the Rolling Stones as the Crawdaddy Club's weekly resident band. Finally, she and Jack were persuaded by Eric to sign him formally into the Yardbirds as a professional musician. 'At Keith Relf's house in Ham, Surrey, it was,' says Rose. 'All the parents of the Yardbirds and the band members were there. We all looked at each other, wondering what we were signing.'

But Rose was quickly hooked by the infectious atmosphere. As Eric's guardian, she countersigned his management contract between Giorgio Gomelsky and the Yardbirds.

Jack Clapp died when Eric was twenty-five. As Eric's career moved ever upwards, and he left Ripley, he constantly kept in touch with Rose, sending her postcards and dropping in on her with his latest record or news of his progress. Often, Rose was moved to tears when he walked out of her house. 'Rick's music, and looking at him, did something to me deep inside. Oh gee, when I first heard him playing "Telephone Blues" with John Mayall that really got me inside here, brought a lump to my throat.

'He was placid, gentle, as a boy, but at the time I thought there must be something inside him. He was a true artist, right down to his drawing pictures in my recipe book. There's something inside him, I used to say to Jack, that's got to come out somewhere. Now, when he got going with John Mayall, the Cream and his own bands, I gradually got to see . . . maybe that shyness, that *reserve* in him as a young boy, was just waiting to come through in this way. 'Course, *he* calls it the blues, but I reckon it's something he's invented . . .'

Eric's mother, Pat, still cries when she hears him play. 'I love his blues sound,' she says. And she adds that she often thinks back as she hears him to the child she never brought up.

Reflecting today on his troubled childhood, Eric says the pain of those years has never left him. As with all great artists, it has been channelled into his creative output.

'I can clearly remember somehow knowing that Pat was my real mother, my natural mother. And when she came to see us in Ripley, back from Canada, I was nine. My first words to her were: "Can I call you Mum now?" So I must have known, in advance of her coming, that she was my own mother. I was excited about seeing this woman, see. And her response was: "No, I don't think you should. I think you ought to carry on calling Rose your mother, because she's the one who's been your mother and will carry on being."

'So I went from being very excited to being very confused. My education just went straight down the tubes. I couldn't go to school any more. I used to lie in bed and think up every kind of disease you can have, to stop having to go to school.

'At that point, I think some kind of barrier dropped down, whereby I swore that I was never going to trust anybody again. No one would ever be able to hurt me like that again. And that's been

In Richmond, aged sixteen

one of the moulding processes in my life . . . and it's a reason for my loneliness and my isolation right up until today.

'And I'm actually still struggling with it at this moment, to find out what I went through and whether or not I can ever redeem myself from that situation and become a normal human being.' He says that after his confused emotions arising from meeting his natural mother again at the age of nine, he 'remembers the affection for Rose coming back in dribs and drabs' in his late teens. 'But from the age of nine, until I was about sixteen or seventeen, I was really hateful towards everybody; very disappointed, unhappy and confused. It took a long time for me to be able to deal on a day-to-day level with my closest family.'

That explained his decision to pour himself into music. 'And also finding a way of making people love me for something that had nothing to do with family or roots or blood . . . but purely by what I did through music.'

He says his feelings towards his mother and his surrogate mother, Rose, are still tinged with problems and deep self-questioning.

'My relationships with Pat and Rose are still very confused. I have a great deal of loyalty towards Rose and a great deal of affection towards my natural mother, which hasn't really showed its true face yet. There is still to come a time when my mother and I will sit down and talk at length about what we feel towards one another. And discover how much it's based on illusion and fantasy. And then we'll be able to get a clearer picture of where my heart and my love really lie.'

3

THE
STAR

'We're the Cream . . . that's the name of the band'

'Where does it say,' asks Eric Clapton, 'that you should stay in one place, or with any band, for a long time? In my youth, and all my time as a player, my attitude has been: pack in as many different experiences as humanly possible . . .'

The true giants of popular music have always had fertility of thought, a quicksilver inclination to change courses in midstream, when their friends and fans least expect it. A deep-seated rootlessness, aggravated by his parents' absence and linked with his own desire for individuality, caused Clapton to embark on what was, in the mid-1960s, an unfashionable route. The quicker, easier path to glory as a performer was in one of the thousands of 'beat groups' whose biggest inspiration was the success of the Beatles.

True, the Rolling Stones flanked the Beatles-led revolution as a gritty, blues-based band. But they forfeited a lot of credibility as musicians through their heavy concentration on their looks, their image and – in John Lennon's immortal words – Mick Jagger's posture as the Charlie Chaplin of rock.

For Clapton, the field was wide open. He did not set out to be worshipped as a guitar hero, Britain's first and eventually the world's finest. But he was able to achieve and sustain the role in the turbulent 1960s, throughout the 1970s and even into the empty 1980s because music always came first, in his mind and in his body. In that ethic, he was unwittingly following the tradition of jazz musicians who thrived mainly because their diaries were full of gigs.

The jazz and blues world's backdrop had been the austerity of the 1940s. Eric, born a few weeks before the Second World War ended, was lucky to have the liberation and creativity of the 1950s and 1960s to help fuel his art.

The jazz and blues musicians who formed Eric's musical herit-age wore suits and ties. Their appearance was not part of their ap-peal; their music won the day. Clapton, born into a different era of artists, adopted a resonant style in his appearance which, during his vital period with John Mayall's Bluesbreakers, added greatly to his mystique.

Just as in music he proved to be something of a sponge – soaking up all the work of players of calibre – in fashion, too, Clapton lifted the most significant aspects from his peers. Bob Dylan had curly, frizzy hair, so Eric went and had his hair permed. King's Road, Chelsea, was the place to be seen and to absorb everything in the mid-1960s. So he made it his first home away from Ripley, and he had a flat there during his Cream period, almost a declaration of young independence. Military jackets were fashionable, so Eric was usually seen wearing a fresh one from his vast collection in different colours on most stage shows – spreading the trend among people who thought that if their 'God' Clapton wore one, it was essential for them. Even as a teenage drinker and sometime guitarist in Kingston while he was at art school, Eric had a reputation for clothes consciousness. He told astonished friends who would listen that he bought his jackets and ties in Shaftesbury Avenue, *London*, and that the best import records from the USA could be found at Dobell's in the Charing Cross Road.

His ballooning white bell-bottom trousers, purple shirts and sharp Italian boots made Eric one of the wildest-looking musicians of the psychedelic era, and later his friendship with the outlandishly dressed Jimi Hendrix was in keeping with his love of style.

'But then,' explains Steve Winwood, another close friend, 'art *is* self-indulgent. What Eric probably did, without realizing it, was transfer his art school background into his career as much as possible. He certainly always cared a lot about appearance from the first time I saw and met him.'

The Clapton of the psychedelic era moved, and spoke, boldly. His resignation from the Yardbirds, his move to the Mayall band 'because I could see integrity in its outlook', and his assertion of fashion consciousness, both on and off stage, marked him out to many players.

Winwood, whose magnificent voice powered the Spencer Davis Group of that period, struck up a friendship with him. Eric, he recalls, was by then rethinking the direction of his career. Win-wood's group, based in Birmingham and with its roots clearly in the rhythm-and-blues camp, played on the same bill as John Mayall at

Follow that, Van. Clapton seems bemused.

Newcastle-on-Tyne's Whiskey-A-Gogo club in 1966. Steve recalls being stunned by his first sight of the much-discussed Clapton on stage.

'There's no doubt that he was definitely something special, from that first moment I saw him. Very special. He had a finesse and artistry on display that no one else at that time, and since, could match. He had an energy. And I remember being struck by the fact that he wasn't particularly a technician.

'I later found, from working with him, that he is not a great student of the theory of music. But his knowledge of other people's music was always fantastic. We talked that first night a little, as young musicians do, asking about other players. He was a great instinctive musicologist – his knowledge of other people's music, especially black r & b, at that time, was enormous.'

As the two men spoke that night in Newcastle, it was clear that Winwood, too, distanced himself from the pop helter-skelter. Like Eric, he sought a career which swore allegiance to the music of black America. Clapton and Winwood agreed to keep in touch, perhaps already tacitly considering the possibility of working together.

'I visited him in London and I was living in digs when I came; Eric had very arty friends and this very arty flat in Covent Garden which I enjoyed going to for the conversation and red wine,' says Winwood. 'He was very much the existentialist at the time. Our only common ground, then and now, really, was music, but that rapport was terrific. We knew we ought to be working towards getting a band together because it was obvious, without either of us saying, that he was outgrowing John Mayall's band and I was looking for something to follow the Spencer Davis Group.'

Those were the rich days of 'sitting in', when musicians would enjoy drifting into another band's session and ad-libbing. The British bands that crusaded for rhythm-and-blues, including Georgie Fame's Blue Flames, Zoot Money's Big Roll Band, Manfred Mann, Alexis Korner's Blues Incorporated and The Graham Bond Organisation, provided the powder for the explosion in rock music ignited by the Cream. At all-night sessions at clubs like Soho's Marquee and Flamingo and the Zeeta in Putney, Eric enjoyed occasional sit-ins with the Spencer Davis Group and many other bands.

The camaraderie generated in the long bar of the Ship pub, in Soho's Wardour Street, increased the talk between musicians of who was good and genuine and who was awful. It was like a rock 'parish', and the moustached, slightly menacing figure of Clapton, by now renowned, was surrounded by admirers.

'Sitting in' helped shape rock history, but still a definite loyalty prevented much interchange of players between bands. 'People leaving groups in those days was a dirty trick,' Eric recalls. 'I don't think it was particularly dirty for me to quit the Yardbirds – I was attracted by the big pop thing at first, and success, and the travelling around and the little chicks! I was seventeen. But, later, when you work in a more serious musical band like Mayall's, you don't quit unless there's a really good reason.'

Steve Winwood continues the theme: 'The reason Eric and I didn't get together in the mid-sixties is because British musicians feel they are committed to their bands, whereas American players will mostly leave and join the next one almost on a whim and especially for money. I mean, I know so many American players who are playing in a band . . . and suddenly they're looking for something else to do.'

Clapton's timing, and rationale, had to be immaculate for a move from the hard-working and satisfying John Mayall Bluesbreakers. But 1966 was a year of great energy, inventiveness and excitement in the world of music and fashion. Eric, aware of this, knew his time with Mayall was limited. The band was well run by a regimental leader, but Clapton believed John's confines were too narrow to hold his own aspirations as a guitarist. 'I just wanted to get further than that band was going, which was in the Chicago blues field. I wanted to go somewhere else, you know . . . put my kind of guitar playing in a new kind of pop music context.' The vibrancy of the period was contagious: he saw broader horizons. While the blues would always be the core of his playing, he could see himself planting that seed within a wider style. A new kind of rock 'n' roll, with a strong blues bias, its potential audience far wider than the club world, perhaps with a nod towards high fashion, and certainly with fresh lyricism, was needed to absorb Eric's energy.

Among the sitters-in on the club scene was an exceptional Glaswegian double bass player with a mercurial temperament. His name was Jack Bruce and he also played harmonica and sang with a well-respected band, The Graham Bond Organisation. He passed the word on Eric's ability to the drummer in the Bond group. That band's great drummer, Ginger Baker, sat in with Mayall's band one night in June 1966. Baker had a faultless pedigree among musicians. Inspired by the jazz greats and in Britain by a prescient jazz drummer named Phil Seamen, Baker rated himself at least comparable with the giants of American jazz drumming (Buddy Rich and Elvin Jones). There was a problem: his Anglo-Irish temperament matched his demonic intensity. And Jack Bruce was not exactly a placid Scotsman. And with Clapton, never a malleable musician, increasing his reputation for moodiness if things went badly on stage, the trio did not at first sight look good bets for a long marriage.

Two forces drove them together to form Cream: their own ambition for adventure was the main reason. And big business clinched it.

The triumphs, the trials and the exceptional chemistry of Cream, and particularly Clapton's role within a band that proved to be a watershed in rock's history, are recalled by Jack Bruce. Today, the articulate, animated musician lives in Stuttgart, Germany, keeping impeccable musical company but content to play to audiences of a thousand.

A musical purist, he admires Eric's unique ability to combine adherence to his blues roots with a canny commercialism. That eye for self-projection, Bruce says, has never been one of *his* talents. But while he respects Clapton, relations between the two men are distant and cool.

Bruce is uniquely placed to paint a portrait of life within Cream. He sang and wrote many of the songs, and assumed the leadership, he says, in the recording studio. On stage, he declares, Eric Clapton was the unassailable leader, 'because he was simply very much *happening* as a player and as a person'. The fractious relationship between Bruce and Ginger Baker, whose personalities clashed, with Eric in the middle as a hapless, often tearful, victim, made life in this great band as electrifying off stage as it was on.

'Great memories – it was a very special kind of time. There was a *feeling* among all musicians drifting around then that hasn't come again. I don't think I was quite ready for it, but I would be now,' says Jack.

What Bruce describes as an 'accidental, organic' partnership that generated the Cream began in the most bizarre fashion.

Ginger Baker virtually ran The Graham Bond Organisation in which he and Jack Bruce were key members. The communication between them was musically compatible but in human terms disastrous. 'One night Ginger fired me from the Bond band,' says Jack. 'He said I didn't fit. But I defied him. I simply kept turning up to each gig, and this went on for weeks. I refused to be fired!

'The next time Ginger and I were on stage, with me technically fired, at Golders Green in London, his drums were too loud. I said "Shhhhhhhhh . . ." and he started throwing drum sticks at me, hitting me on the head. So I took my double bass, lifted it, and chucked it at him. That demolished that, and we were rolling around the stage fighting, and the audience was loving it. We punched the hell out of each other on that stage.'

Hair-conscious poses . . . Eric as he looked in 1967 during his earliest period in Cream (*London Features International*)

After that, Bruce concluded that he had indeed left the Graham Bond group. He went on to join the bands of Manfred Mann and then John Mayall. He turned up at the Ricky-Tick club in Windsor for a jam-session alongside Eric Clapton . . . and found the drummer in the band was Ginger Baker.

The night went well, musically, with Bruce and Baker calling a truce on past battles.

A few weeks later, Baker phoned Eric with the idea of forming a band. Clapton's reply was stunning to Baker: 'Well, yeah, okay, let's form a band,' said Eric. 'But only if Jack Bruce is in it.' He could not then have known, says Bruce today, 'that he had just mentioned Ginger's mortal enemy.'

Bruce and Baker decided to bury their hatchets. Here, after all, was the opportunity for a unit in which a superb bassist and an outstanding drummer pulled in the hottest, most talked-about guitarist in Britain.

If the whole idea was Ginger's, the surge of the band, the presence and the direction of it was shared by Clapton and Bruce, with Eric towering over them in personal magnetism. It was during his cynical period with Mayall, when he was poking fun at the leader's theatrics, that Clapton developed the spark that ignited the idea of forming his own band and which led to Cream.

'I first thought: well I can do this! You know, I can do what *he*'s doing. And when John Mayall let me sing one song on his album, I thought, I can sing as well . . . God, I should get my own band! Who shall I get? And while I was thinking about this, Ginger came to see a gig, when I was with John, and asked me if I'd be interested in forming a band with him. So I thought, well, Ginger's a good drummer, Jack had once played with John Mayall for a bit and we got on very well. So I thought – a blues trio! And I would be the slick, front man, the Buddy Guy type, a white Buddy Guy, the guy with the big suit, baggy trousers, doing straight blues. The other two would be the perfect back-up. And this was typical of me. I often have all these mad fantasies in force, but never say anything about them. I just imagine that it's going to work out that way – without me having to do anything or say anything. So I never did. When we had our first rehearsal, that just went completely out of the window and they took over. Jack brought in the songs that he'd written and I just had to go along with it. Because it was very interesting and because Jack's songs are so good and the combination of the musicians was interesting, I found that I let my idea take a back seat and actually die in the end. My fantasy probably wouldn't have been very good anyway at that stage in my proficiency. And so from there we went to the concept of playing mad music, wearing mad clothes and having a mad stage set and all that. That dissipated too, because the music itself and the dialogue took over and that became enough.'

Adrian Clapton recalls driving Eric in his Ford 8 to a John Mayall appearance at the Plaza, Guildford, in 1966. Afterwards, when they adjourned to the Prince of Wales pub nearby, Jack Bruce and Ginger Baker appeared to discuss with Eric the formation of a new band. The venue for the first rehearsal was agreed: in the front room of Ginger's house in Neasden, London.

There was some early wild, enthusiastic talk by Clapton of calling the band Sweet and Sour Rock 'n' Roll. But the clinching name was struck by Eric in Ginger's house during that first rehearsal. 'He just came right out with it,' recalls Jack Bruce.' "We're the Cream – that's the name of the band," he said, and we just said, yes. It was *right*. Eric always had this great knack for the right touch, the finishing gloss, if you like. I admire that in him. It has stayed right through his career.'

Clapton was faced, says Bruce, with an unsolvable dilemma. While the promise of good music was powerful, he was sandwiched between two men who fundamentally loathed each other. 'Ginger and I never got on, ever,' says Jack Bruce. 'But perhaps because of the very pain of our relationship, we were the hottest rhythm section I've ever played in, and I've played with the best since then. Name the top drummers in the world, and I've played with them all. And yet . . . there was something between Ginger and me that was a *fire* burning. He brought out some amazing stuff in me. And he is a wonderful drummer. If you have respect for someone as a player, you set out to impress them.

'That's how it was between the three of us. Eric, Ginger and I wanted to turn each other on. We weren't playing for the audience at all. That's always a big mistake, a trap so many bands fall into. The only good music is when good musicians play for each other – for yourself first, for the other musicians second. And if the audience are there, they're quite welcome to listen. That was my philosophy, still is, and I believe that's what made Cream so *different* from the other rock groups. It was like a jazz band playing in a rock setting. And that's what frightened Eric about it. He doesn't have the roots I have in jazz. He has his own, different roots, which I respect. But coming from jazz, I loved the accidents, the limitlessness, the improvisation of the music. I think that's precisely what ultimately turned Eric off the Cream.'

Jack Bruce remembers that shortly after they were launched, Eric said he was sure they would 'never make it' as a live band. They would do well in the studio, but never achieve their goals on stage. 'I don't think Eric ever thought of it as a good group, but he was right when he said it was two bands. He led on stage, me in the studio. But all the time, wherever we were, the atmosphere between Ginger and me made it impossible for Eric. So many times I'd have to go up to Eric and say: "Look, I'm sorry, it's no good, y'know, between Ginger and me." And he'd be in tears, or very, very down because of it.' The rows were musical as well as personal. 'Instrumentally, Ginger didn't have the vision to see what I was trying to do. Eric was caught in the crossfire. I remember Ginger shouting at me across the stage somewhere: "You're playing *too busy*." He couldn't see that in a three-piece band, with no keyboards player holding down the thing harmonically amd melodically, it was up to someone like me to do that. What has since become normal was being done by me in Cream. Ginger couldn't see that then. It was difficult, and not surprising that it created terrific tension.

'Once, in Copenhagen, we were in the car going to a gig from the airport and Eric actually burst into tears because of the slanging match between me and Ginger. It was impossible.' During another gig, Jack Bruce actually ran away. 'We used to travel around with very little equipment in America, and being the main singer I found it a great strain on the voice if there wasn't an adequate public address system. At one baseball stadium I said to Ginger: "Look, we've been given a hundred watts for the guitar, a hundred watts for the bass, and a hundred watts for the p.a." Nothing was miked in those days. I asked Ginger to get it improved but he just said: "No, we're not gonna do that." And I just got a taxi to the airport and bought a ticket. The roadies caught up with me and dragged me back, my feet not touching the ground. I was sitting waiting for the plane to take off and I went back. The sound was awful. You can imagine the atmosphere when I returned. But all these problems were part of Cream.'

The band took flight in the days before sophisticated sound systems enveloped rock and later gave birth to heavy metal. 'We were overworked in bad conditions with very often inadequate equipment, and the relationship between Ginger and me was one of constant bickering and dislike. It's a miracle that so much good music came out of Cream . . . but perhaps that's one of the reasons it did,' says Jack Bruce.

News of the formation of Cream, exclusively reported in the *Melody Maker* in a mere three-paragraph story on 11 June 1966, did not capture the imagination of the frenzied world of pop. The rhythm-

and-blues scene watched expectantly as Clapton, the 'musician's musician', as he was now called, made yet another interesting move.

This was a month before the group's second rehearsal, in a church hall in Putney, southwest London. There was no indication of the band's name yet and the news of the launch of the band read like this:

> A sensational new 'groups' group' starring Eric Clapton, Jack Bruce and Ginger Baker is being formed. Top groups will be losing star instrumentalists as a result.
>
> Manfred Mann will lose bassist, harmonica player, pianist and singer Jack Bruce; John Mayall will lose brilliant blues guitarist Eric Clapton; and Graham Bond's Organisation will lose incredible drummer Ginger Baker.
>
> The group say they hope to start playing at clubs, ballrooms and theatres in a month's time. It is expected they will remain as a trio with Jack as featured vocalist.

In the week of that news, Frank Sinatra was at the top of the record charts with 'Strangers in the Night', and the pop world was still gripped by the Beatles and the Stones.

One man, though, reacted to the news with astonished delight. Up in north London, now heavily into wood carving and blissfully departed from the music world, Eric's warm friend from his first band, the Roosters, Ben Palmer, read the newspaper story with interest. 'Ah God, Clappers is starting a band!' he said to himself. 'This might be good.' Palmer mused that Eric had been unhappy with the Yardbirds, Brian Jones was dissatisfied with the musical route of the Stones, and Palmer didn't care for Eric's work in the Mayall band. With company like Bruce and Baker, though, Palmer thought there might be better prospects.

He phoned Eric: 'If you ever need someone to do some driving, I'd quite like that.' Clapton arranged for his old friend to meet Robert Stigwood, the manager of Cream. Stigwood was concerned. 'Do you feel you can do this? I have to be sure you're serious, because I've invested a lot of money in this band . . .' Palmer, believing that to be appointed a 'roadie' meant simply driving the band around, said yes, of course he could do whatever was needed.

'I must have impressed Stig enormously as a confident, competent road manager. In fact, I had no idea what was involved. Eric didn't think about it beyond the driving. He told Stig there was "absolutely nothing to worry about" with me.' So began the initial Cream shows, for what was then the exorbitant fee of £400 a show. But a big shock awaited Ben Palmer when he drove the three men, all feeling on the crest of a new life, up the motorway in the black Austin Princess for their first public appearance. Joyful and optimistic, they played records on the small car record player bought by Jack, and sang as the car headed to Manchester for the gig at the city's Twisted Wheel Club. Ben Palmer takes up the story.

'I parked the car at the back of the club and Eric, Jack and Ginger went in. I went off to the nearest pub. I thought I'd give them an hour and pop back to see how they sounded. I went back an hour later and all the amplifiers were still in the car. Ginger said: "You've been a long time. Is it all ready?" I asked him what he was on about. I said I'd not been long, just for a drink. "But you're the bloody *roadie*. You're supposed to set up our gear," boomed Ginger. I told him I hadn't a clue how to do it. I was totally out of my depth. I expected a fiver in my pocket for driving them, and "see you next week". I hadn't realized what I was taking on, having to build amplification equipment into a kind of architectural finish! I mean, in the Roosters we used to put everything through two 30-watt amps which we carried like suitcases. This was something else.'

But when Palmer got involved in it, he became thrilled with the pioneering aspect of Cream. He learned to do the job properly, went on their first US tour and many others, and sealed a brotherly friendship with Eric.

There has never been a band with so much *gristle*, says Ben Palmer. And if anybody ever *stretched* Clapton as a musician, it was Bruce. 'On those long Cream numbers, when each played a solo, sort of answering each other over a period of threequarters of an hour, Eric was pushed by Jack as far as anybody pushed him. If Jack is bitter, it's because of the way his life has been. I don't think it's traceable to a jealousy of Eric. Jack's too big for that,' says Palmer.

Bruce, unstinting in his admiration of Eric, says he not only liked Eric, 'I *loved* him in the early days.' His memories of their great days of personal and musical brotherhood are punctuated by flashes of insight into Eric's make-up. He might not have realized it at the time, but Clapton was even then a rare survivor. Bruce remembers going with Eric to witness the squalor and horror of the youth of America high on acid in Haight-Ashbury, San Francisco, in 1967; he recalls the bleak look on Eric's face when Eric said to him what he still believes today: 'Black musicians start things . . . and white musicians make money out of it.'

'Eric is fortunate,' Bruce ponders. 'He's blessed with a realization, a vision, of what's going to be commercially acceptable, on his level. But it's still musically good, which is why he feels okay about it.

Eric with Ginger and Jack at the start of Cream's meteoric rise (*London Features International*)

That's a very special touch, which I don't have. When I write songs, say even "Sunshine of Your Love", it never crosses my mind to relate it to commercial possibilities. Eric does, and I admire that. But in Cream we were doing fresh things and I've continued to do so, playing with the world's finest musicians. The difference between us is that Eric records and I don't any more . . . but his new stuff is just pleasant middle-of-the-road music.'

Chaotic, turbulent and exhausting though Cream was, it was a vital period for Clapton. As a group, they broke barriers, and were a significant part of the change in emphasis in popular music records from singles to albums. They made musicianship hip. But for Eric, above all, they saved him from the stagnation he felt in a Britain where there seemed little future.

'I was a loner when I reflected that America was the only place I could go to get anywhere,' Eric said immediately after joining Cream. 'I was really out on my own at the time, mentally. Now I'm with a band I really dig, I don't want to go to America – other than to see the place and find out what's happening.

'My whole musical outlook has changed. I listen to the same sounds and records but with a different ear.' And, in a telling commentary on his own view of himself as an emergent star: 'I'm trying to listen from a listener's point of view. Whereas before, I'd always put myself in the guitarist's place, I now think it's the overall effect I must listen to.

'I'm no longer trying to play anything other than like a white man. The time is overdue: people should play like they are and what colour they are.

'I don't believe I've ever played so well in my life. More is expected of me in the Cream. I have to play rhythm guitar as well as lead. People have been saying I'm like Pete Townshend – but he doesn't play much lead!

'A lot of biased listeners say that all we are playing is pop numbers. In actual fact, closer listening reveals that none of us are playing anything that vaguely resembles pop, although it might sound deceptively like that.

' "Wrapping Paper" is an excuse for a twelve-bar blues. That's all it is – a good tune, very commercial, with the sort of feel that represents *us*. We do exploit this kind of feeling, but we retain the beaty feel as well, all the time we play. Although we might play a number very loudly, and it might appear violent, in fact the tune and lyrics are very sweet.'

How did Eric think, at the birth of the group, that audiences would accept Cream? 'I don't believe we'll ever get over to them. People will always listen with biased ears, look through unbelieving eyes, and with preconceived ideas, remembering us individually as we used to be. The only way to combat this is to present them with as many facets of our music as possible.

'Some people might come to see Ginger, or to hear Jack's singing, or to look at the clothes I wear! Therefore we have to please them all – we have to *do everybody in.*'

Here, indeed, was a new Clapton talking. The air now filled, if not with compromise, with an awareness that a delicate tightrope could, and should, be walked to reach out for audience recognition – while not pawning any musical values.

Asked whether he felt in a period of transition, he said, three months after the formation of Cream: 'Sure, I've changed. Jack Bruce has had a tremendous influence on my playing – and my personality. It's a lot easier to play in a blues band than in a group like this, where you've got to play purely your own individual ideas. You have got to put over a completely new kind of music. This needs a different image.

'Jack, Ginger and I have absorbed a lot of music and now we're trying to produce our own music. This naturally incorporates a lot of ideas we've heard, and we've all had. It's hard. It's original. It's satisfying. And it's worthwhile.'

'Blues Ancient and Modern', as Eric Clapton described Cream after a mere three days of rehearsal, had their first major debut in daylight the day after the club warm-up in Manchester. It was in pouring rain at the open-air sixth National Jazz and Blues Festival at Windsor on 3 July 1966.

The audience response was enthusiastic but not ecstatic. Among musicians, the vibrations were cynical. Three musicians with a very high pedigree were getting more advance publicity than many bands who had demonstrated their popularity to audiences throughout Britain; there was also great envy of the machinery surrounding Cream, fuelled by the entrepreneurial Robert Stigwood as manager and mentor.

Against that backdrop, and with the players clearly nervous, the debut was a qualified success. Their extemporizing solo work, and Jack's affinity with jazz, scored with a crowd which applauded the improvisational 'feel'.

Eric enjoyed the vigour of it all but privately believed that British audiences would never warm to the Cream. America beckoned, but not before the tenacity of the band was tested. For several months the

trio achieved a chemical togetherness, travelling up and down
Britain's first motorway, the M1, and learning the hard way. The
business artillery behind Cream, however, had its sights firmly set
on the US. In planning its exhausting schedule, there was a big ace:
the three players, though still all in their twenties, were hardened
veterans of the London club scene, revelling in all-night sessions.
Little did they realize what gruelling days lay ahead.

The Clapton of the Cream period hardly smoked and never drank
excessively. Both came later with a vengeance typical of his obsessiveness. Had he indulged himself during Cream days he would
never have survived the punishing schedules that awaited the band
in the US.

For young British musicians like these three, America was literally
the promised land at that time. It was the birthplace of their
inspiration, and Eric's spiritual Mecca. But the schedule that awaited
Cream when they stepped off the plane in New York in April 1967
was more suited to a circus act than to three musicians seeking to
extend their credibility.

The zany New York disc jockey Murray the K hosted a show at the
RKO Theater on 58th Street and Third Avenue. In this non-stop,
fast-talking, fast-moving affair, the curtain went up at 10 a.m. each
day. Each of several acts did just one song, in five shows a day.
Cream were among the acts paraded by a beaming Murray the K to
undiscriminating audiences: thirteen-year-old schoolchildren on
holiday formed the morning audiences, empty seats the afternoon,
and adults in the evenings. Murray the K's 'Fifth Dimensional Show',
so named because it ran five times each day, was perhaps the most
soul-destroying show imaginable for a group hoping to break a pop
image and the treadmill of chart-based performances.

The Who, with whom Eric struck up a firm friendship, were also
on the bill alongside Mitch Ryder and the Detroit Wheels, Wilson
Pickett, Simon and Garfunkel, the Blues Project, and Jan and Dean.
There were dancing girls and a daily film show on surfing. But Pete
Townshend remembers being jealous, underneath his bonhomie, at
Cream's rocket to popularity; he resented their 'overnight stardom'
compared with the Who's three-year slog to success.

Cream and the Who had one thing in common, though: they
became totally disillusioned, especially when Murray the K said he
could not pay the acts because he had lost £27,000 on the week. 'He
hadn't bargained for our casual English approach and expected us to
be leaping around doing a James Brown thing,' says Eric. 'It just
wasn't our show.

'The best moment came when we had these fourteen-pound bags of flour and eggs we were going to use on stage on our last night. But Murray the K heard about it and said we wouldn't get paid if we did. So instead we spread them all round the dressing rooms. Pete Townshend ended up swimming round in his dressing room, fully clothed, in a foot of water when his shower overflowed!

'We took the actual show as a joke. There was no chance for Ginger to play his solo, and we had to use the Who's equipment because we couldn't take any with us – there was none provided, as usual.

'The best musical times we had were in Greenwich Village. It was like an English Musical Appreciation Society. I sat in with a couple of the Mothers of Invention and Mitch Ryder at the Café Au Go-Go where Jimi Hendrix used to play. I liked the Village the most. The shops stay open all night! I made a lot of friends there, including Al Kooper who played on a lot of Bob Dylan tracks.' Life as a freewheeling musician, jamming and taking in the communal atmosphere of New York, made a big impression on Eric.

'New York's incredible,' he said while he was there. 'I'd love to live here. Everybody is so much more hip to the music scene. My taxi driver talked to me about James Brown! Can you imagine that happening in London?'

If the New York shows were a fiasco, San Francisco proved the turning point for Cream. The world capital of the hippie philosophy was uniquely prepared in 1967 for their kind of freewheeling rock. Like much of the West Coast sound, Cream's music, with its long, headstrong solos and assertion of individuality, proved the perfect backdrop for the marijuana smokers in the audience.

A major factor in helping the Cream to happen in San Francisco was the far-sighted promoter Bill Graham. Eric told him they felt frustrated at not getting enough time to 'build' in their work. Graham's calculated gamble, knowing his audience would be enthralled anyway at having Britain's top guitarist on stage, gave Cream carte blanche to have an 'open-ended' programme. 'Go on and play and do it your way,' said Bill Graham, the first promoter to show such vision. 'If you want to play "Spoonful" from night until dawn, do it. We've never done it before. We'll see what happens.'

For the next two weeks at the Fillmore, crowds went wildly enthusiastic. The good vibrations were contagious, wafting back to Britain where the Cream had scarcely had time to make much impact. At the end of it, Eric intoned: 'England could use a little more maturity. In San Francisco there is more encouragement and less competition from musician to musician. The scene in London thrives wildly, often because everyone is jealous of someone else's success.

In the States you are encouraged. Everyone digs everyone else and they don't try to hide it. It seems the English market has been bred on immaturity. What they could learn from San Francisco is to be open-minded to what's *not* Top Forty, and grow up a little.'

He loved San Francisco audiences, 'the best anywhere. They're so obviously critical. Every little move you make, every note you play, is being noticed, devoured, accepted or rejected. You know you have to do it right. You do your best because they know if you don't.'

'We seem to be a lot more popular in San Francisco than I'd imagined. I knew the Cream had been heard of through the underground scene but I didn't imagine we'd be this popular.'

Cream played on the same bill as Paul Butterfield's Blues Band and another band Eric rated very highly, Mike Bloomfield's Electric Flag. 'It's amazing that a band like Butterfield's can go to England and just die,' Clapton observed. 'It's not like that here, not competitive and jealous. I think English musicians are afraid that American music is too far ahead of them.'

The spirit of West Coast music and the philosophy of the players deeply moved Eric. When he heard that the Grateful Dead were playing a series of shows for nothing, he remarked: 'I'd never heard of anyone doing that ever before. It really is one of the finest steps ever taken in music. What the Grateful Dead are doing sums up what I think about San Francisco. There's an incredible thing that the music people have towards their audience – they want to *give*.'

After the Fillmore, the Cream went on a gruelling coast-to-coast US tour lasting twelve weeks. Although nothing equalled the San Francisco experience, they were swept along on a tidal wave of popularity and respect; there were standing ovations in many cities. And back in London, where word spread that Britain had sent America a trendsetting band, readers of the *Melody Maker*, in their annual popularity poll, voted Eric Musician of the Year. Clapton ruminated that he had entered Cream as a blues guitarist and inside it he became a rock 'n' roller. He was not sure about the desirability of that, but was intoxicated by his success.

Cream returned home, triumphant. But, very ironically, they were so successful that there was nowhere they could comfortably play in Britain. The burgeoning campus concert circuit could not afford them; the clubs were far too small to hold a band with such a reputation – a club booking would disappoint many more fans than it would please. The band was at a critical crossroads. And they were increasingly at loggerheads. On several concert dates, the three men actually did not speak to each other, but just played and went their separate ways afterwards. At one Wembley show, Jack Bruce left midway through the show, and Eric and Ginger completed it. Now, the three insisted on travelling separately and staying not merely on separate floors in their hotels, but in three different *hotels*. They met up five minutes before the show, in the dressing room. The end of Cream was on the horizon.

They went off on a European tour, and their hit singles, 'I Feel Free' and 'Strange Brew', and best-selling albums, *Disraeli Gears* and *Wheels of Fire*, had given them great self-confidence. The public saw a band on a perpetual adventure, apparently finely balanced, too: Jack's soulful singing and harmonica wailing, Ginger's explosive drum solos and Clapton's shimmering solo work on tunes like 'Steppin' Out'. But that title was more accurate than anyone could have known at the time: the band that promised so much was indeed stepping out from itself. It was difficult enough to adapt to hit singles, adulation and big money but the non-stop aggravation of battling personalities clinched the decision to find a way out.

Clapton was the first to want a split. 'I've had enough. I'm leaving,' he would say to manager Robert Stigwood, in person and by telephone, on many occasions. Eric's irritation at the acrimony within the band, the constant bickering between Bruce and Baker, reached a peak in Europe. But Stigwood always managed to paper over the cracks and repair the problem temporarily. Cream were, after all, a vital backbone of his show-business empire. He needed the money they were generating to subsidize his investment in other long-term properties, like the Bee Gees.

In personal terms, too, Eric was changing. Uncharacteristically, he allowed the rapid fame to seduce him into behaving like a pop star, almost crossing the division between musician and idol. With his ever-present shades, monstrous collection of fashion rings around every finger, leather jackets, colourful shirts and menacing, drooping moustache, he now lived in a rambling studio in the King's Road with his girlfriend Charlotte Martin, a model, amid an 'artistic commune' which included Martin Sharp of the London 'underground' magazine *Oz*.

Says Eric: 'I remember thinking the music wasn't going anywhere. We were just ad-libbing all the time, not planning any changes. It first hit me when I heard The Band's album, *Music From Big Pink*. I realized we were already out of date and there was no way of trying to get the other two to move forward. I thought, if only we had a keyboard player, or could play a bit differently. What I should have been was more satisfied with what we had, instead of wishing for more of other influences. It was incredibly difficult. I felt I wanted to change Cream but it wasn't up to me. I wasn't the leader of the band

and I didn't know how to change it even if I could persuade Jack and Ginger. I was frustrated. That's why I faced up to a split.'

The non-stop verbal lashings between the other two finally clinched it. 'Their anger was so vicious. I'd never experienced any words like it. It never reached blows in my presence, but the language, the venom was so powerful that it would reduce anyone to tears.' During a European trip, Eric was, in fact, tearful about the friction. 'I was a stripling of a lad, remember. It really got to me. This was a big band going out of anybody's control. Between Jack and Ginger, it was pure love-hate.'

What probably also lay at the root of Eric's discomfort in Cream were the utterly different musical backgrounds from which the three men sprang. Jack Bruce, born on 14 May 1943, was a multi-instrumentalist, an ex-student of the Royal Scottish Academy of Music, who went to London in 1962 as a capable cellist, electric and upright bassist, harmonica and piano player. He became immersed in the thriving blues and jazz scene, playing with Alexis Korner's famed Blues Incorporated and The Graham Bond Organisation before impressing Clapton in John Mayall's band.

Peter 'Ginger' Baker had a similarly structured background in a world of music more 'legitimate' than the casual beginnings of Eric Clapton. Born in Lewisham, London, on 19 August 1939, Ginger had begun as a fourteen-year-old trumpeter with the Air Cadets. Two years later he had transferred his allegiance to drums and then moved through several prominent traditional jazz bands in London – the Storyville Jazzmen, Acker Bilk's Paramount Jazz Band and Terry Lightfoot's Jazzmen – before spreading his wings into modern jazz and the blues. For a period, he was the resident drummer at Ronnie Scott's world-famous Soho jazz club.

Having renounced the Yardbirds for their brazen commercialism, Eric believed that with two mature colleagues he need have no fears. But he reckoned without the reality of the music business: despite Cream's visual and musical trendiness – they were, like their friend Jimi Hendrix, pioneers of psychedelic fashion – Cream were quickly under great pressure to make a hit single. Jack Bruce and his lyricist partner Pete Brown, who were together to write some of Cream's best songs, came up with 'Wrapping Paper', a superficial if catchy effort which did not reflect the band's real style. Nevertheless, it reached number 34 in the British charts, and was followed by the more aggressive 'I Feel Free', on which Eric dominated with a vibrant solo indicative of what was to come. That single rose to number 11 in the British charts.

The singles, and their success, were only remarkable because they

Above: Cream posing in their manager's office just before their split in late 1968 (*London Features International*)
Below: With a cluster of rings and a keen sense of psychedelic fashion, this is Eric in 1967 (*Barry Wentzell/ Melody Maker*)

were the work of true musicians, rather than conveyor-belt pop stars. They were, however, perfect curtain raisers for Cream's debut album, which appeared on manager Robert Stigwood's new Reaction label. *Fresh Cream* proved a resoundingly triumphant statement, soaring up the British album charts to number 6 in January 1967, a stimulating promise from this band of future anthems for the counter-culture of hippie philosophies.

With two hit singles and a much acclaimed debut album, events now moved rapidly for Cream during that heady flower-power year of 1967. They went to America for the Murray the K concert season, and while there recorded some tracks for their second album, *Disraeli Gears* (the title was again Eric's, a stream-of-consciousness notion gleaned from a cyclist who boasted to him about his machine's uniqueness). The American tour that year was immaculately timed for the turned-on generation, the flowing solos allowing Cream's heavily stoned audiences to turn off their minds, relax and float downstream. The band were not ready for the tumult but their egos were handsomely fed at last.

By the autumn, with the release of that second album, the warring factions within the trio were already simmering, but such was their momentum that they knew they had a band that was perfect for its time. Martin Sharp, Eric's Chelsea flatmate, who had designed much of the controversial magazine *Oz*, gave the cover of *Disraeli Gears* such a stunning psychedelic impact that it might serve for ever as Cream's most telling memento: a glorious fusion of pink, turquoise and green imagery, with peacocks symbolically preening beneath the cut-out faces of Baker, Bruce and Clapton. Musically, the album was equally urgent, featuring 'Strange Brew' (their third single, which had been a moderate hit) and 'Tales of Brave Ulysses', which Eric co-wrote with Martin Sharp. Also on the record was 'Sunshine of Your Love'. It was the clincher for a band who had soared so quickly, and went into the top five in both the American and British album charts.

But as that year of achievement neared its end, it was obvious to Eric that, despite some fine gigs, Cream could not continue. Of Jack and Ginger, he says now: 'I was outside them. They couldn't agree on *anything*. The vibe was horrible. It had even begun at the very first rehearsal, where I thought up the name. We weren't rehearsing, just *talking* about the rehearsal, when it turned out that Ginger had leaked the news of the band's formation to a newspaper. Jack flew off the handle. They were into one another's throats at that first meeting.'

Eric's first public sign of disenchantment and frustration came when he announced that Cream would not make any more single records. 'The main reason is that we are very anti the whole commercial market,' he told the *Melody Maker*. 'The whole nature of the single-making process has caused us grief in the studios. I'm a great believer in the theory that singles will become obsolete and LPs will take their place; singles are an anachronism.

'To get any good music in a space of two or three minutes requires working to a formula, and that part of the pop scene leaves me cold. I hate all the rushing around, trying to get a hit. As long as the pop scene is geared to singles a lot of people will be making bread who shouldn't be making bread.'

It was at that point, he says, that he finally sat down and said to himself: 'Okay, I own up. I am Eric Clapton, a guitar player, and now I'll just stop mucking about and make my career under my own name.' The idealism of the musician would remain, but the belief that he could submerge his stance into that of a sideman would have to disappear from his thoughts.

'We were fighting success, but it happened against our will. It really did. We were desperately trying to be jazz musicians and lived that life and role. I fought success because I could see the traps and pitfalls. When Cream became acknowledged as virtuosos, that's when the rot set in, because *we* started to believe it, and became very cynical about success.' It had to end, he declares.

Musically, he enjoyed it while it lasted. 'It worked like a jazz group. We started with a theme and improvised on it, and because there were only three people, as long as we got back to the same place in the tune at the same time, it was okay. You can't do that in a band structure where there are more than three people. So it worked pretty well and we all bounced off each other on stage in an interesting way.

'But we worked too hard and we didn't get a chance to sit and reflect on where we were going or what we could do to change, to keep up with what was happening, musically, outside us. We were cocooned, on the road for seven months of the year just doing the same old stuff. We were still improvising, but in a repetitive way. Towards the end of Cream's life, there was a great revolution taking place, led by The Band. And when we all opened our eyes to that, we found ourselves miles off course. And we made the *Goodbye* album by Cream with all of us trying to establish a new face for the group. By then it was too late.'

He remembers Cream with both affection and regret. 'It was very intense. I don't meet many people with that kind of intensity any more, with that serious musical intention.' In February 1985 he once again met Pete Brown, who had written many of Cream's song lyrics. 'I hadn't seen Pete for fifteen years, and it really struck home how much I missed those days.'

On Christmas Eve, 1967, Eric, Jack and Ginger trailed wearily back into Heathrow Airport, London, after another tiring American tour. They were hardly speaking to each other, so dismal had been their relationship. Although they had many commitments, including a return to Chicago just after Christmas, the band was doomed. 'It was,' says Eric, 'just a question of how and when we could split, not whether we should do it.'

Musically and personally, Eric felt at sea. The band had lost direction. The route taken in the company of Bruce and Baker had strayed too far from what Eric regarded as his natural blues playing. 'I got really hung up. I tried to write pure pop songs and create a pop image. It was a shame because I was not being true to myself. I am, and always will be, a blues guitarist.' The same warning bells that rang in his ear when he walked out of the Yardbirds, astonishingly only two years earlier, now pulled Eric back from the precipice of musical dishonesty.

Cream had peaked in San Francisco, he declared. 'From then on, we all went on such huge ego trips.' Making it so big in the States had proved 'a big bang in the head'. The three men were exhausted, he said, and needed privacy and independence from each other. 'I want to perform contemporary blues. With the Cream, solos were the thing, but I'm really off that virtuoso kick. It was all overexposed. We died the death from playing too much.'

They had also become a money-making machine, selling millions of records and catapulting the three men into a lifestyle hitherto undreamed of. Their final six-week American tour, which began in October 1968, earned the trio $650,000. Around the world Eric in particular was discussed by all other musicians with almost hushed reverence. He struck up a promising partnership with George Harrison. The Beatles had stopped touring and George was busy producing albums by such fine artists as Jackie Lomax for the Beatles' idealistic Apple label. Eric played guitar on that session, and even played on one of Harrison's Beatles songs.

In the post-psychedelic haze of London, 1968, a new breed of confident musicians had emerged. The survivors of the pop explosion that had erupted five years earlier had absorbed the rich tapestry of sounds that had come from America. Clapton loved the raw, fiery energy and bluesy feel of Jimi Hendrix and even admired his gimmickry, like playing guitar with his teeth. From America's

West Coast, the rock revolution had thrown up a fascinating cross-section of styles and players who interested Eric and opened his mind to new formulae of bands: the Mothers of Invention, the Grateful Dead, Buffalo Springfield and the Lovin' Spoonful. Cream had been singing 'I Feel Free'. Now Eric intended to implement the phrase.

Attempts by manager Robert Stigwood to keep the group together failed. Said Eric: 'Our management have come to realize that unless we are allowed to do what we want to, we can kick up a bigger stink about it than them.' The farewell concert at London's Royal Albert Hall on 26 November 1968 sold out all seats within two hours and a second performance was added. As they played, Jimi Hendrix went on television to say Cream's farewell was a sad day for rock 'n' roll; he dedicated a song to Eric, Jack and Ginger.

In a highly emotional send-off, fans climbed on to the stage and showered Eric in confetti. They played three encores, and their programme favourites like 'White Room', 'I'm So Glad', 'Sitting on Top of the World', 'Crossroads', 'Toad', 'Sunshine of Your Love' and 'Steppin' Out'. And the meteorite that was Cream had fallen to earth. Few bands had combined such innovative music with the role of signposting rock's future.

But Eric was pleased it was over. His reputation as a guitarist and as an intelligent songwriter was now legendary. The security of a lot of money gave him the cushion of freedom. And his appetite was whetted for new ventures.

If the Beatles had dragged pop out of the fifties, then Cream had progressed it into the sixties and beyond and were instrumental in changing serious music fans' thoughts from pap and singles into imaginative solos and albums.

The memory of Cream is strong enough with Eric, but for millions, particularly in America where their impact was colossal, he will for ever be remembered as part of the trio, just as Paul McCartney will always be 'ex-Beatle'. Eric has mixed feelings about the historic aspects of it, and living with it is a millstone around his neck.

'I look at it both ways. Looking back, I really enjoyed it and saw a great deal of life during those three years. I met great musicians and learned a lot. On the other hand, we started a ball rolling which I don't like being responsible for – people say we started the heavy metal thing, which is quite an indictment!

'But Cream *had* to fizzle out. It was the first time I'd felt really disappointed, though. I had been glad to be out of the Yardbirds situation, with John Mayall I'd been pleased to be moving on to something new. With Cream, at the time I felt disillusioned. I felt then that I'd wasted three years. I now know better, but at the time I was down.

'There were times when I felt like I had the right direction, but I never felt confident enough to take the initiative from the other two, because their musicianship was more experienced. In Jack's case, and Ginger's too, to a certain extent, they had a wider scope. They had played jazz for money, you know, they had literally *done it* on the road. I felt that maybe they were more entitled to know what was right and wrong. But if we were going to do a blues song, then I felt pretty confident, I knew how to do it. So there was the introduction of material too that I would be responsible for. But other than that, I wouldn't tell them how to try to play. I'd have to leave it to them.' Cream certainly did not prepare him at all for bandleading.

To Eric, Cream seemed to last for an eternity. He quickly tired of the role of mediator preventing Bruce and Baker from fighting. 'I managed to be in the middle of them and my mellowness, my delicacy in some of the situations, probably stopped them from actually tearing one another to pieces. It might have been because of their concern for me, or because I was the youngest of the band. And I was also helping to make the band. They didn't want to lose me. At first, I had a great time. It was only towards the end that I started seeing the faults as being a reason for ending the band.'

Eric's verdict on the musical frustration that forced the end, as well as the bad chemistry, is succinct. 'Instead of growing, we used the same material on those long tours. We played the same stuff over and over again and really worked ourselves into a hole embellishing it all. And that, in the end, becomes very hollow. There was no core left at the end of it. We were just empty.

'There were a lot of telephone conversations taking place, transatlantic, with Robert Stigwood. We were all calling him for different reasons. Jack was calling him because of Ginger, Ginger was calling him because of Jack and I was calling him because of both of the other two! I was getting the most favour from Stigwood. He was saying in so many words, "You're the one I pick. So if you don't like it with them any more, don't worry, I'll look after you. I'll take care of them later. But you've got big things ahead of you, so if you want to break the band up, don't worry about it, because we can go somewhere else." I was getting a lot of strength from that dialogue, enough strength, probably, to break the band up!

'We all loved one another in a way. That's the heavy thing! If you put the three of us together now, the same things would happen. That's why we live so far away from one another, probably. I remember having a reunion with Jack and Ginger in the mid-

Above: London's Royal Albert Hall in November, 1968. The occasion was Cream's farewell concert (*Barry Plummer*)
Below: Towards the end of Cream's life, Jack, a sheepskin-coated Clapton and Ginger play aboard a float during a Scandinavian tour in 1968 (*Jan Persson*)

seventies at my home. The three of us met in London in the office by accident and tore the place apart and came back to my house flying – really flying – on cloud nine. Took acid and just started talking. It was a summer's day, people were arriving – like they sometimes do in a country house – and we were out there, sitting on that terrace, in chairs, facing the same way, the three of us, almost as if we were expecting people to come. And people were arriving and sort of walking round the corner, down round the side of the house, walking round there and stopping, as if they were approaching a *court*. And this buzz was coming off of us. Ginger would get up and address whoever it was. It was amazing, just bizarre, and the three of us were like a unit like that. One of us would take care of one angle, one would take care of another angle, one would address the remainder. It could happen again. If you put the three of us in a room, we would immediately find our level and function on it perfectly. Very strange. We haven't changed that much. Jack's still basically the same, Ginger's still basically the same and I'm still basically the same. Those two fought like dogs, but the triangle made it work.'

While Cream were disintegrating, it occurred to Eric that if they added a keyboard player they might be able to reassess their musical outlook, and perhaps continue with a fresh approach that would also curb the clashes of personality within the band. 'That person, to me, was Steve Winwood. I thought if he joined Cream, it would be great, so I went looking for Steve after Cream broke up. And we hung out in each other's houses for several months, playing together and having a good time. Then Ginger joined and we looked for a bass player, and suddenly we were taking ourselves too seriously. We were nudged into the studio, nudged on to the road, and I nudged out when I saw Delaney and Bonnie. I was slipping out of the back door, really.' Looking back, he saw that decision as consistent with everything he had done up to that point.

'I'd left the Yardbirds because of success, and Cream ended as a direct result of its false success, or what appeared to me to be a hypocritical form of success. So with Blind Faith I wanted no more to do with success. I wanted to be accepted as a musician. Derek and the Dominos was what that was all about. We went on tours of England when nobody knew who we were. We played to punters who came to see what they thought was probably a local band. And it was great, because they were knocked out by the fact that we were good. We had no expectations to live up to, and no trappings. So that succeeded for a while.' But he says that because some members of the

Dominos were 'younger than me and from the hills of America', the money went to their heads 'and that all went wrong. It's the same old story . . .'

In the prelude to Cream's split, Eric had met Steve Winwood several times. Then part of a successful band, Traffic, Steve and Eric exchanged confidences: there were deep-rooted personal and music-al differences within each man's band. 'Neither of us believed the difficulties could be resolved,' recalls Winwood. 'We both knew Cream and Traffic would split. One day, Eric came down to the house in Berkshire where I was living and we had a play. I said it would be nice to try to get back to the old feeling when he jammed in my first group, the Spencer Davis Group. He said: "Yeah, I think we should form a band." And that was it. It had been a long time coming; we both hoped we'd be free of our bands one day and it happened naturally.'

Winwood says that Clapton described Cream to him that day as 'too self-indulgent'. He believed they had strayed too far into the area of jazz-rock. He wanted to play more *songs* rather than leave each player virtually undisciplined. Only three months after Cream's farewell concert, by February 1969, Eric and Steve had agreed to partly form the new band. 'Eric named it Blind Faith because that's exactly what he had in the project,' recalls Winwood.

The first idea was to be a trio, like Cream. Just as the two founders of Blind Faith were casting around for a likely player, Ginger Baker arrived at Winwood's house. 'You need a drummer,' he said. 'Look, I can play pretty good. There aren't many people who can play better than me.' Clapton was now in a quandary. True, Baker was a majestic drummer. But he didn't want him in his new band. As well as the danger of clashing personalities, he told Winwood, he was looking for a change of scenery in his musicians. And two former members of Cream would leave Blind Faith wide open to accusations that it was Cream Mark Two.

Steve wanted Baker in the band. He was mightily impressed by Ginger's dynamics and persuaded a very reluctant Eric that the music would benefit. It was, as Clapton predicted, the single biggest factor in sealing Blind Faith's fate. The public did see it as a reincarnation of Cream. As the ballyhoo surrounding the formation of a 'new supergroup' which included two ex-Cream men, one great singer who came from Traffic and the respected bass player Rick Grech from the band Family grew, Blind Faith had a lot to live up to.

Blind Faith's only major British appearance was a free concert in London's Hyde Park on 7 June 1969. Among the crowd of 150,000 were scores of eminent rock stars, curious to see Clapton's new guise. Mick Jagger and Marianne Faithfull were backstage and, as a gesture, Blind Faith played the Rolling Stones' song 'Under My Thumb'. The band's music was subdued and bore little resemblance to that of any other band; Eric smiled happily when one voice from the crowd beneath the stage boomed out: 'It's not Cream, Eric, it's Blind Faith. Play what you like!'

The band was judged with cautious optimism by most of the cognoscenti. The big achievement of the day, reported London's *Daily Mirror* in an editorial, was: 'There aren't many countries where 100,000 youngsters could get together so peacefully and give the police no real worries . . . [it was] one of the most remarkable and amiable gatherings of young people ever seen in this country.'

Within the band, the storm clouds already loomed. After a spectacular response from a crowd of 20,000 at their first New York concert at Madison Square Garden, Blind Faith ran into controversy in the US in July 1969. American record dealers who saw the cover design of their debut album described it as 'obscene and salacious' and said they would refuse to stock it unless it was redesigned. The cover showed a naked eleven-year-old girl holding a silver spacecraft. As reaction against the picture grew in America, the Robert Stigwood office in London was told that 70 per cent of American record dealers had decided against stocking the album, so a fresh cover was essential. Faced with advance orders of a quarter of a million for the album, there was little choice: a new, acceptable cover showed a harmless picture of the musicians in Blind Faith, a stronger sales pitch anyway in view of the fact that it featured two thirds of the mighty Cream. A note included with the album said that buyers could obtain the original, controversial, sleeve on request from the record company, Atlantic, who released the LP as planned in Britain.

Eric faced questions all the time about why Steve Winwood was allowed to dominate the band. 'I think he's the most talented guy in the group, and as a result he deserves to be out front,' Clapton invariably answered. 'But we're not just backing him up. We all play an incredibly big part.' Other factors, however, quickly militated against the band. As they went on the road, Eric frequently became annoyed by Ginger Baker's insensitivity and it looked like the clashes between Baker and Bruce in Cream might be re-enacted by Clapton and Baker in Blind Faith. And, finally, in America, according to Winwood and Clapton, the fate of the band was obvious.

A combination of greed for the big money that was around, plus a lack of material – astonishingly, this band could only play for just

A study of Eric, clean-shaven again, during his short-lived period in Blind Faith in 1969 (*Barry Wentzell/Melody Maker*)

over an hour without running short of original material – sowed the seeds of the band's demise. In America and in Britain, many members of the audience were Cream or Traffic fans; faced with the easy applause and constant demands for Cream or Traffic favourite songs, and their lack of other material, Eric and Steve succumbed to the easy option. The band became exactly what they had hoped to avoid: a mirror image of their previous groups. And because they were so rapidly thrust forward, they did not get the time to reflect on their musical identity or produce enough new songs to sustain it.

'The management and the record company joined our own greed,' says Winwood, looking back on it. 'You can't really blame them or us. There was a multimillion dollar time bomb out there. We wanted to work, so we said: "Oh, let's go and earn the bucks!"

'There were pressures left, right and centre to go out and earn the money. Never was there a moment to develop the character of the band. Who would let a million-dollar-a-week potential in a band sit around and rehearse? It's understandable. And we thought it was more sensible to go out and work rather than sit around. We decided to make our mistakes in public. But when it came down to it, we failed because we couldn't resist requests for the hits. Ginger did a drum solo and they thought it was Cream, so we chucked in an old Cream song, then I put in a Traffic song, and the identity of the band was killed stone dead. If you have 20,000 people sitting out there and you know you only have to play one song for them to be on their feet, you *do* it! We were only human. But that was the end, really, when that began.

'Soon there was a realization that this was a bit of a cop-out. We should have started Blind Faith by insisting on playing 1000-seater halls. There was serious pressure on us not to do that because it would be a retrograde step. And our egos might have been a bit of a problem ... Eric had been playing 20,000-seater halls around the world and Traffic had done pretty big shows, too. That was the root of our unrest – the audiences, the planning, and the fact that we didn't get away from who we had been before the band began.'

Eric agrees with Steve that Blind Faith lacked an identity. But there was a more deep-seated reason for his conviction that Blind Faith was doomed from the start. 'Steve couldn't see it this way, but when Ginger walked in, I lost interest. I was freshly grieving from Cream and I wanted no more part of Cream again. I found Steve and he was loose.

'The pair of us were living in the country and we were developing lifestyles which were very similar. Steve would come here, or I would go to his Berkshire cottage and we'd do some dope. We'd play and hang out for days on end without forming an idea of what we were doing – just enjoying one another's company. And then somehow word leaked to someone to someone to someone . . . and next thing I knew, Ginger was knocking on the door. Now I love Ginger very much, but at that time I didn't really want him around! But I didn't have the heart to say no.

'That loyalty went back to a situation that happened during the end of Cream when I gave Ginger my word that if he did something to prove a point for me I would always be his friend. It was a very emotional scene. And I felt obliged to let him move into this situation with Steve and me. At the same time, I felt that destiny was taking an upper hand. And it was doomed from that point on.

'And then Ginger took the reins because Steve and I were both so laid back! We were in no hurry to get anywhere, whereas Ginger could see . . . zoom, the bucks. So could Robert Stigwood. Before we knew it, we were into the harassments of making a record and with a tour lined up which we weren't ready for and had no desire to do.'

Blind Faith became, to Eric, Son of Cream – and he says: 'I was looking for a way out, subconsciously, from the minute we hit the road. And Delaney was there . . . so I jumped straight into that Delaney and Bonnie Bramlett band scene for a while.'

Just as America had been the scene of the demise of Cream, it also proved the country where Blind Faith's coffin was nailed. 'Look, this is ridiculous,' Eric said to Steve after one show. 'It's a successful group all right, but we're getting applause for all the wrong stuff. It's not the group we planned, is it? It's Cream stuff and long drum solos!'

Winwood's theory is that, despite the collapse of Blind Faith after only a year, Eric gained enormously from the experience. 'In a way, the jump from being inside John Mayall to being the star of Cream was too big. He wanted to learn a little more about what happened in between for a musician . . . that role of accompaniment. I think he learned that role inside Blind Faith, whatever our failures. But we didn't even have to talk the end of the band through. It was perfectly obvious to Eric and me on that tour in America that it couldn't last. As we had put the band together, so we just split it up. In fact we didn't split formally. We just drifted away . . .'

As throughout his life as a musician, Clapton had absorbed the experiences of the period like a sponge.

'Inside Cream, I felt I had to live up to something all the time. With Blind Faith, I didn't. The audience did, but I didn't! In Cream, on those long solos, I found myself repeating myself night after night.

There never seemed any time to stop and think. I was totally exhausted in Cream.

'The only thing that doesn't change is that I'm changing all the time. The consistency of my character is that I'm a paradox. The only thing you can count on in me is that I'm going to keep changing. And that I'll always be playing guitar, five and twenty-five years from now.'

He added that while he might have proved himself to many thousands of listeners, he had not proved himself to himself. He felt restless again.

'Looking back,' reflects Steve Winwood, 'it's obvious that Blind Faith, just like the Yardbirds and John Mayall, was a stepping stone for Eric. He was just moving from band to band, taking lots in each time, but it was all leading for certain to where he is today. Eventually, he could not remain a member of any band. He'd have to go solo.'

Clapton weathered strong criticism over his handling of Blind Faith. Many fans and musicians thought he had appeared too subservient to Winwood, and should have assumed the leadership more aggressively; he was, after all, the bigger name. But Eric wanted different things from the band. He was not ready for the leadership job at that stage. 'It's easier to be led than to lead . . . I felt very insecure sometimes inside Blind Faith, and that was my own hang-up that had to be cured in its own time.'

Fights in the audience had also marred the band's American tour. In the worst scenes, in New York, Los Angeles and Phoenix, Arizona, Eric reported that 'the crowd came prepared for the fact that there would be cops there, and were prepared to be bugged from the start. Their main thing was to heckle the cops. The cops replied with violence.

'Our main thing was to appease them both. And that had nothing to do with being a musician. That's being a politician. The violence happened everywhere we played. Partly because of that, we played too loudly, which is the very thing I wanted to avoid with Blind Faith.'

But at least two satisfying aspects of the American tour had been the band's album jumping to the top of the charts . . . and the money which came from playing such big venues. The band might have failed to fulfil Clapton's hopes, but behind his biblical beard and thinner frame, the man who returned to Britain was more mature as a twenty-four-year-old, robustly confident of his future as a musician who could take his time before making a firm move. He was also very rich.

The changing image of Eric Clapton, in 1967 (*London Features International*)

4

THE
ADDICT

*'I was trying to prove I could do it and come
out alive'*

The rollercoaster of the Cream had brought the twin compensating factors of money and freedom. After months of searching for a permanent home to replace his succession of flats, Eric bought, just after his twenty-fourth birthday, Hurtwood Edge. The beautiful twenty-roomed mansion, deep in the Surrey countryside, occupied sixteen acres and bordered National Trust land. It cost Eric £40,000 – expensive in 1969 – and with its history, ornamental ponds, swimming pool, vast grounds with the donkey grazing in the fields and even an observatory, it had more character than the mansions usually bought by rock stars.

Eric bought the house after seeing a photograph of it in the magazine *Country Life*. Built in 1910, it had a distinct flavour of Italian architecture which appealed to Eric. 'I fell in love with it immediately on my first look at it,' he says.

Eric enjoyed his money and bought himself a Ferrari, and a vintage 1929 motorcycle for his girlfriend, who moved into his house with him – Alice Ormsby-Gore, the daughter of the late Lord Harlech, former British Ambassador to Washington. As president of the British Board of Film Censors, he was one of Britain's most respected peers. He died in a car crash in Britain in 1985.

Eric and Alice had met by a quirk of fate. A Chelsea friend, Ian Dallas, who would later be the catalyst for Eric's love song for his wife, was instrumental in causing their meeting. When Eric bought Hurtwood Edge, Ian Dallas recommended an interior designer to him. The designer was David Mlinaric, who was just starting to make his mark but who has gone on to design interiors for castles and stately homes. There was also Christopher Gibbs, an antique dealer, friend of Mick Jagger and described by Eric as 'an aristocratic visionary'.

'At that time,' says Clapton, 'there was a set of aristocratic hippies who were all into a sort of gypsy way of life. David Mlinaric, because of his aristocratic connections, knew the Harlechs and their daughters.

'So Alice came down with him to look over the place. She was sixteen at the time, but I did fancy her a great deal. I asked her if she was free – at sixteen years old!' They had 'a very innocent courtship' for about a year. 'I had other girlfriends bouncing around, but no one steady.' Eventually the tall, willowy Alice, born on 11 April 1952, went to live with him at Hurtwood Edge.

The transformation from a determined but struggling blues guitarist, sleeping rough on railway stations after missing the train home after a gig, to a superstar living in the grandeur of a country retreat had happened quickly. Clapton adapted easily. Others found it hard; on their first visit to Hurtwood Edge, Eric's grandparents cried. They found it very difficult to grasp the changed lifestyle of the boy they had raised in their modest terraced house. Quickly, Eric demonstrated that if the surroundings had changed, he was the same man. He told them he was determined to enjoy his cash. One of his first gifts to them was a six-week first-class world cruise.

The new house, the redecorating, the enjoyment of life in the country again after the world tours and living from suitcases, suited Clapton perfectly in 1969. After three relentless years of some great music, much adulation and lots of friction, a period of no responsibilities appealed to him.

He was, of course, in great demand by his peers. A telephone call one night from John Lennon asked Eric if he would go, next day, to Toronto to guest with John and Yoko Ono's Plastic Ono Band at a big rock festival. The infectious enthusiasm of John soon persuaded Eric. They had no repertoire and actually rehearsed on the plane. 'It was a great gig. We did an hour of solid rock; numbers like "Blue Suede Shoes" and "Dizzy Miss Lizzy",' says Eric. He had great affection for Lennon, which was reciprocated. After the Canadian show, John said that the Plastic Ono Band was his successor to the Beatles and Eric was vital to it. He wanted Eric and the others in the band, particularly the fine bassist Klaus Voormann, to go on a concert tour. Eric's empathy with Lennon was based on Clapton's simple belief: 'He was sincere.' The murder of John in New York in 1980 devastated Eric.

Eric defended Yoko's controversial singing: 'Yoko has the same effect on people as a high-pitched whistle has on a dog. Her voice is spine-chilling, very weird. John and I played some feedback guitar while Yoko was singing. I think she was amazing. Her style of singing requires a technique, like anything else. If you try it, after ten minutes your voice will break. She is doing something unique – it has never been done before. She doesn't really need a backing but it's more entertaining to work with a foundation. The drummer just sets a beat but he can go into very abstract rhythms if he wants to. Toronto was tremendous fun.' Lennon gave Eric, on Apple Records writing paper, five drawings in lieu of payment for the Toronto show. They were typically witty and Eric has them framed.

He felt calm at home and was happy with Alice, who had a highly developed sense of humour.

Now his career followed a jagged, self-indulgent path. As if to exorcise his past roles as other people's 'God' inside Cream and Blind Faith, Eric virtually buried himself as a sideman. He appeared in the never-seen Rolling Stones' *Rock 'n' Roll Circus* film; he jammed with the greatest players in a supersession at Staines, just outside London (jazz multi-instrumentalist Roland Kirk, guitarist/drummer Buddy Miles, guitarist Stephen Stills and others); and he guested on George Harrison's hugely successful triple album, *All Things Must Pass*.

He went on tour with Delaney and Bonnie Bramlett, the gifted husband-and-wife team whom he had first seen in America when touring with Cream, and who had opened the concerts for the Blind Faith tour. On the road, Delaney and Bonnie and Friends seemed like one long jam-session, with some of the cream of American musicianship inside the band: Bobby Keys and Jim Price (horns), Carl Radle (bass) and Jim Gordon (drums). George Harrison chased them for the Beatles' Apple label, and for about a year, among the top rock musicians, they were the most fashionable name around.

People began to mutter darkly that. Clapton was submerging himself alongside others too much, particularly on his first solo album. This bore the title *Eric Clapton*, but most of the songs were co-written with Delaney. Only when he was allowed to stretch out on his own, in a song called 'Easy Now', with a light, appealing vocal, did his identity come through.

Even deeper moves into solitude followed. Next, inexplicably, Eric decided to go on tour incognito as Derek and the Dominos to test the reaction of audiences in small clubs throughout Britain, who would not guess that the leader was famous. The musicians were the same as Delaney and Bonnie's good-time boogie unit: bassist Carl Radle, organist Bobby Whitlock and drummer Jim Gordon. The music was good, if unspectacular, and the grassroots return to the club circuit achieved what Eric wanted.

But the disguise was a failure: everybody knew it was Clapton

In December, 1969, Eric joined the Plastic Ono supergroup for an all-star concert at London's Lyceum. Clapton, on the right is flanked on the opposite end of the photo by George Harrison, and the other players include the Who's drummer Keith Moon, Delaney and Bonnie (top right) and, next to Eric, Billy Preston (*Barry Plummer*). *Below:* Eric and George Harrison, backstage after a concert with Delaney, Bonnie and friends in December, 1970 (*Syndication International*)

playing games. His record company, wanting maximum publicity, even showered 'Derek is Eric' badges on the music industry. By the time the band hit the road, people were talking and writing about 'Eric Clapton's new band, Derek and the Dominos . . .'

One autumn afternoon in 1970, Eric was wandering around London's West End and went into an instrument shop. On the wall hung a left-handed Fender Stratocaster guitar. Eric bought it on sight as a gift for one of his dearest friends, Jimi Hendrix. That same night, Eric went to London's Lyceum Ballroom to see a show starring Sly Stone. Jimi was expected to sit in a box opposite Eric's box. Clapton took along the special Stratocaster. But Hendrix was not at the concert; next day, Eric learned that Jimi had died that night.

'I was heartbroken. We had a very close, intuitive friendship. People weren't so demonstrative in those days, so we didn't go around saying "I love you, man," but the sad thing is that we both acknowledged that we'd be around as musicians and friends for ever and so we didn't have to rush to talk about anything. We never had the serious conversation we both wanted, but there was a great empathy.'

The two men had spent magical jam-sessions together in Greenwich Village during Cream's tours. 'We'd virtually take over a club for a guitar duel, then move on for a jam to someone's house. Great days.'

The rock world bitterly mourned the loss of an original, shining star whose work, like Clapton's, was rooted in the blues. Although Hendrix's death was linked with drugs, the London inquest recorded an open verdict. It was stated that there was no evidence to suggest Hendrix had been a drug addict or that he had been depressed. Medical evidence showed that death had been caused by inhalation of vomit due to barbiturate intoxication. Eric, badly hit by the death of a musician friend, nevertheless did not attend the funeral. He feared that it would be a 'showbiz event'. Throughout his life, Clapton's mourning for close friends or relatives has always been very private and swift. But that should not be misconstrued as heartless; it is his own way of handling his grief.

After Jimi died, Eric felt 'very, very angry'. He says: 'Nobody could be blamed, but I felt incredible fury. I just had this terrible, lonely feeling. I loved Jimi, and his music, and I'd played with him . . . and because everybody was talking about him, I'd keep running into these young kids playing guitar like him, saying to me: "Have you heard this one? I can do a Hendrix." It made me feel sick. I just turned away from them and said to myself: "Forget it, mate. It's all been *done.''* I don't ever want to hear anything said about him again.'

*

Six weeks after the death of Jimi Hendrix, Derek and the Dominos were on tour in America when a phone call from Robert Stigwood gave him the news: Eric's grandfather had been taken to a clinic in Guildford with suspected cancer. Clapton cancelled a press reception for his new group and flew home; Jack Clapp died shortly afterwards, aged sixty.

'It was a traumatic experience,' recalls Eric, 'mainly because of what it did to Rose. Not me so much, because I'd departed from Ripley and I felt my role in their situation was more of a benefactor than anything else. But my love had always been there, very deeply, for Rose. I was very broken up for her when Jack died.

'My caring was purely for her and not for me, in a cold sort of way. From my early teens, I felt I'd established a way of being, and thinking, and staying, *alone.* I severed all my home ties when I went to live with John Mayall. I had no real attachment to Ripley in my late teens and early twenties. I felt gratitude to Rose and Jack for raising me, you know, but little more. But when Jack died, it cut me up for her.'

It would be too simplistic to say that Eric plunged into his long, silent reclusive period after those two deaths. But is is certain that they contributed to the deep-seated soul-searching that was affecting him. Aged twenty-five, with the world at his feet, he went home and closed the door. From the end of December 1970 until the beginning of 1973, the only time he ventured out with his guitar was for the all-star Concert for Bangladesh, organized by George Harrison, at New York's Madison Square Garden on 1 August 1971. The attraction of playing with a band of old friends, including Bob Dylan, was a contributory factor in forcing Eric out of hibernation. But his playing at the concert was unsteady. The miracle was that he was on stage at all. I attended the concert and remember thinking that Eric had, in a sense, achieved what he wanted: he had become a sideman in a band of stars. Yet the New York audience's applause for him was loud and clear.

Eric's descent into the long, three-year darkness of hard drugs and silence will haunt him for ever. He and Alice were barricaded from the world. He and hundreds of other people both close to him and distant will always attempt to explain why and how he became a recluse at Hurtwood Edge, insulting and rejecting his dearest friends and relatives. Eric is both the best and the worst expert on the subject; the wide-eyed, alert Clapton of today looks back on the period as an essential – if dangerous – diversion. He *had* to experiment and over-indulge himself in drugs, he says, for several reasons: as a kind of heroism, to push himself to the brink and to emerge having proved to himself and others that he could survive; because the rock lifestyle, the headiness of Cream and fame, and the fashion of drugs in the late 1960s had endorsed it; because of his unrequited love for Pattie Harrison, as she was then, married to Beatle George. These things, compounded by the deaths of people close to him on different levels – his grandfather and guitar star Jimi Hendrix – seemed to hammer home to Eric at that time the pointlessness of rock stardom. But he greatly regrets the loss of time in a heroin vacuum.

Paradoxically, Cream had been a reasonably clean-living band. 'We were incredibly hard-working and, apart from the occasional acid trip and the mild drugs, we were certainly not a group of doped musicians,' says Eric. 'We worked more in the old jazz tradition, I guess; living for the next gig.' He ponders the big question about why he felt the need to go so far down the road with drugs. American musician Leon Russell and George Harrison once went to see him when he was 'smacked out of his mind' on heroin at Hurtwood Edge. 'Leon was angry. He demanded to know what the hell I was doing and the only answer I could think of was to say I had to go into the darkness to find out what was in there, and I didn't know what light meant.

'There was definitely a heroic aspect to it. I was trying to prove I could do it and come out alive. At no time did I consider it being suicidal or a shutting down on life. The rejected love affair, the apparent non-availability of Pattie, was certainly a factor. I had to prove to myself that I could do this thing on my own – that I could forget Pattie, survive, and come back from the dead. I still functioned, even though it was not in public. I mean, I had a box full of cassettes at the end of that period. There was me, playing guitar, and I hadn't remembered doing them at all. But I'd been churning out the music; some was usable later . . .'

The road to heroin addiction began almost accidentally. In 1970, with Blind Faith an unsatisfactory memory, the whole of the Derek and the Dominos band lived at Eric's house.

'We played music twenty-four hours a day and then we'd stop and go to sleep, whatever the time, and to live this kind of life, you tend to want a stimulant. We were taking all kinds of mild drugs: marijuana and acid and uppers and downers, and cocaine. And that's where the heroin came in, because the dealer we were usually getting the coke from was insisting that we buy a little bit of heroin with it,

Clapton just before he began his long period of isolation from 1970

because that was his stock-in-trade as well, and he couldn't off-load it. So he said we'd have to buy a gramme of coke and a gramme of heroin as well.

'No one wanted to go near the heroin. And from being close to other musicians I knew it was dangerous. But the problem was that I had a drawer with most of the drugs in, and this pile of heroin was building up and up. And so, one day, I just became too curious for my own good. And I liked it. I was a quick learner. I didn't puke. In fact, I thoroughly enjoyed it and I thought, well, this isn't so bad. When it wore off, I didn't feel too bad either, and so I did it for maybe a year, very infrequently, also doing lots of coke and lots of other drugs and drinking as well.' The heroin habit grew, though. 'It became once every two weeks, then once a week, then two or three times a week, then every day . . . so it was insidious. It crept up on me without me really being aware of it.'

All the negotiating with drug dealers was done by Alice, something she now regrets. 'I remember when we went to New York in 1971 for George Harrison's Bangladesh concert, I was desperately running around that city trying to score some heroin for Eric. And I remember thinking how stupid it was for me, even then. I did that for him, and for myself, for three years. It was probably childish to be over-protective, but I thought it helped him not to have to face the full horror, himself, of scoring his own heroin supply. It might have been better, I can see now, to let him do it and learn the difficulty of it first-hand. Then he'd know, like I learned, the degradation of the dealing. But then, you see, Eric's able to give himself into other people's hands for a limited spell of time, and give himself *totally*, if he thinks it will tide him over a problem. If it hadn't been me doing the scoring for him, it would have been someone else. And if you love someone, as I did, you do anything . . .'

As the Dominos drifted apart as a working unit, and one by one left Hurtwood Edge, Eric and Alice sank even deeper into an addiction to heroin. The cost was high, financially as well as in human terms; before long, Eric was operating a 'cover-up' system with his office. The hundreds of pounds he was getting from the office, legitimately, was not enough to buy heroin, since he was spending about £1500 a week on it. Gradually, he began pawning his precious guitars, through the drug pusher.

At Hurtwood Edge, the house so aptly named for Eric's period of addiction, the phone rang continuously and nobody answered. Eric was seldom seen for two years, even by his close friends and relatives. The word was out that he was ill, heavily into drugs, or just wanted a retirement from the dizziness of being hailed as the world's greatest rock guitarist. All three theories were correct.

His old friend, Ben Palmer, back in wood-carving but surprised at the lack of postcards which used to arrive from a 'normal' Eric, decided to visit Clapton Towers to find out why the phone was not answered. 'I had no experience of drugs and wasn't prepared for the vehemence. I went in virtually saying: "Well, Eric, you're not going to live long now. You're going to die soon." I felt impotent, but he was furious that I had even broached the subject.

'It was the worst experience I'd encountered. I saw a man who was very dear to me, and he was clearly killing himself. I felt I had no part to play and I also felt guilty at not having gone down there before, when he began with drugs. Eric had *always* been lonely as a man, even though he had good friends – but nobody, dare I say, like me who went back a long way and he knew loved him as a bloke instead of as a famous rock star. I felt terrible guilt that I'd not been around to stop him going down. I probably couldn't have achieved that, but I'd have tried. First time I went to Hurtwood, I couldn't even get inside. No reply from the front door. I knew he was in. Second time, Alice opened the door, but Eric made me feel like an intruder. I've since heard this is a typical heroin user's behaviour. Very anti-social, very cross with anyone who's straight.'

The guilt caused by his deflating of one of his closest friends will stay with Eric Clapton for ever. 'The surprising thing about heroin,' says Eric, 'is that you believe you can make yourself invisible. The minute your eyelids begin to droop, there is no one else in the room. You may be in a room full of people, and they may be concerned about you, but you neither care nor feel anything about them.

'Yes, I do remember the situation Ben describes. I can see him now, coming down the drive, and presumably he'd come all the way from Wales. I think I was on my own, upstairs, and I was stoned on smack. I was annoyed he'd come to see me because he required a me that wasn't there, a straight me, a compassionate me, a friend. He wanted to see his old friend, and his friend wasn't here. And I was desperately ashamed of this. So I hid upstairs while he stayed for a long, long time. By instinct, I knew he stayed downstairs for hours and I couldn't face him. I've lived with the guilt ever since and always will. Even though it was a small thing, I now realize what that rejection meant to Ben. Actually, it's amazing that I can think back and remember that shame, because heroin should have blotted that out as well. But it doesn't. People can look at you with fear, concern and pity . . . and their grief means nothing to you, because you feel all right, you're in this shell. You don't need anybody. All you need is that powder.'

He never injected himself with heroin. The survival instinct told the inner man that injection was the most slippery route of all. But heroin in powder form, for inhaling, costs much more than that bought for injection. 'Heroin,' Clapton continues, 'feeds on the nerve centres that make you selfish. You don't take the drug because you're selfish, but you do become selfish because of it.'

Another unwelcome visitor to Hurtwood Edge was Eric's mother Pat. Visiting England from Germany, where she lived at the time, she too was puzzled by the hermit-like behaviour of her son. She went to Hurtwood Edge, got inside, and sat talking to Alice in the kitchen for several hours. Eric, upstairs, did not feel he looked physically presentable enough to meet his mother. 'I cried a bit on the way back to Ripley,' says Pat. 'I thought he was killing himself, and what could I do? I sat for hours and hours and hours waiting to see him. But nothing.'

It was tough, too, on Rose. He visited her infrequently during the two years, and when he did occasionally arrive, with Alice, she could not believe her eyes. 'He'd stand in the doorway, looking tired out. "Hi," he'd say. It didn't seem like Rick. I thought, oh God, he's drunk. Then my daughter said: "Mum, he's on drugs. I can see it in his eyes."

'I used to really pray, get down on my hands and knees and say my prayers for Rick. I tried to talk to him once when he came round here with Alice. He just laughed, and that made me feel a lot worse.'

'Most of the family guessed what was going on, but Rose didn't,' says Clapton's Uncle Adrian. 'Those of us who went to Hurtwood Edge, like his mother Pat and me, felt aggrieved because every time we arrived Alice would say sorry, he's upstairs in bed asleep.' Eric occasionally made the effort to visit Rose, who had by then left Ripley for a house in another Surrey village, Shamley Green. 'I saw him there a few times,' recalls Adrian Clapton. 'We knew he wasn't well. He was in a vague dream most of the time. It was sad to see him like that.'

The relationship between Pete Townshend and Eric Clapton has always been musically grudging but personally respectful. Eric liked the Who, but it wasn't strictly his kind of music. Pete's early view of blues playing by white people was cynically dismissive. 'I was never interested in hybrid white blues,' says Townshend. 'I thought John Mayall was an idiot and that any white performer, particularly a London white performer, trying to play blues was nothing but a joke. I thought that young British white boys emulating black American music was too funny for words. So I always felt a bit superior, and

Eric felt a bit superior to me, I believe, in the mid-1960s.' Still, they were both articulate and committed, and a kind of trust developed. 'During the psychedelic period we started to see quite a lot of each other because of the atmosphere that prevailed in London' recalls Pete. 'We were mixing with a lot of the same people. We socialized a fair bit and went to see Pink Floyd a couple of times together because we both had a passion for Syd Barrett. Then we got a bit closer during the Murray the K show in New York, when the Who and Cream were together on the bill. But in 1969, after Cream finished, he disappeared completely from my life.'

One year later, the two men met when Derek and the Dominos were recording at the Olympic Studios in Barnes, London. 'It was strange. He obviously had some cash-flow problem, because he was *selling guitars*. Actually *selling guitars* to people who would buy them. Then I heard why – from Bob Pridden, the Who's senior sound man whose wife went to school with Alice Ormsby-Gore. Bob said Eric had a drug problem. That's why he was selling guitars, to raise ready cash to buy dope.' Townshend had no such problem. He had renounced drugs in 1967, in favour of the spiritual teachings of Meher Baba, who reached out to Townshend in the way that the Maharishi Mahesh Yogi's transcendental meditation had briefly captivated the Beatles.

Clapton's guitar-selling incident preceded his three-year period of seclusion at Hurtwood Edge. Townshend would be the last to claim that he alone pulled Eric back from the precipice – 'The only person who can stop a person being a junkie is the junkie,' Pete says forcefully. But while Eric was down, he was one of the few visitors allowed access to Eric's home. Townshend was appalled by the indignity of the slope down which Clapton was sliding. And by now, Pete, always a conscientious spokesman on the force of rock, had witnessed the rapid casualty toll: Rolling Stone Brian Jones, Beatles manager Brian Epstein, Jimi Hendrix, American singer Janis Joplin, and too many others.

In late 1971 and throughout 1972, Townshend endured what he describes as 'the terrible strain of seeing what was happening with Eric and feeling pretty powerless.' Townshend had never used heroin; he had had 'a couple of belts' at cocaine, which had done nothing for him; but he knew enough of heroin addiction to realize that Eric was in a deep mess.

'I was having to answer hysterical phone calls from Alice practically every night. She always wanted me to go over there. It was an hour and a half's drive, and always at awkward hours of the night. When I got there, usually she just wanted to explain what was happening.

Eric would be asleep somewhere and she would be running around hysterically.

'What was worrying her, what she needed to talk about, was that she was giving Eric all of her heroin supply, most unselfishly. And then she was having to deal with Eric's extremely selfish outbursts accusing her of doing the *reverse*. He kept alleging she was keeping the best for herself.

'It was a typical junkie scene,' Townshend continues. 'It was despicable. But even through all that, you know, I got to like and love them both very much. It was the first encounter I'd had with heroin addicts. I wasn't prepared for the lies, I wasn't prepared for the duplicity . . . but even through all that, I decided they definitely seemed to me to be worth the effort.'

Says Alice: 'I always thought Pete was one of the most extraordinary, intuitive and intellectual people around. I needed him so that someone besides me could see what Eric was like in his attitude towards me.'

Eric and Alice were together for about five years, but Eric says 'three of those were spent under the influence of heroin, and we never communicated at all – only to have an argument. And although we had some good times, I'd never describe it as head-over-heels in love. All the time I was with Alice, I was mentally with Pattie. My love for Pattie began almost the first day I saw her, and grew in leaps and bounds.' Before Alice, he had had a brief fling with Pattie's younger sister, Paula: 'That really was a case of a surrogate Pattie in my mind. Alice was really on the rebound, when I was waiting to build up some plan of action to get Pattie.

'But it was a very solid, good, working relationship. Alice understood me very well and I understood her. We worked together to be happy. In spite of the fact that a good amount of the time we were stoned, we still managed to function together as a couple. We had a very good rapport. She's a very intelligent girl. The one thing that kind of kept us apart was her low estimation of her abilities, which I always find difficult to deal with in other people. If people have a low opinion of themselves, I get very short tempered. Because I often think that it's a front or that it's an adopted stance to gain attention. And often it isn't, obviously. It's deeply based. But I've never got any patience with that and that was one thing that kept us very distant,' says Eric.

Alice agrees that her lack of self-esteem infuriated Eric so much that it created a barrier. But she does not agree with his theory that their relationship was not a love affair. 'I can't go along with him on

The beard has returned for Eric, alias Derek, during his leadership of Derek and the Dominos in 1970 (*Barry Wentzell/Melody Maker*)

that,' says Alice. 'Maybe because I was only seventeen I wrongly thought of it as mutual. My extreme youth made any rational analysis of the situation impossible.' She had been attracted to him from the first time they met at a party in Glebe Place, Chelsea, in November 1968. When she subsequently went to his house as part of the interior design team, she sensed a chemistry between them, and believed that Clapton reciprocated her feelings. Whatever Eric's verdict now on their relationship, Alice declares, 'I was in love with him, most definitely.'

She moved into Hurtwood Edge in March 1969. Eric, meanwhile, had begun his two-month affair with Pattie's sister Paula, and Alice moved out. They reunited in March 1970 but their relationship became stormy very quickly. Alice feels now that Clapton's treatment of her was insensitive: she was after all only seventeen and he was twenty-five. In April, Alice left to spend the summer alone in Israel, while back at Hurtwood Edge the house assumed the air of a musicians' commune, with the players in the Dominos living in and taking it in turns to cook. The air was thick with drugs ... and Clapton gave full rein to his passion for Pattie, writing *Layla* for her during Alice's absence.

Soon after her return in the autumn, by which time the Dominos spree was over, Alice took on all the shopping and cooking for the house. She recalls that she was 'subliminally' aware that Eric was thinking of Pattie for a great part of her time with him. 'When he first fell in love with Pattie, he was very open to me about it, but as the years went by he was very quiet on the subject.' But Alice remembers knowing that Pattie was still very much on his mind.

It would be wrong to think of Clapton's three-year self-imposed monastic existence as that of a junkie incapable of assessing what was happening. 'Mentally, I was totally aware of what was going on, what I was doing to myself, and I was not lying in bed all day long taking H.'

Alice says that Eric often rose at four in the afternoon and casually played his guitar most days. They were not a reclusive couple for the entire three years: 'We went to London quite often, and made weekend trips to Rose at her home not far away and Eric would enjoy a game of badminton in her garden. It wasn't all sitting at home getting full of smack. We were both completely aware of ourselves.' They even flew, at Pete Townshend's invitation, to a Who concert in Paris in October 1972. 'Eric's condition was much more worrying to outsiders than it was to him. I could see that he knew he was all right and going to come through it all. But anyone seeing him would think he was on the road to being finished. That was the difference.'

One afternoon in 1972, a surprise phone call from Eric asked Pete Townshend to come and visit him at Hurtwood Edge. He had an eight-track recording studio, he said, at the house and he wanted Pete's help in completing some work he had begun with Derek and the Dominos. 'They'd done four or five tracks, which we sat and played through, but they weren't quite *there*,' says Pete. 'My job was to try to revive his interest, engineer, produce, finish the records off. But by the time I got there, he was very, very unwilling. He vacillated tremendously. He gave me all sorts of excuses. He sent me off to write lyrics for the songs, look for new material – anything to stop me doing what he knew should be done.

'Then he took me into the little sub-sitting room, the room where he used to listen to short-wave radio all night and where I'd sat with him on many occasions for hours and hours, talking.' Eric's only real diversion during his two years of 'retirement' had been making models of aeroplanes and cars. But such was his condition that he had trouble focusing his eyes on the intricacy of the work.

'Finally, in that little room, he announced it to me: "Look, I'm a junkie. That's why I'm having such difficulty."

'I answered: "Look, I *know*" – and Eric was flabbergasted.

' "God, did you *know*?"

' "I know," I replied, "that's why I came down here so often – to try and help you get active again."

' "Oh God," said Eric. "I thought I was hiding it really well." '

He seemed, recalls Townshend, dismayed that *anybody* knew – mostly because his dignity had suffered.

Eric's manager Robert Stigwood played a role of 'discretion, wisdom and benevolence' during the three years of addiction, during which Eric hardly moved out of his house. 'He had been a very big part of my life and career. He was the mirror we looked into when we went to him with the Cream idea, and he said yes, it would work. I love him as a man, and he must have known me well to handle my drug period so carefully.

'He stayed totally in the background and made sure I got enough money so that I didn't end up selling all my possessions, or hit the streets. I made very open appeals to the office for money, which was obviously for drugs. Sometimes, someone in the office would go and pick up the drugs and he would turn a blind eye. I can never know what his motives were but I imagine it was because he felt I was going to come through it and that the only way he could handle the situation was to let me get on with it.' Eric says that Stigwood did not visit his home once during his smack period.

Lord Harlech, Alice's father, played a particularly supportive role. Eric said in 1984: 'He'd appealed to Alice many times and I think he'd tried to appeal to me, but he was a perfect gentleman and a sweet human being. He did write me a threatening letter which must have cost him a great deal. It said that if I didn't either leave his daughter alone or give up the drugs and make sure that she gave up the drugs, he would turn me in to the police. And for someone like him to say something like that must have required a great deal of effort. Then after that, he was very supportive. He was always the kindest man. We got on very well.'

Lord Harlech masterminded the major step towards public rehabilitation. He asked Townshend to put together a concert in London which would benefit a charity which Lord Harlech supported. Eric would be persuaded to take part, as a major return to work; it would be the ultimate cure.

Pete remembers that Eric was particularly cooperative when the idea was put to him that he should appear at a special concert at London's Rainbow Theatre on 13 January 1973. Ten days of rehearsal were arranged at the house of guitarist Ronnie Wood, at Hampton Court, Surrey. Many people believed Clapton had not touched his guitar in two years; in fact he had strummed it often, alone at his home. Despite Eric's pretence, the players – in fact most of the music industry – suspected that he had been in a private hell for two years. The villagers near his home said he had not been seen for more than two years.

Eric's ability to tune himself mentally into disciplined rehearsal work surprised Townshend. 'The drugs were flowing very freely among the musicians, and I think Eric upped his intake of heroin – he stopped trying to substitute it with other things, which he had been doing to try to pull himself round. But his togetherness was a surprise and a great pleasure to see.

'He was very, very strong, authoritative and confident,' says Townshend, 'and when anybody voiced any doubts, like "Oh God, how am I going to remember all these chords," he'd say: "Oh, don't worry, it's easy, you know. They're simple songs." Somebody said: "This song isn't going to work live," but Eric was positive in attitude. "Yes it *is*," he'd say. "Don't worry. It's going to be *good*."

'He retained his dignity for the rehearsals. We were all very impressed. The only pushing I had to do at the rehearsal was of Steve Winwood. He came the first day, played beautifully and Eric was absolutely inspired to have him around. Everybody was. He was an important catalyst. Second day, he didn't come.' Townshend, furious, berated Winwood on the phone: 'Listen, if you don't want to come, don't, but don't piss us about. Get over here now, or tell us all to fuck off. We can take it either way . . .' Townshend says there was stunned silence at the other end. 'Maybe I'd taken a sledgehammer to crack a nut, but Steve does have to be bullied. Anyway, he came back.' Winwood's presence was crucial to Clapton's continuing confidence.

The word was out for the concert: Clapton's comeback after two years of hibernation which people would not discuss was going to be tense. Could Eric still play? What would he look like? There was an all-star turnout for the band of young veterans: Clapton, Townshend and Ronnie Wood (guitars), Rick Grech (bass), Steve Winwood (keyboards) and Jim Capaldi (drums).

In the audience sat George Harrison and Ringo Starr, Klaus Voormann, Elton John, Rory Gallagher, Joe Cocker, Jimmy Page and

Ahmet Ertegun, whose Atlantic Records had championed Clapton through happier times.

Backstage, the tension and worry by the organizers was palpable. Five minutes before the start of the first show, Clapton had not arrived. His manager, Robert Stigwood, said to Pete Townshend: 'Pete, pray.' Townshend recounts the story:

'I said: "No, Robert, *you* pray. He's your artist."

'Robert said: "Look, if I pray, He won't listen."

'So I went out on the stairs alone at the back of the Rainbow and I said, twice: "Please God, make Eric come before the show . . ." '

That morning, Eric had woken up thinking he had lost his voice. But it was sheer nerves; he knew too much depended on his arrival that night.

One minute before the start of the concert, Eric arrived with Alice. Breathlessly, Stigwood asked him why he was so late. His white suit, which he hadn't worn for two years, needed letting out, said Eric. He had to wait for Alice to get out her sewing machine and let out the waist of his trousers. Clapton had, surprisingly, gained quite a lot of weight during his addiction. 'I ate like a horse, mostly junk food and chocolate, especially.' On stage, his waistcoat buttons would not meet.

The security arrangements were intense as the crowd leaving the first show met the second house crowd. Even Eric's mother had trouble persuading the backstage officials who she was. A mighty roar went up when a confident Eric, showing none of his nervousness, took the stage. From the opening wail of 'Layla', it was evident that Clapton was not going to be a passenger in an all-star band. When Winwood sang 'Nobody Knows You When You're Down and Out', Eric played a solo that almost wept with emotion. They drew powerful applause for Jimi Hendrix's beautiful song 'Little Wing', and played other Cream, Traffic and Clapton solo songs. During the much loved 'Let It Rain', one of Eric's strings broke, but he ploughed on relentlessly, the string swinging from the neck of his guitar. At midnight they played 'Key to the Highway' and 'Crossroads', an apt title and song to match the occasion, and they encored as the show had begun, with 'Layla'. On every level – creative, organizational and as an event packed with emotion – the Clapton comeback was a triumph. Inwardly, though, Eric hated every moment of it . . . because it was just a 'showbiz occasion' such as he usually shunned.

Addicts of any kind of drug stand in a doorway at a certain moment, and have to decide whether to retreat and continue with their habit, or whether to step out of the doorway into the daylight.

The Rainbow Theatre concert did not cure Eric; he was still addicted to drugs when he went on, and came off, the stage. But it was a powerful axis on which he could think about reshaping his life. The performance had renewed his confidence in his ability to play. From the stage, above the applause, Eric said of Townshend: 'Thank the man who got me to come up here because I wouldn't have done it without him.'

Eric says now: 'Pete has been very close, and I owe him a lot. The reason for that is that he really took a lot of time to help out, because he thought I was worth it, and I didn't think I was. He gave me faith in myself again.'

Townshend, though, is typically analytical about his role in Eric's return. 'He knew it was not something I'd done for him alone. He knew it was something I'd done partly for me, and partly for the dignity of the British music industry. That's why, quite rightly, he's never got down on his hands and knees and thanked me. He knew I'd get lots of credit in time, and that all I'd done was respond to a bit of a crisis. I don't pretend to have been any more humane, caring or compassionate than any of the other people involved. There was Lord Harlech; Alice, who we all realized later on had practically given her own life through using any substitute for heroin that she could lay her hands on, rather than deprive Eric of any of his drug. There were so many other people in the background . . .'

Eric believed that, musically, he had lost nearly three years of his life. But soon after he saw daylight, he found the pile of cassettes at home on which he had recorded some of his idle strumming. One song, particularly, which ended up as 'Give Me Strength', demonstrated both the turmoil and the faith within Eric during his lost period.

Give Me Strength

> Dear Lord, give me strength to carry on.
> Dear Lord, give me strength to carry on.
> My home may be out on the highway,
> Lord I've done so much wrong,
> But please give me strength to carry on.

All Eric and Alice's friends knew that several urgent moves were crucial if they were to gain permanent advantages from the initiatives taken by Lord Harlech and Pete Townshend. First, Eric would have to be willing to undergo a medical cure. Secondly, a split from Alice would be essential if both were to survive.

Lord Harlech moved determinedly. Eventually Eric arrived at the Harley Street home of Dr Meg Patterson. The quietly spoken doctor, a

thursday salt lake city gig

nigel has apologized for not being on duty last night, although i'm not sure he hasn't got his fingers crossed behind his back, anyway he has said that he will write one hundred lines, saying 'i promise not to let barry forget to take the rothmans off the plane" later ~ we watched the buddy holly story on the tele, excuse me for a minute, but roger has just come for a chat, now, we all know what that means ~ 'have you had anything to eat today" so my reply is: well i was just going to have a shower, so he says 'ave you sure you can fit both things into the same day" what a lovely man ! anyway as i was saying, we watched the buddy holly story on the box, and i got very unhappy about it, i suppose i knew it would be wrong, but i was curious to see how far they would go to earn a buck. later ~ the gig was okay although after two days of kicking our heels we played a bit stiff, i couldnt get that film out of my mind either, i felt like an anachronism on display.... i mean by that, that i am something left over by the past, a sort of museum piece ~ you see; for all of the really young rock fans, who didnt grow up with rock and roll, gary busey, is buddy holly ! i know i am a purist at heart, but any damn fool over the age of thirty knows the words to 'thatll be the day", to top it all they changed jerry allisons' name to jesse, and then went on to introduce a mediocre sax man as king curtis, who had already been dead for at least two years when that film was made. fuck 'em, they made their bed and now they got to sleep in it ~ and i dont wish 'em luck. the high point of the night was getting olivia de havillands autograph, me and albert went and knocked on her door, and although she was probably already in bed, she passed her signature under her door, and her voice was just the same as i remembered it, so sweet ~ selah ~ 🐖 ~

no-nonsense Scot with a medical degree from Aberdeen University, a Fellow of the Royal College of Surgeons and holder of the MBE for outstanding medical work in India, seemed an unlikely ally for Eric Clapton. Many requests for him to go and seek treatment for his heroin addiction had been stonewalled: the obstinacy of the addict, combined with guilt and Eric's inborn suspicion, made him reluctant to offer himself for help. After the Rainbow 'comeback' concert, a full year passed during which Eric virtually retreated into his old habits of seclusion and addiction.

Alice has kept the letter from her father to Eric in which he pleaded with Clapton to seize control of his drugs problem before it was too late. Written in August 1973, Lord Harlech's letter ran:

> I love you both so much that I cannot bear to see what you are doing to yourselves. For all that you can do and all you can have in your lives, please let me help you . . . you can paint and draw art, you can travel the world. Look what you have before you. I will probably never know how much courage it will take, dear Eric, but for your own sake, please do it.

The sincerity of the message from this man whom he admired enormously struck home with Eric, but he was addicted. He was inhaling a minimum of two grammes of heroin a day, sometimes double that amount – an extremely large quantity. He drank very little, perhaps wine with dinner, but physically he was in no state to respond instantly to David Harlech's supplications.

By February 1974, Eric knew that he was plunging back down in the abyss. Heroin was costing him incalculable sums and he was drifting aimlessly, squandering his resources and his talent. His financial mess was exceeded only by his physical state. He sat around Hurtwood Edge for days, weeks, months on end, eating vast amounts of the chocolate which addicts crave. He vanished upstairs when anyone arrived. Nobody, particularly his family and best friends, was allowed to see him at his worst.

An unusual feature of Meg Patterson's treatment was that she practised neuro-electric therapy as she called it, a new form of acupuncture in which electric current penetrates the ear lobes.

The doctor's memory of her first encounters with Eric and Alice are insightful into the mind of Clapton the addict. First, Meg said she would have to establish whether Eric was willing to be treated; a time was set for Eric, then twenty-eight and Alice, then twenty-one, to visit the Harley Street home and base where Meg Patterson lived with her husband George, who worked with her, and their three children. Meg and her husband had little idea of Clapton's fame, having only recently returned from ten years in Hong Kong.

Predictably, Eric and Alice were half an hour late for their evening meeting with Meg. 'Drug addicts are nearly always late,' says Meg. 'And they're usually so terrified of even thinking about treatment that they always come full of their particular drug. And, to some extent, unless they've got their drug, they can't behave normally. So, of course, they were stoned on arrival at my home.' The couple found refuge from their fear by playing on the floor with Meg and George's two sons, Shane, twelve, and Lloyd, ten.

'Taking drug addicts into a home where there are children is one of the most therapeutic things you can do,' says Meg. 'The children treated them as if there was nothing exceptional about them, and they were at ease very quickly. So we chatted . . .'

Over a cup of tea, Meg explained to Eric and Alice the concepts of her treatment. 'I told them the techniques were still fairly rough. The only stimulator I had at that time was one that was made in Communist China but which I'd bought in Hong Kong. At that time, I was also still using tiny acupuncture needles. They were applied, I told them, into the saucer-shaped hollow, the contour, of the ears, on a little clip. The Chinese stimulator I used on Eric was about ten inches by five inches by two inches deep. You could carry it in your hand, and it is connected by wires to the clips, which I'd invented myself. It was like a clip-on earring. But because there was a needle in it, I could still only use it for at most an hour at a time, three times a day.' It wasn't painful, but not comfortable either: no night treatments were possible, because 'you couldn't sleep with that thing stuck in your ear,' says Meg. The nights, therefore, used to be very bad, because they received no treatment at all.

Guardedly, Eric agreed to a next step after Meg's exploratory conversation: she told him she would have to move into his home with him for an intensive week of treatment.

The first problem came from a nurse who accompanied Meg to Hurtwood Edge: an evangelical Christian, she began preaching at Eric and Alice, who nearly ejected her and Meg on the spot. After she had been reproached by Meg, the nurse stopped preaching. 'The first day we were there, things were very tight. But I think Eric realized we had gone there with a genuine desire to help, and he became more open and responsive. Initially, he had been very very cautious indeed towards us.'

Alice loved Eric so deeply that she was giving him as much heroin as she could get hold of. To compensate herself for the heroin she was missing, she was drinking heavily: at least two bottles of vodka every day. Meg's first demand was tough: Eric and Alice would have to stop using heroin immediately and totally. 'All drugs were banned from the start of the treatment,' she says. 'I knew there was no heroin in the house because I saw Eric and Alice scraping among the fibres of the carpet to see if they could pick up a few grains. We had the cooperation of Lord Harlech, and Eric's manager Robert Stigwood, who said he wouldn't give them any money to buy it; Eric and Alice didn't have to leave the house to do anything.'

Eric loosened up in conversation with Meg and her husband George, who went down to Hurtwood Edge to reinforce her efforts. 'He was desperate, and wanted to try to cure himself,' recalls Meg. Two days after the nurse had tried to lecture him on Christianity, Clapton said to Dr Patterson enigmatically: 'You know, I was converted to Christianity a few years ago . . .'

Eric bared his innermost soul to George Patterson, especially when they discussed religion. This was when Eric revealed that he had become a Christian some years earlier; a Scots-born disc jockey whom he had met in America had converted him. The disc jockey had travelled on a concert tour of the US with Clapton for several months and Eric was particularly grateful that he cared enough for him, and his spirit, to travel with him and nourish his desire to embrace a faith. Eric's friendship with the man, and acceptance of his conviction, was dented when they went together to a New York music business party. Part of the man's Pentecostal beliefs dictated that whenever the spirit moved him, he had to say prayers, there and then. At that party, he announced: 'I feel God wants me to pray.' An irreverent rock star chipped in: 'I feel *I* want to pee.' At which point, Eric's 'guru' lost his temper and stormed out. The incident was a major turning point for Eric: he felt that if God could not hold on to a committed believer in that situation, he was no longer so sure of his own wavering faith.

Within a couple of days of Meg and her nurse moving into Hurtwood Edge, Eric was opening himself up to her as well. He clearly realized he needed treatment but his customary guardedness, and Meg's inhibition at being in his home for the crucial early stages, made the beginning difficult. Eric baulked at Meg's first instruction that they cut out all drugs immediately. 'Eric's physical condition was getting worse,' says Meg.

'I make all my patients stop taking drugs totally and immediately. Neuro-electric therapy is so different from just coming off the drug that within two or three days the addicts' minds are so clear that we can start our psycho-spiritual counselling.' There was a fear that Eric might sell his last guitar to get cash for dope, but Meg and George

The face of a recluse: a rare photograph of Eric in 1972 (*London Features International*)

became alerted to this just in time. Says George: 'It was agreed that the symbolism of selling that last guitar would be so important . . . life would be finished and he would commit suicide.' No money, no dope and no guitar would be too much. Within three days of Meg's arrival, Eric had changed from desperation for heroin into formulating a new attitude: 'I will do something about my condition.' He drank a little brandy and whisky, but his mind stayed clear. Alice, however, leaned increasingly on neat vodka.

Eric denies that sales of guitars were ever on his mind, despite the recollections of George Patterson and Pete Townshend. Says Eric: 'There were so many guitars here, getting on for two hundred downstairs and in storage, that selling my last guitar would have been out of the question. I recall some talk of selling one of my four cars. That would have made more sense, because selling guitars wouldn't have produced enough money.'

When he eventually conquered heroin and 'saw daylight' in 1974, the full irony of his financial needs during those years came before him in a bizarre discovery. For years Eric and Alice had opened none of the mail arriving at Hurtwood Edge. When Pattie moved in in 1974, she discovered 'mail everywhere, with lots of brown envelopes containing about £5,000 in out-of-date cheques'. Eric had not touched any of the letters arriving at his home during that period.

The days were long but Eric busied himself making models. The nights were complicated. 'Neither Eric nor Alice could sleep,' recalls Meg. She and George decided, five days after Meg had taken up residency at Hurtwood Edge, that complete separation of Eric and Alice would be essential if both were to benefit. With some persuasion, Alice went off alone to a clinic for individual treatment, and Clapton went back with Meg and George to their Harley Street home.

There, Meg took delivery of the first model of her self-designed stimulator. But there was an early hitch: before leaving his home, Eric had, unknown to Meg, taken a large dose of Methadone, a liquid substitute for heroin.

Then came a technical problem: Eric, who was negative and passive all the time, told Meg he had felt no current from her new machine throughout the first day. Alarmed, she traced the fault to a broken wire. Within half an hour of giving him proper treatment, he felt better after a day of being violently ill.

'We check a patient's pupils all the time, and his pupils were large so I knew he couldn't have had heroin,' she says. But she had not reckoned on Eric's slipping Methadone into Hurtwood Edge. 'Whether they kept it as a fallback I don't know, but I didn't find out until much later that they'd got it. That did set him back a bit, but apart from sleeplessness and his craving for the drug, he responded well to the treatment.' Eric stayed with Meg and George for two weeks, sleeping in the same room as their two young sons on a fold-down bed.

'His sleeplessness was so bad that sometimes I did give him a sleeping pill, which I almost never do because addicts have such a tolerance for drugs that you have to give them a huge dose to make them sleep. So you're in danger of overdosing. Mercifully, he had my two sons with him as supportive company, but he was so utterly passive. One day, in my consulting room when I was seeing other patients, I said: "Eric, could you just make coffee for yourself this morning because I'm so busy?" And he said: "Meg, I don't know how to make coffee." He wasn't fibbing. There was nothing there but passivity.

'He wasn't interested in life at all. But it was very strange: the children stimulated him. He would play toy soldiers with the children and spent hours talking to them about music, playing records to them. He even brought up some of his records and tapes and took the boys out and bought them the first rock records they ever possessed. He came to life with the children, but not with anyone else.'

One day, the inquisitive Pete Townshend arrived to visit Eric. He asked for a demonstration of Meg's stimulator and after half an hour he said: 'Yes, this really is doing something to me. I really feel the effects of this.' To which Eric replied: 'It's funny that it's affecting you, yet it doesn't do a thing for me.' So while Pete was there, Meg told Eric: 'It's time for your treatment.' Eric connected the stimulator to his ears and within twenty minutes was sound asleep, snoring. Because of his night-time sleeplessness, Eric often fell asleep during his machine treatment.

'We tried very hard to ban alcohol,' Meg continues, 'but we had alcohol in the kitchen and you couldn't watch Eric day and night. George and I were busy and Eric was often around on his own. The only time he really had a lot was when George and I had to go out and we left him with our young sons to look after him. We weren't out for long and we had given them our telephone number . . . but Eric had wandered through to the kitchen and had quite a lot of whisky to drink. Poor boys – by the time we got home, Eric was so drunk that when he wanted to go to the bathroom they had to take him, holding an arm each. Eric and the boys were both upset about it afterwards but this is all part of the experience.'

Inside a month, the week at home followed by slightly more than two weeks at Harley Street with Meg and George, Eric Clapton had withdrawn from his heroin addiction. Just before Meg Patterson concluded that Eric was ready to leave her daily care and return home, he shattered her with an eyeball-to-eyeball statement: 'You know, Meg, even though I'm cured of my heroin addiction just now, the moment I leave this house I'm going to go back on it again.'

She begged him to rethink his attitude. 'Eric, it's as if you're in a prison just now and you're seeing things from inside your own prison. All I'm asking you to do is come out of your own prison and view it from the outside instead of the inside.'

He plucked up courage and said: 'All right, I'll go on with it.' And almost as quickly, he contradicted himself: 'I just can't live without it.' That day, the craving was really bad. 'Look, Meg, I feel that I've just . . . there's something I feel urgently, and that is . . . I've got to feel what heroin is like, again. Already it's so confused in my mind. You know, if you don't let me try it, I'm going to go out and get it somewhere. I've just got this compulsion. I've *got* to try it again.'

Meg says: 'I felt he was at the stage when he would walk out if I didn't let him have it. Remember, I had to balance things the whole time. Treatment of Eric was very difficult at that moment. I said: "All right, Eric, go ahead. Phone the dealer and get some." Eric replied, "Meg, when you were out of the room I phoned my dealer and he wouldn't give it to me." '

This, says Meg, was most unusual. 'Dealers usually come running to give anybody the drugs, because they want the money. But Eric explained to me that the dealer was a very good friend of his and he'd said to Eric: "I'm not going to give you any heroin unless I have Meg's permission." So I said, "All right, I'll phone your dealer." '

'So I phoned him and he brought one dose of heroin to my house. Which Eric took. And after that, there was no more problem. He said: "Yes, it was good." But they always say that, those who have done this with or without my permission. In fact, it's always been without my permission. Eric's the only one I gave permission to have a dose.'

Meg Patterson explains that she was partly calling his bluff in allowing him to have a dose, and partly applying logical psychology. 'I felt he really would walk out if I didn't give in on that point. I couldn't be sure, anyway, that he was going to stop taking heroin for ever. You just live one day at a time with addicts. And you get used to the fact that they are liars. I knew that one dose might slow down the process of withdrawal because he was setting himself back again, chemically. But at that point, the greater danger was that he would walk out.' Later, after his initial enthusiasm, Eric said to Meg: 'Well it was good, but it wasn't like it was before. Okay, I'll go on with the treatment.'

She has no doubt that if he had not gone for treatment, Eric would have killed himself. 'The impression I got from him was that he was surprised he hadn't already killed himself, but he just hadn't had the courage to do it.' It might not have been heroin that would have killed him, unless he overdosed. 'But Eric had already almost killed himself,' says Meg, 'because in his own effort to come off heroin, he'd taken a very large dosage of Mandrax, which is a powerful sleeping pill and a particularly dangerous one. It is banned in Britain now, although you can still get it in America. He very nearly died from that large dose. And I'm sure that either by doing something like that, by overdosing on a more dangerous drug or actually overdosing on heroin, he would have killed himself.'

Significantly, Eric had taken with him to Meg's clinic his acoustic guitar. He told Meg and George he had not touched it for the three years of his drug isolation. This was untrue; but he might not have realized just how much the guitar had helped him pass the time during those long, hard days of heroin-induced torpor. More importantly, his triumph over heroin during his time with Meg heralded another tough crisis inside his head.

Eric firmly believed that through heroin he had lost all his talent, and also all his friends. 'He started strumming his guitar, and whenever he started I used to stop whatever I was doing just to listen to him. Just his strumming was so exquisite, so beautiful. But he really was in a spiritual trauma,' says Meg.

'Part of my treatment was very much instilling in him the will to live. It was desperately difficult. He'd lost all the confidence in his creativity.'

It fell to Meg's husband George to deal directly with the mental torment inside Eric that followed the successful departure of heroin from his life. George found himself face to face, night after night, with a man empty and defeated. George Patterson had studied the world's religions and worked as a missionary and preacher; he had travelled throughout China and Tibet before meeting Meg in India and joining forces with her. He had studied occultism and parapsychological phenomena – and had worked as a journalist for thirty years. 'As far as talking to Eric Clapton went,' says George, 'it was merely a one-to-one situation for me. Here was someone with problems related to how he coped with life. When he said "What's the point of living?" he was talking to someone who had been asking that question for forty years.'

With Clapton, however, there was a difference: Eric said he only wanted to live if he could make music. If he couldn't make music, life offered nothing for him.

'He didn't feel his music was there any more. This was compound-ed by a guilt complex. Another level of his problem was this: he said the greats of music, who got into the same problem as him, chemically with alcohol or drugs, when they reached the place he was at in life, killed themselves. Jimi Hendrix had died, Janis Jopin too. Charlie Parker, the jazz player, had done it and some of the others in early rock had also done it in their own way. So Eric had a kind of professional as well as a personal guilt complex. He ration-alized that their deaths must have come because they felt the same as he did. Artistically, they had exhausted their experience and there was nothing else to give, he said.

'That's the message he gave me. I rejected it on several levels. Ever since I went to China I had moved among people who took drugs . . . opium, especially. Again, in Tibet, opium was used lightly and I had to become very skilled in detecting what it meant, because my life depended on it. If I was travelling and I got a cook who was on drugs, I wasn't going to live very long! You learn never to trust them, ever, anywhere. They're all liars. Totally. Meg is more gentle and better natured than me. I learned the hard-headed way. So Eric to me was just a liar. And I can deal with liars. So when we got talking about it, I knew his argument wasn't strong. I began probing.'

To try to rationalize his negativity, Clapton said drugs had entered his life as a cumulative effect. Three years previously, when he began, he seemed to be losing his gifts and he took more and more drugs to try to stimulate himself and bring back his creativity.

'But when he took drugs and then played back his performance on tape, when he listened objectively, he realized his performance was not so good. So he became increasingly despairing, and this led to tension and contradiction.' The only exception was the performance of 'Layla' by Derek and the Dominos when the band were stoned out of their minds. 'That was the only time he ever thought that under drugs he performed better than when he was not on drugs.' The sheer animal-like power of that song, containing as it does Eric's passionate cry to Pattie Harrison to listen to his love for her, would anyway cloud any objective judgement of his performance.

Put simply, Clapton was telling himself drugs would improve his performance. The reality was that they didn't; that factor, and the consequent distrust of drugs, caused the problem fermenting in his mind.

'It was all tied up in a mesh of personal guilt, and nothing was clear in Eric's mind. Fear certainly came into it. He had been trying to justify his indulgence to other people as well as to himself. Under-neath his conviction that drugs were good for him was a suspicion that this was wrong, so he had been trying to repress that conviction. My conversations with Eric, every day, every night, were on the basis that I knew, and I knew that *he* knew, that the rationale of drugs being good for creativity was bullshit. So when I talked with Eric, I hammered away at that point: "Hey, you know, I don't *believe* you. You *know* you're not doing as well with drugs!"

'I said no aesthetic gift ever came from nothing. It comes from a spiritual experience. I argued that the art produced by Charlie Parker, Beethoven, Bach, Haydn and Mozart came from a spiritual tension, and *never* from a chemical, like a drug. It never did and never will. It might give a whip to a horse, but all it does is give a spurt to something that's already there.' Gradually Patterson's argument won through.

The departure of drugs had stripped away Eric's inhibitions so much, and he spoke so honestly to George Patterson during those two weeks, that it's possible he will never recapture that moment of transparent soul-baring. Repeatedly, Patterson hammered across his point to Clapton that art and talent came from the spirit, the suffering, the aesthetic, and not from chemical input. 'He'd lie to me about his background, he'd evade everything. But I knew there was much to come from him,' says Patterson.

Clapton led Patterson to believe that the circumstances and events of Eric's early childhood underpinned his problems with drugs.

'His illegitimacy had an impact on him and he felt embarrassed that other kids might get to know about it, or even that he felt they did know. So he withdrew more and more. In fact, he concentrated more and more on learning and he learned music by listening to it. Basically, this was the big thing in his life that had produced various reactions. There were three: one was that he hated his mother; the second was that he wanted to be the best blues player in the world; the third was that he wanted to lay as many women as possible – he wanted to lay a thousand women.

'Now about his statement on his mother – I said the most significant statistic was that all addicts had a bad relationship with their father, or the father was nonexistent or weak. That's how his statement came about – I said this meant the mother took the role of the father and became domineering or indulgent. Eric became fascinated at the unfolding of all this. Nobody had ever talked about or dealt with his feelings.

'I said: "As far as I'm concerned, this is where true Christianity comes in, or true religion. It's not a question of whether you become Pentecostal or whether you forgive your mother. That's where healing starts. You hate your mother, but what do you want to do?

Lay a thousand women? But with every woman you lay, it will be worse. You get more distant from a real relationship because you're laying them for the wrong reasons – hate, not love. You'll end up not knowing what a relationship is.' (Before his liaison with Alice, Eric's associations with girls throughout his late teenage years had been concentrated mostly into the year when he was with the Yardbirds. Most had been short-lasting physical flings. His confused attitude to women had been gnawing away at him ever since he had realized his dual loyalty to his mother and his grandmother.)

Confronted with George Patterson's cold, hard facts, Eric bristled. He put up some resistance to Patterson's argument, and said he still could not find a way of dealing with the suffering he had endured as a child. The next stage of Patterson's persuasion process advanced this theory: Eric's music had nothing to do with his technical ability to play guitar, or compose, or with taking heroin. It was what Eric *did* with his suffering that would be transmuted into his work. 'I told him the biggest composers in the world had always been the people who had the least in the world. The Jews painted and sang. Why? Because they're always under persecution. They, and others, develop the capacity to survive under it. Mozart produced the greatest stuff under persecution. Beethoven too, and he was deaf. It's the spiritual quality of how you cope with suffering that does it.' Eric pondered that one long and hard.

These deep conversations, with Eric conceding very little but listening attentively, took place as George Patterson prepared the evening meal in the kitchen at Harley Street or when Eric was lounging around between treatments. Eric still couldn't sleep and it usually fell to Meg to talk to him at night when he wanted company and conversation. He tended to wake after four hours' sleep.

One night, Eric tapped on George and Meg's bedroom door and George opened it. Eric told him he had been having a 'black scene' alone in his bedroom and could not sleep. Sitting on the side of the bed, the two men talked about religious beliefs and George Patterson confessed his own scepticisms. Then he added: 'God has just told me to pray with you.' Open-eyed, he said prayers with Eric while Meg went out to make hot drinks and offer Eric a sleeping pill. He refused. 'Okay,' said Eric. 'Where do we go from here?' Patterson's reply was simple and direct: 'There's you and your guitar and there's God. I can only think of two lines: "Lord, for tomorrow and its needs I do not pray, Give me, dear Lord, give me strength for today." ' Patterson said he knew of no other solution to life than that. A pensive Eric retired to bed on that note.

Flowered shirt, white suit and eyes closed during a guitar solo . . . this was
Eric at his 'comeback' concert at London's Rainbow Theatre in January 1973
(*Melody Maker*)

Next day, Eric spent hours strumming his guitar. George and Meg noticed him crying. 'He went inside himself, just strumming, never playing a song.' After that night marked by a prayer, Eric was particularly quiet and emotional. Soon afterwards, he went back alone to his Surrey home. Meg and George noticed that the man who had arrived on their doorstep several weeks ago with a world-weary shuffle and a slight stoop now looked more positive. If he wasn't exactly radiant, he had at least responded to their medical and spiritual treatment extremely well, and the future looked more hopeful. Still, the Pattersons knew better than to predict that all his problems were over. 'Dealing with addiction,' they point out, 'you're dealing with underlying resentments and bitterness and hatred. You have to pick your way through a minefield of insincerities and deceits. The chemical is the least important, by about 49 per cent to 51 per cent, and you cannot deal with the person at all until they are detoxified and thus deprived of the *excuse* of a distressed mind or body.

'The excuse all addicts use is that they can't get it together – too much pain, a thick head, stomach pain or sweats, you know. We have to eliminate that. After three days of treatment, they have an ice-cool head because they are allowed no drugs. So we strip away the façade and then they hate themselves for having lied!' Eric's fertile mind had become bored at Harley Street. 'Drugs had filled his mind for so long, now his mind was crystal clear he needed to get back to activity,' says Meg. She sent him away with a portable stimulator machine so that he could continue his treatments. He insisted, against Meg's wishes, on her giving him some sleeping pills, and off he went. He told the Pattersons he needed to find somewhere to recuperate.

Eric's rehabilitation, planned by Lord Harlech and Meg Patterson, called for a month of farming near Oswestry under the eye of Frank Ormsby-Gore, Alice's brother. 'I drove myself there and took my acoustic guitar,' recalls Eric. 'I was very unfit, and very low in spirits and the agreement was that I would semi-work, according to my condition.' But he struck up an immediate friendship with Frank. 'We had a lot in common in terms of taste, and intellectually we were on the same wavelength.' On a less intellectual level, they also went to the local pub and got drunk several times. 'I came straight off heroin into drinking. It was essential. Woke up most days with a hangover, and Frank said that if I didn't want to work, that would be okay, but I couldn't stay around too long in that case.'

But as a piece of motivating therapy, it worked perfectly. Frank set an example as a hard worker and within days Eric was up at dawn. 'He was running a farm which barely managed to break even. It was all manual labour, with hardly any machinery. So there was a load of hard work to be done, mucking out and baling hay, chopping up logs, sawing trees and God knows what. It was up to me to pull my own weight. And within a month I was very fit, brown from windburn and ready to take on the world. All that time, I had a guitar and I was playing.' He took occasional breaks most days, went back to the farmhouse and played and sang – 'dreaming up ideas of the kind of record I'd come back with'.

Alice, meanwhile, had entered a clinic for treatment of a different kind. 'They had come to the conclusion that not only was she suffering from drug addiction but alcoholism as well. Whereas I was a more simple case of just drug addiction. She stayed in the clinic after I came out of Meg's.' Eventually, Alice joined Eric in Wales.

Says Eric: 'We tried to form an understanding friendship again but we were told by Meg not to sleep in the same room together, not to start any emotional relationship right away because it could turn us back into what we'd been.' In fact, the medical instruction to freeze the relationship with Alice only confirmed Eric's personal decision.

Alice says she believed then that their separation was temporary and physically essential while she underwent detoxification.

After the farm experience and her own treatment, Eric and Alice returned, however, to Hurtwood Edge together, although it was agreed that it would be a temporary arrangement. During the three years of addiction, Eric hardly mentioned Pattie to Alice. 'Pattie was dormant, almost dead, in my mind during those years. But as I gained consciousness again, she came right to the forefront. And I told Alice of my passion and determination to see her. I'd go and see Pattie and tell Alice I'd been to see her.' The final separation from Alice was 'painful'.

Touchingly, Eric sent as a departing gift to Meg Patterson the gold spoon which he had worn around his neck most days for the past three years: it was the spoon from which he had sniffed heroin. With it came a simple handwritten messsage: 'Thanks, Meg. I won't be needing this.'

Today, Eric looks back on this three years as a drug addict with mixed feelings. He can rationalize what led him down the road, but feels remorse and regret at the loss of time, the wasted years and the self-deception in which he told himself he needed to do it for his art's sake.

'I conquered drugs,' says Eric, 'through my own wish or will to survive, with the help of Meg Patterson and her husband and family. They gave me love, and I found that was the medicine I needed as much as, if not more than, the actual acupuncture which she was practising. Mine was a totally self-centred way of getting better.

'It's very irresponsible. I do think that if I hadn't jumped off the path into the mire, I may have had a fuller career at this stage. It would have been a lot different. I do think that there are gaps in my life which needn't have been there, and drugs took a lot out of it. Although I carried on functioning. And who's to say that I couldn't have become even better, if I'd been practising, or if I'd been concentrating on making music or working with other people, or building healthy relationships instead of indulging my own pain?

'I don't believe you play better under dope. I think it helps you to perceive it in a more pleasant way, but that's because you perceive everything *else* in a more pleasant way.

'If you put me in a kind of laboratory situation, with drugs and then without drugs, and made me play two identical pieces of music, or even ad-lib or improvise over a certain amount of time, I would not be able to say that one is better than the other, or even different. It's just that when you're on drugs, your *perception* of what you're doing is far more rose-coloured. That's all.'

'He repeatedly said that to play the blues, which was his music, you had to *be something*,' Alice remembers. 'Long before we took smack, he would talk about the great jazz musicians, and his favourite bluesman Robert Johnson, living the right kind of lives to create his kind of music. So yes, it was definitely an act of heroism to go down that road and find out what it was like.'

Alice has her own views on Eric's battle with drug abuse, and subsequent victory. 'As it was with heroin, so it was with drink: Eric always waits for the other person, or in this case it was the other article, smack or alcohol, to make a mistake. In the case of heroin, the drug's failure for Eric was not to live up to his expectations in helping him create some work of genius, or help him towards some profound recognition of life. So when heroin did not provide any answers, he could kick it and say "I've conquered it! I've won. Because I've met heroin head on and I've come out on top – and I can *still create!*" So yes, heroin was a major reason he went down the road. Because deep inside him, he knew that he could find the way back.'

Clapton says he never took drugs with his mind on suicide, even at his lowest ebb: 'I don't believe I ever did. I don't think you go to the brink unless you actually want to end it all. I think as long as you're enjoying life, no matter what you're using to enjoy it with, you've still got a chance of survival. I don't remember ever, during that period, feeling so distressed that I wanted to die. The thing about heroin is that it makes you feel *good*. It looks terrible to everyone else and you *look* like you're dying. But in your little shell, you feel great. The only trouble is that if you're mainlining [injecting], then you can die from an overdose, but if you're snorting it through the nose, as I was, it's difficult to actually injure yourself *fatally*. You do your liver and everything a lot of damage, but that can be repaired. The biggest problem you've got is the addiction itself and how to break it.'

Alice is adamant that Eric was never in danger of killing himself with drugs. The real danger, she maintains, is that he might have killed himself in a car crash, or in an accident in the house, as a result of slow reactions or over-confidence. Alice says his driving was appallingly erratic during his three years of addiction: 'His driving really was frightening. I distinctly remember removing the rotor arm from the Mercedes once or twice, to immobilize it so that he couldn't drive it away from the house.' Inevitably, that provoked another argument between them.

'No, there was never any question in my mind of his being close to death, or suicidal, or at death's door from drugs. There was a totally different certainty, to me: that he would *survive*. Everything pointed to that. If anything depressed Eric during our time together, it was me, and what he saw in me and kept on hammering across to me . . . my low opinion of myself and my lack of confidence and self-respect. *That* brought him down much more than the drugs.'

On injection, Eric says: 'No, I never did. I did, at one point, *ask* to be injected, because I was going through heavy withdrawal . . . but it was denied and that was by Alice . . . and I think that was very clever of her really to see that that was a big step. And once you took that step, you were in a lot of trouble.'

'I don't think Eric would have injected,' says Alice. 'There was never a complete guarantee, because of the junkie's twenty-four hours-a-day, seven-days-a-week, 365-days-a-year preoccupation with wondering and worrying about the supply of the next dose. And when you fear it's not going to be around, you're in so much pain you just want to die. On a couple of times it was available by injection I said no for Eric, but he would have said no anyway. He hates injections of any kind, and he'd never have become a habitual injector of heroin.' Confirming Eric's recollection that she steered him away from the needle, Alice adds diffidently: 'Yes, I urged him not to. Because I knew that it would have been a very different and dangerous slope.'

Throughout the three years, he was eating fairly abnormally: 'Oh yeah, very heavily. I was overweight. Mainly junk food and sweets . . . chocolate, because that all goes along with any kind of morphine addiction. And so I was bloated, quite grotesque, really. I was not healthy, but not unhealthy.' Eric's assessment of his condition may be an overly positive one.

Paradoxically, while he was mentally introverted during his years of addiction to drugs, Clapton retained his sense of sartorial pride. He continued to amass hundreds of shirts, shoes and suits and Alice recalls that on most days he was 'meticulous, almost fanatical' about his appearance. 'He would change his whole outfit up to three times a day, just to sit around the house. He was potty about how he looked and loved the exercise of changing his clothes.'

On Christmas Eve 1974, Eric threw a small party for his family and friends at Hurtwood Edge. When he got up to dance with his grandmother, he said: 'Rose, I have a confession for you . . .' He was about to tell her of his drug addiction, and his renunciation of dope, when Rose interjected: 'I know, Rick. I know all about it. Don't you ever do that to us again.'

'Don't worry, Rose. I won't.'

Clapton is realistic when he talks of his lucky escape from heroin addiction and when asked for his advice to potential heroin users. 'I had a craft to go back to from the word go. I was sure that I would come out the other end and that I was having a kind of holiday. And Alice obviously recognized this too: it never looked to her as if I was getting anywhere near a danger zone. And I never felt that way, because to me, it was incidental to being a musician.

'Really, taking heroin never became my life. It was a very heavy habit, but it was a case of: "Well, I'm a musician, and this is what musicians do." It took over and it was an illusion for me to think I could get away with it. But I did.'

His message to today's drug users is based more on practicality than on a lecture. 'If you have no root to hold on to that will get you through, like being a great writer or being a great bricklayer or a great musician or an artist or *whatever*, as you were before you considered getting involved with it, then you obviously cannot do it, because it will kill you. Unless you are really sure you can make it with something else in life, you can't look to heroin. I was absolutely lucky.

'And despite the fact that neither I nor Alice thought that I was close, I *may* have been close a couple of times. I might have got killed in a car crash or an accident at home . . . so really, it's not just a question of having something like a career to hold on to, either. That's a good way of looking at it idealistically, and made sense from my standpoint. But obviously heroin can kill you in many different ways, even if you are taking it only for the first time.'

5

THE
SURVIVOR

*'I never saw the tunnel. It's still hard to believe how
close I ran to mortality'*

Drink followed drugs. It stormed into his life, scarcely less of an
addiction than heroin and with an equally devastating, ruinous
effect on his behaviour, his relationships, his work and his health.
Once again the obsessive streak in Clapton, the soar to the peaks and
the plunge to the depths, made him take to heavy drinking with no
half measures. He eventually became an alcoholic.

Returning to Hurtwood Edge from a month of fresh air and
energetic farming in Wales, a tanned and healthy Eric felt a surging
confidence in himself. After the two months of therapy, he saw
daylight. He tore into his work with a manic enthusiasm. At the back
of his mind, though, the question that had nagged at him for four
years would not go away: how to deal with his other obsession, his
love for Pattie, wife of George Harrison. There had been little contact
between them for three years; the spectre of failure to win her love
was emphasized by an even greater, unacceptable humiliation. His
stunning anthem to her, 'Layla', had manifestly not, so far, worked.
George and Pattie had surprised Eric by visiting him in Wales during
his therapeutic month of farming. The couple made the journey as a
gesture of friendship, to encourage Eric to return home fighting fit.
But Clapton told Alice bluntly that he wished Pattie had arrived
without George. It was a remark that dampened still more the dying
embers of Eric and Alice's relationship. In Wales, Eric also told
George and Alice that he was in love with Pattie and that he sought
her as his partner. But the woman he wanted remained at the side of
her husband at Friar Park in Oxfordshire. There were problems in
that marriage, and unknown to Eric she had been thinking of him.
But even the butterfly character of Pattie could not then contemplate

escaping the net around her. She remained loyal to George.

After the Welsh trip, Alice left Eric's life. Both of them realized that a complete split was essential if they were to reject the degradation of the past. But they have stayed in touch with each other and Alice has a firm friendship with Rose, who enjoys her company. Alice remembers her birthday every year. And Eric invited Alice to his fortieth birthday party at Hurtwood Edge. Within a few weeks of convincing himself, and everyone around him, that he was 'clean', Eric was on a plane for Miami, Florida. There, in a month of free-flowing creativity, his rebirth could be judged from his resonant vocal work: he found a real bluesy voice to join his plangent guitar. Incredibly, in only two and a half weeks, he recorded the album which will stand as one of his finest: *461 Ocean Boulevard*, named after the address of the house in which the musicians lived. He agrees that his new voice came from a new, clearer, inner consciousness.

He knew on his return home that he had to get busy, and quickly. He went straight into Robert Stigwood's office and asked him to book him a studio and asked particularly for the fine producer Tom Dowd to be booked with him. The result was Eric's biggest-selling album ever and marked a crucial turning point in his career and his life.

Stigwood had, all along, been a staunch believer in Eric's talent and his will to survive. He needed little convincing by Eric that he was totally serious about a comeback, and wanted to make an impact. But neither man could have guessed that it would be an album carrying such weight. And Eric had no prior hint that the musicians who would be assembled for him would have such empathy with his new style. The line-up was begun when Eric telephoned Carl Radle, his friend from Derek and the Dominos, and Carl put together the band with the help of Tom Dowd.

Eric did not drink particularly heavily during those sessions. But a cripplingly long concert tour followed. It re-established Clapton's musicianship and credibility. But it was so exhausting that he needed some kind of prop. Brandy was his answer.

Confidence and determination, combined with shyness and diffidence, had always been in his make-up. When he left drugs behind, he simply found that their absence fuelled an emotional turmoil inside him. A superficially 'up' person, powered by nervous energy and still discovering fundamental truths about himself at the age of twenty-nine, Clapton took to that most punishing of institutions which all rock musicians love to hate: the American Road.

'When I came off drugs,' says Eric now, 'I was left with a huge vacuum, a huge hole, which I couldn't fill because at that time my belief in anything other than myself wasn't really very adequate. The only way I could fill it was with booze. So I went from one vice to another. I stopped taking drugs but went for the drink, and like everything else in my life, I did it one thousand per cent.'

His confidence, he said, never left him: 'I still had that, even throughout the drug taking' (Meg Patterson disputes this) 'but there was something missing in terms of an emotional or spiritual yearning. That was killed, or muted, by the heroin, which makes you believe in yourself to such a degree that you don't need anybody else. After a couple of years, the awful feeling of not needing anybody else becomes so important that if you stop taking the heroin, you're faced with an awful pain of shame and guilt, with the terrible reality of how many people you've turned away from your door, of how many loved ones you've neglected, simply because of your own desire for comfort. And that's what I was left with when I was weaned off the heroin ... this awful pain, but also a great amount of joy at being able to *feel* the pain. Being able to cry, which had been denied me for so many years because I didn't want to, didn't *need* to, with that drug. And so, coming off heroin, I turned around from being very introverted to being very extroverted. Suddenly, you want to be part of the world again. Be loud and noisy!'

He found an early drinking companion in Pete Townshend. They developed a reputation in London's clubland as fearsome drinkers; Townshend's own excesses led him to build up to two bottles of brandy a day, and Eric was on the way to that, diluted with lemonade, by the time that the massive American concert tour began in 1974.

The twenty-six week coast-to-coast trail would have taxed the stamina of anyone. America, which had had a love affair with Clapton throughout Cream and Blind Faith, reacted feverishly to his return; Eric Clapton and his Band, as it was now officially named for the first time, was booked into the country's biggest sports stadiums with between 60,000 and 70,000 at most venues. In some cities, there were two sell-out concerts on one night.

Tom Dowd, the producer who masterminded the comeback album, had assembled musicians sympathetic to Eric's state of mind: bassist Carl Radle, drummer Jamie Oldaker, singer Yvonne Elliman, keyboardists Albhy Galuten and Dick Sims, guitarist George Terry.

On stage, a celebratory atmosphere prevailed. This was, indeed, a milestone in rock history. The music, as well as those musicians, had a correct mixture of melancholia and jauntiness, from the raunchy 'Mainline Florida' and Bob Marley's 'I Shot the Sheriff', through to the plaintive 'Please Be With Me'. The musicians and fans were jubilant at Clapton's return.

The astonishing commercial success of the album and the tour fed Eric's considerable but confused ego. After the lost three years, he had returned to work with spectacular success. And drink was, he reasoned, not a bad substitute for drugs.

By the time the long American tour of 1974 had begun, Eric had satisfied an underlying obsession that proved far more significant in his life than either drugs or drink. He had persuaded Pattie Harrison to leave her husband, George, and go and live with him at Hurtwood Edge.

Once Eric had surfaced, and split with Alice, his quest for Pattie became an obsession. She moved in with him between the completion of his *461* album and the start of the US tour, when she went around America with him. 'We were not good for each other on the road on that tour,' reflects Pattie now. Partly because she was releasing the tension of making the decision to break her marriage with George, and partly because Eric was relieved at overcoming his drugs habit and reconstructing his career, the couple leaned on each other's fallibility. And they drank. 'Neither of us was a support for the other,' says Pattie.

Eric and Pattie's relationship went in five-year cycles. It was in 1969 that Eric first fell in love with her at Esher, Surrey, where she and George often entertained Clapton. George was enormously impressed with Eric's guitar supremacy and the two men's friendship grew naturally. There were several clandestine meetings between Eric and Pattie during 1971; she felt guilty but he pursued her vigorously and says that his drug addiction was partly caused by his frustration at her inaccessibility. Wide-eyed and clear of narcotics in 1974, he finally won her over. But it was another five years before they married, in America, in 1979. Five years after that, in 1984, they hit serious problems. Throughout their partnership, Eric's clear love of Pattie confounded any theories that his woman would have to be in love with his music to win his reciprocated affection; although Pattie was aware of Eric's status, and enjoyed his work, she has never been uncritical of him. She has, though, mingled with musicians for more than twenty years and understands them. What she found difficult to come to terms with in Eric was his odd sense of humour. 'It's a typical Ripley wind-up,' she says, evoking the temperament of the people in Eric's birthplace. 'He likes to see how far he can push me before he can change anger into laughter.' One such episode occurred when Pattie bought a record of Marianne Faithfull, *Broken English*. She put it on the jukebox at Hurtwood Edge and played it a lot. 'Eric threw it out of the window,' she says. 'He knew damned

Pete Townshend was among the guests at a party in April, 1974, to mark Eric's return from seclusion (*London Features International/Keystone Press*)

well I loved that record and this was his way of teasing me, seeing how far I would go.' She was irritated by her husband's cavalier attitude. 'It was his joke but it also annoyed me because of his generally careless way with records. I loathed the way he treated his vast collection, never putting them back in their sleeves. It always upset me but it amused *him* that such a thing got me worked up.'

The *461* tour and album as it was called, had been masterminded by Robert Stigwood, the Australian-born impresario who had established the mighty empire and recording organization RSO. In the 1960s Stigwood had been a business partner of Beatles manager Brian Epstein; although music was not his hottest subject, and he would eventually move into films, he tended his artists with flair and flamboyance. It was Stigwood who had invested in Cream, and he had an avuncular affinity with Clapton. Eric and all of Stigwood's artists of the period, including the Bee Gees, were regular visitors to his mansion, the Old Barn at Stanmore, Middlesex.

Working for Stigwood, as agent and booker, at the time of Cream's formation, was Roger Forrester. Although the two men worked well together, their characters were utterly different: Stigwood was the entrepreneurial, persuasive stylist moving ever onward; Forrester was the hard-headed, practical, hard-nosed, assiduous, gruff businessman. Forrester was also a dedicated enthusiast of Clapton's, going to nearly all his shows. When Stigwood told Forrester of the multimillion dollar, record-breaking American tour to follow the *461* album, Forrester opposed the idea. He regarded it as both greedy and physically unhealthy for Clapton to be plunged into such a gigantic schedule, so soon after returning from death's door.

He argued strongly but lost the battle; Stigwood was still Eric's manager and had the final word. But it was probably the last decision about Eric's career that Robert Stigwood made. By the time a triumphant Clapton returned from America, Stigwood had delegated all decisions about Eric's future to Forrester. Within a few years, Stigwood's management contract with Clapton lapsed and, in 1979, Forrester became Clapton's official manager, having been associated with him for twelve years.

Their relationship now is intuitive, almost brotherly. Tough, aggressive and conspiratorial in manner, Forrester is super-protective and over-defensive of Clapton, reassessing his moods, his tantrums, his abilities and his capriciousness almost hourly. This most extraordinary manager–musician relationship is essential, says Forrester, because he is dealing with a man impossible to predict from day to day, sometimes hour to hour. And he attributes much of the problem he inherited to the 1974 American tour.

'Fantastic pressure was put on Eric, and many of the problems inside him amassed from that tour,' says Forrester. 'Eric was keen to get back to work and proved it by recording that *461* album so quickly. It could have been done in an even shorter time, he was performing so well and at such a speed. But the tour was another thing. He leaned on the drink, and that caused major problems later on. Eric's never been that ambitious, to want to play the major halls across America flat out like that. Eric had always been lazy. When he had to face those big stadium audiences every night, it wasn't natural for him. He'd stopped all that with Cream and suddenly – here he was again, straight out of a three-year problem as a drug addict, into these big halls. It was all too much.

'For him to return to the studio was enough; he needed six months' rest to find himself again – and then he should have gone into the 3000-seater halls instead of the 70,000 capacity stadiums.'

'When I got back from the farm in Wales,' reflects Eric, 'and the rehabilitation from heroin, I felt I could take on the world. Unfortunately I picked up a bottle at the same time. All the musicians and friends were using a pint glass. So I felt I *belonged* in the same little club. It was comfortable. I felt no compulsion to stop.

'It was full road work on that tour and I have great, great memories of it. I remember I was so drunk on some stages that I played lying on the stage flat on my back or staggering around wearing the weirdest combination of clothes because I couldn't get it together even to dress properly.' He caught conjunctivitis from singer Yvonne Elliman – 'I did half the tour with no eyes, too. But mostly, it was full-tilt drinking, morning till night and after the show. And I don't regret it at all. It was essential for me, as a kind of release.'

There had been two songs recorded by Eric which began with the phrase 'Let It . . . ' With the Yardbirds, he had said 'Let It Rock', and his first solo album contained 'Let It Rain', a perennial favourite. Now, with *461 Ocean Boulevard*, came 'Let It Grow', his most plaintive paean carrying feelings of optimism and a refreshed, positive outlook:

> Standing at the crossroads, trying to read the signs
> To tell me which way I should go to find the answer
> And all the time I know,
> Plant your love and let it grow.
>
> Let it grow, let it grow,
> Let it blossom, let it flow.
> In the sun, the rain, the snow,
> Love is lovely, let it grow.

Looking for a reason to check out of my mind,
Trying hard to get a friend that I can count on,
When there's nothing left to show,
Plant your love and let it grow.

Let it grow, let it grow,
Let it blossom, let it flow.
In the sun, the rain, the snow,
Love is lovely, let it grow.

Time is getting shorter, there's much for you to do.
Only ask and you will get what you are needing,
The rest is up to you.
Plant your love and let it grow.

Let it grow, let it grow,
Let it blossom, let it flow.
In the sun, the rain, the snow,
Love is lovely, let it grow.

'From my side,' says Eric, 'looking back, it all seems like a series of steps rather than a severe turn to the right or left, or an upward or downward movement, which is how a lot of people must view it. By 1974 I'd been absent for a long time. I went into the studio, but not with any earth-shaking ideas. I just had a couple of songs I'd always liked, like 'Willie and the Hand Jive', a Robert Johnson song, and a couple that I'd written.' The producer, Tom Dowd, was partly a coach and mentor in the studio, patient and painstaking but quickly sensing the rich mood that Eric was generating from his voice, his soulful playing and the texture of the song material. 'It seemed to me a bit of a hotch-potch as we made it,' says Eric. 'When it was finished, I liked it. And now in hindsight, it is a great record. But at the time, it never seemed to me that much of an earth-mover. It was just coming out of hiding . . . '

Eric disagrees with Roger Forrester that the tour was totally responsible for starting his heavy drinking period. 'The alcohol was going to come in anyway,' says Eric.

By the time Eric came back from that tour, he looked weak and wasted. Backstage, in hotel rooms and when he was travelling by air, he hit the brandy bottle. And his moods dipped and soared. Home at Hurtwood Edge, he could hardly last a day without going to bed for the afternoon. Many of his friends thought he had returned to drugs. Two who did not, and who fully understood the substitution, were John Hurt and Pete Townshend.

Eric's comeback took him on a coast-to-coast tour of the U.S. in 1974. He is
pictured here at Nassau Coliseum (*London Features International*)

Says John Hurt: 'With Eric, there was always something I recognize in myself . . . if we are going to do something, we overdo it. There's a certain love of danger in both of us, and it's always been apparent to me in Eric's work. The *danger* is what makes it electric. It follows that the person making that music has to live on the edge just a little bit. There is a self-destructive streak in both Eric and me which I've always known about, and it's always been getting on top of it, keeping it at bay, which has helped Eric survive and got him through the worst brandy period. He is a survivor . . . '

Townshend's relationship with Clapton has had peaks and troughs since the drugs and drink periods. This is partly because Pete insists on often talking about the heroin and alcohol periods when they meet; Eric dislikes being reminded of it by Townshend and prefers to look ahead. But Pete clearly remembers Eric's own interpretation, during one alcoholic night, of why he kept pushing his body to the limit of its endurance. 'He had this feeling of heroism about the relationship with heroin and booze. It's the star fighting back. He obviously identifies greatly with the underdog, but perhaps felt he wasn't enough of one. So he turned himself into a piece of shit so he could come back from the dead,' says Townshend.

'He once told me that in order to be able to play in the way some of the great ghetto blues players had played, he really felt he had to experience life at that level. And he was prepared to undergo that for music. And that's why Eric allowed himself to go down. So that he, and virtually he alone, could pull himself back.'

And yet Eric was never a morose, introspective drinker. Another close friend, Phil Collins, the solo singer and drummer with Genesis, recalls all-night snooker sessions at Hurtwood Edge with the drink flowing freely among a crowd of old schoolfriends from Ripley, and companions who went with Eric to football matches – Eric had developed an interest in West Bromwich Albion. Clapton was the life and soul of the party, with no self-examination or self-pity, says Collins.

Having a pub very close to his home accelerated his drinking habits. 'It didn't just escalate it – that fact just galloped my drinking along!' says Eric. 'I used to be the first one there in the morning, at half past ten, even though it didn't open until eleven. I liked the social part of being in a pub, because there was always enough drink in the house. I didn't need to go there, but I enjoyed being at the bar.'

He risked his and others' lives by driving his car 'in various degrees of dangerous states' after he had been drinking. 'I had several crashes. The last severe one was ten years ago when I came back from Australia, and got off the plane drunk and jet-lagged.

Came home, got into a Ferrari, drove it down the hill and hit a laundry van head on. I had to be cut out of the car. It was a bad crash. I was taken to hospital suffering from concussion and stayed in for a couple of days with a broken nose. I'd bashed myself about badly.' After that, he took it a little easier. But Eric has never been one to heed the warning signs: he continued to drive when he had had too much to drink. 'Sometimes I was pretty reckless . . .'

A contributory factor to Eric's prolonged alcoholism was his innate acting ability. 'Only the people who were very close to me had any inkling of how bad it was,' he admits. 'Unless you came close up and smelled my breath, I could appear to be sober and rational when in actual fact I was ten sheets to the wind. I could go all day like this . . . even at lunchtime, I'd be stoned out of my brain but would appear to outsiders to be fairly *compos mentis*.' In the pub, Eric always chose to drink in the public bar, rather than the saloon bar, so that he could mix with 'real people'. They were always less monied than him. The complexity of his character showed in his enjoyment of driving away from the pub, and waving goodbye to the workers from the comfort of his Ferrari. He regards this as classless behaviour.

'I had the ability to let my drunkenness out of the bag only when it was in an appropriate setting. In the pub, where it was okay to be drunk, I'd behave twice as drunk as I was! But most days, I was generally much drunker than I appeared to be. My manager and my close friends knew the problem, but they were frightened of telling me they knew because of the rage that would ensue.' He became very defensive and aggressive whenever anyone touched on the subject of his drinking habits: 'Don't tell me how to live my life.'

But Pattie says drink relaxed Eric. 'Basically, he's a very shy person and he felt he could unwind through drink. I thought that after his ulcer in 1981 he might have treated drink as something to take in moderation, but I should have known Eric doesn't do much in moderation! It was brandy before the ulcer, scotch whisky afterwards because the doctor had said an occasional scotch would be all right.'

For a man who capitulated so readily to drugs and drink, Clapton has often displayed an iron, ruthless streak. The characteristic may contrast with the warmth and sensitivity of his music, but he has a low threshold of tolerance when things are not working his way.

Around him, he has always needed familiar, friendly faces. He runs a 'tight ship' in the management team, and since 1978, when he formed an all-British band, he has been polishing his style as an uncompromising, decisive, if low-key bandleader. He is acutely aware of his status and loathes packed dressing rooms after the show.

The job of protecting Clapton on the road falls to Alphi O'Leary, whose giant frame keeps unwanted visitors at bay in dressing rooms and hotels around the world. His entry in 1973 into the trusted Clapton inner circle was not easy, and told much of Eric's distrust of fresh faces. In 1975, Clapton had been away, tax exiled in the Bahamas and touring America on concert dates. O'Leary was sent to keep Hurtwood Edge safe for nearly a year. On his return, at 3 o'clock one morning, Eric had to climb up the side of his house and in through a window. Eric became irritated by O'Leary's obsession with security, locking all the windows and doors. 'If you're at my house,' Eric roared, 'it takes me two weeks to open the bloody place up again. Leave some of the windows and catches open!' O'Leary answered: 'If they are left open there's no need to have me here. I might as well go then.'

Eric was annoyed, too, at O'Leary's decision to paint a fence white during his absence. Clapton dislikes familiar sights interfered with unless he approves first.

'You walk on thin ice with Eric, for a long, long time,' says O'Leary. 'He's a perfectionist as a musician but he's no fool and he will not be taken for a ride without giving out a lot of stick very quickly. I've seen him with musicians who he didn't think were giving their best. He'll swallow it for so long, and then it's "Right, axe!" '

O'Leary feared that very axe falling on him during a marathon American tour. At 7.30 one morning, Clapton phoned Alphi in his Chicago hotel room. He asked him to go along to his suite. 'Uh, can you do something for me?' asked Eric.

'Sure,' said the half-asleep O'Leary.

'Get rid of this,' said Clapton, handing him a plastic bag.

'Now when Eric says do something I usually do it,' smiles O'Leary. 'I didn't look to see what it was and just took it downstairs and put it in the hotel incinerator. Two days later, I got a phone call from Roger Forrester. "Where's Eric's laundry?"

' "What laundry?"

' "He gave you his laundry to have cleaned, two days ago."

' "No, he didn't."

' "Yeah, his best jeans and his favourite Hawaiian shirt. He's had them both for years."

' "Well, he told me to get rid of this bag, so I put it in the incinerator." '

The repercussions went on for four days on the tour. Every time O'Leary went near Clapton, even to apologize, Eric rasped: 'Piss off.' They joke about it now, but Eric has the last word. Alphi says to him,

my room is starting to look like a dust bin, and needless to say, my presence in it doesn't help very much ~ a perfect day, very, very hot with all the loonies out in droves ~ then later caught a little bit of the olympia marching band, they don't usually come out much these days, so i suppose its because it's easter sunday ~ anyway they were great, and i also found the gumbo cafe that mac recommended years ago, it's called 'felixs', but it was closed today, so i'm looking forward to some good cajun food tomorrow ~ an otherwise perfect day spoiled by yet another tantrum from roger, i think our friendship is walking on a very thin wire, he thinks i am out of order, and i think he' is sticking his nose into my personal life a little too far this time, and his answer is always "alright, ill go home then", knowing full well that i can't do the same thing ~ take it from me, it's close to the edge ~ the gig was excellent, thanks to bobby charles, who was the first person i saw. afterwards, back at the hotel, me and roger got drunk as rats together (honest!) and made up, i think he is just going through an insecure patch ~ and then, and then, we teamed up with the roadies and hit some dirt en masse, and by eight o-clock on the other page i decided i had made enough of a fool of myself for one night (dancing with vogan etc.) and went back to the hotel, there was a chick in this club who actually wanted me to go with her and watch the banks of the mississippi overflow, i told her i hadn't got any wellies, but she still seemed to ~~think~~ think it was a great idea ~ madness! ~~they are all~~ loonies down here, i really can't wait to get moving ~
see y'all later ~   G

often: 'Cor, Eric, lovely jeans you're wearing.' And Eric's reply is always the same: 'Yeah, but not as good as my old ones.'

In the seven years during which Clapton had an increasing drink problem, those close to him found him as prickly on stage as he was when he came off and hit the bottle. He was particularly vulnerable when fans in the audience received heavy treatment, as they did once in Austin, Texas.

'Without those kids,' says Eric, 'I'm out of work.' So when the security team in front of the stage at Austin began billy-clubbing exuberant kids, and spraying Mace on their faces, as well as on Clapton's own crew, the guitarist took dramatic action. He laid his guitar down on stage, stopped the band, and walked off. When the confrontations between the security men and the fans had subsided, they returned. But to all those around Clapton, and the promoters, it was a sharp warning, from a superstar, that he would not play at any price.

Surprisingly, Eric's heavy drinking years did not colour his judgement of others, or his decisiveness, or, crucially, his ability to play. 'But I was on automatic pilot most of the time,' he says now. On stage, or when he rationalized his career to himself and even to his guardian Roger Forrester, Clapton was lucid, cool and objective. Chris Stainton, joining him near the end of his drinking period, found him a 'natural bandleader, whatever he says'. Stainton observed immediately that Eric 'loved or hated, people or things, cities or countries – everything. There was no in between, no shade of grey'. The total definition in Eric made for a leader who knew a bad audience, or a bad night's playing, and did not want, or expect, to be bolstered by false persuasion to the contrary.

Fifteen years of performing had given him an ability to judge an audience quickly. Stainton recalls casually saying to Eric after one European concert: 'Good one tonight, Eric.' Eric snapped back: 'Nah it wasn't. It was like playing to a load of fucking corpses.' The quality of his music, and that of the musicians, was lost in the absence of Eric's more important 'fix' – the warmth, the instant response, the empathy of the crowd.

Only twice did drink seriously affect his playing. Both concerts were, strangely, in a country he loves, Japan. He had stopped drinking but sneaked back on it that day when nobody was with him. He thought he was able to have an occasional drink, but his body rejected it and he went on stage with a combination of pain-killing tablets and too much Cognac inside him. He played a whole solo a semitone out of tune. His musicians, and the road crew cringed, but he survived, blissfully unaware that although he was hitting the right notes, the key was wrong.

Chris Stainton, a war veteran of rock who saw service in Joe Cocker and Leon Russell's bizarre Mad Dogs and Englishmen tour, views the Clapton drunken walk along a tightrope with a glance back at his own drugs problem. 'What happens is that *you think* you're playing better, but you're not. You're usually coming out with a load of rubbish.

'I think there was a little bit of the culture of jazz and the blues players he idolized. So many of the black players Eric loved used to get through a bottle of scotch before they went on stage. So maybe there was a bit of that romance in it for Eric. I know, from experience, and Eric does now, that if you want to deal with music properly, you must do it straight.

'But the determined, stubborn streak inside Eric makes for a very complex attitude to drugs, and drink, and that's why he went right to the edge with both. You know, he actually had to be at the point of death, looking the angels in the face, before he gave up. Now he's kicked everything, I know he will never, ever go back to it. He's a survivor.'

Now Eric particularly enjoys one aspect of being 'dry' – watching people drinking too much, talking too much, 'and generally making a complete idiot of themselves, while I'm sober enough to stand back and watch it happen.'

The 'pub-crawling Herbert', as Pete Townshend so inelegantly described Clapton, alienated all but those who recognized the deep-seated cause of the drunkenness.

His immature, custard-pie humour and practical jokes have often been at odds with his seriousness as a man and as a musician. Once, he pushed his jokiness too far even with loyal aides like Roger Forrester and Alphi O'Leary. On tour, Forrester knocked on Eric's hotel room to be told from the other side by a mocking Eric, sleepy from brandy: 'Oh *go away*! I'm not going *on* tonight. Don't feel like it.' Forrester and O'Leary literally smashed the door down, thinking Clapton meant it . . . to find him ready to go to the concert.

At the local pub, O'Leary called the joking Eric's bluff one night. Under the influence again, Eric began systematically kicking Alphi under the table. O'Leary, whose physical size and strength does not invite argument, said: 'Eric, if you do that once more, I shall take you outside and knock the shit out of you, whoever you are. You're not a big enough boy to kick me.' Clapton turned to his other drinking friend and said: 'I think he means it.' He stopped, knowing he had pushed the joke too far, and not wanting to take issue with the six-feet three-inch giant body of a sober O'Leary.

Another dangerous confrontation came in the Bahamas after O'Leary had hired a Toyota car and a playful Clapton snapped off all the chrome fittings and placed them inside. Then he jumped up and down on the roof. 'Now,' recalls Alphi O'Leary, 'he could say he paid the hire car money, but that wasn't the point. He was treating me like a moron. I didn't want to drive around in a car looking like trash. I picked up a paving slab and threw it at him. It missed him by half an inch and shattered on the floor. He said: "You're mad." I said: "Fair's fair, Eric." '

He went through a period of winding people up, seeing how far he could push people. 'I'd never been used to that,' says O'Leary. Deep down, though, Alphi O'Leary has massive respect and love for his boss. 'He's sincere, there's a ton of love and tears inside him, and he really is a god of the guitar.' Talking to fans at stage doors around the world, Alphi O'Leary is convinced that many really do idolize Clapton as a seer.

Among those who saw the unhappy years of Eric from close quarters was Gary Brooker. The ex-leader of Procol Harum, the group that ran for ten years from 1966 and recorded the international psychedelic anthem 'A Whiter Shade of Pale', bought a pub, the Parrot Inn, two miles from Clapton's house. The year was 1976, bang in the middle of Eric's drinking years.

Clapton and Brooker had first met in the sixties. Cream were playing 'Strange Brew' and Procol Harum 'A Whiter Shade of Pale' on television's 'Top of the Pops'. Later, Brooker's band toured America in the footsteps of Cream, and he says they were 'staggered' at the breakthrough Cream had achieved. 'Before them, bands like the Animals and Herman's Hermits had played the big cities, but now Cream were breaking records in places like Akron, Ohio! They were *everywhere*.'

After Eric had wandered into Gary Brooker's pub one night to find him behind the bar, the two became friendly. Two years later, when Procol had ended, Gary had gone solo as a singer-songwriter-keyboardist. Eric asked him if he wanted to join his band, complementing the rocky piano work of Chris Stainton.

'The day he asked me to join, I saw that he had a problem,' says Gary Brooker. 'He said he wanted someone strong in the band.' Brooker's role was to be twofold: as an experienced bandleader, he was expected to help knock the band into shape and take some of the leadership responsibilities from Eric; and he was also to help Clapton emerge from the shroud of bleary boozing.

'Eric's condition was very worrying,' says Gary Brooker. 'Often

At the Crystal Palace Rock festival in July, 1976, Eric jams with Freddie King and faces a sea of fans who swam up to the stage through a specially-built moat (*Barry Plummer/Paul Canty/London Features International*)

we'd get drunk together, but I was surprised that he'd flake out, or be drunk many times in addition to the ones when we had a drink together. And he'd crack up, in tears. I tried to get to the bottom of what it was . . . and Eric would say things like: "Oh, I just want to play the blues." This wasn't just the drink talking, it was something very deep that was troubling him. It was distressing.'

Brooker tried to convince Clapton that part of the problem was that his musicians at that time – Chris Stainton, Dave Markee (bass guitar), Albert Lee (guitar) and Henry Spinetti (drums) – didn't behave like a *band*. 'We should all get together more often, get to know each other,' said Brooker. A stiff attempt to do so, a formally arranged jam-session in the barn of Brooker's home, did not ignite; the others failed to understand why Gary had been brought into the band in the first place. 'I think the others revered him, and didn't mix, whereas he'd enjoy coming round to my hotel room, or me to his, at eleven in the morning for a chat. He seemed removed from the band and I don't think that helped.'

In a vivid recollection of the days he saw Eric behaving emotional-ly, Gary Brooker says: 'There were tears in his eyes on some occasions. He'd say to me: "I'm cracking up." He didn't like what he was doing to himself but he couldn't get out of it. He said it was such a slow process, winning himself round to saying: I don't want to be this person any more. It definitely seemed to hurt him to realize he was ruining himself.' The worst periods, predictably, were when there was no concert tour on the road, no album to prepare, and consequently no responsibilities to work. Clapton always performs best, as a person, when he faces the prospect of putting himself through the hoop. 'The other time I saw Eric cry was when we all went to see the film *ET* in America. There wasn't a dry eye among the whole band,' says Brooker.

On 20 February 1979 the inner man surfaced in a particularly emotional entry in his diary: 'I realize today that I am a very nervous and bitter man. I've been reviewing some of my records to help Nell [Pattie] put together a programme for the tour and I felt it come through the music . . . God bless all, I'm scared stiff and I don't know how to deal with it yet. I know I'm good, but good enough for you? I drink too much and I lie, mostly to myself, I write this to you because I need your help. All I know is your gift and you can have it back any time you like. You see, I lie. Dear Lord, please give me strength to stop drinking all the time and please grace my hands with the beauty that we all know. I am yours, E.C.' Two days later came a short entry summarizing the whole day, and what was to be a continuing problem surrounding his forthcoming tour: 'A lot of trouble today,' wrote Eric, 'concerning the itinerary clause about no women on the road. Still not much done.'

Pattie's memories of her husband's seven years as a drunk are vivid. Warning lights had flashed before her during the 1974 American tour; Pattie was acutely aware that he had just kicked heroin and needed a prop, but the quantity he drank, about two bottles of brandy or sometimes bourbon a day, shocked her. 'Meg Patterson located his hotel occasionally and talked to him about his drinking; she warned him there was a possibility that he would replace drugs with brandy and it could become a similar problem. He insisted to her there was absolutely no problem and she wasn't to fuss over him. But he was drinking a fantastic amount,' says Pattie.

Back home, he became 'unbearable to live with. He just got worse and worse. I'd never know what mood to expect him to be in. He was aggressive, loving, vindictive, everything. He woke up to drink brandy and lemonade which was left in the glass from the night before and slept only in five-hour cycles. His body needed drink every five hours. There was no set pattern to when he'd go to bed.

'I tried several different ways of letting him know I thought he was drinking too much. He told me not to be silly. I purposely nurse-maided him and got his drinks for him. There was a good reason. He said: "Get me a drink" and I'd sometimes say: "No, wait a couple of hours." He'd get very cross and say: "All right, I'll get it myself." And he'd pour far too much brandy. At least when I prepared it, I could control the amount of alcohol and put more lemonade in it.

'Then I tried another way: I'd sometimes not drink at all. I thought he might notice that I wasn't drinking for a few days and copy me. Then I'd get bored with that, drink far too much and be terribly drunk and very silly, which of course he loved. But I felt dreadful the next day, so that wasn't much fun either. And there was nothing really I could do. It steadily got worse. We went on holiday one year with Guy Pullen and Nigel Carroll to Portugal. Eric was drinking so much that we were all nervous to go out to the beach, or go out shopping, because Eric was still asleep and we dare not leave him. He'd been up half the night drinking, so he'd come down like a bear with a sore head, get himself more drinks and then become more like a human. That was the daily pattern. Then we could go off and do whatever we all wanted to do. But in England Eric wanted to stay at home, near the drink.'

A frightening event, emblematic of Eric's drinking came when he and Pattie were driving to Rutland to spend some time with the family of Bob Pridden. 'I was driving because Eric felt so ill on the way up,' says Pattie. 'He hadn't had his usual bottle of brandy that day and felt awful. He was sick in a phone box in the village when we stopped to phone for directions to their house. When we arrived, we all suggested he went to bed. He insisted that he wanted to take a brandy and lemonade with him to bed. I said he was absolutely mad. After he went up, I went to check on him. He said he was shaking inside and he felt the same as when he was coming off heroin, because he hadn't had any alcohol.'

Next evening, they went with friends for dinner to a smart restaurant. 'I was talking to somebody on my left and Eric was sitting on my right, when suddenly he leaned on me terribly heavily. My immediate thought was: Oh gosh no! He's drunk again and the evening hasn't even begun! And then I realized, he hadn't had anything to drink. He'd only had one drink all day and the waiter had only just taken everybody's order. I turned round and looked at him . . . As I was turning, I noticed all these faces looking and listening to him with their mouths wide open. He was shaking all over, with his mouth open and was sliding down the sofa on to the floor. Everybody left the room and somebody called an ambulance. One person said he was having an epileptic fit, that I was to try and grab hold of his tongue. Somebody else said, "Undo his tie." Somebody else said, "Undo his trousers." We just made him very loose. And I tried to hold him, but he was shaking so much and convulsing. This lasted at least three minutes. Finally, he stopped shaking and he looked at me, but he couldn't see me. He wasn't focusing. Then, gradually, his eyes came into focus and he was wondering what on earth he was doing, lying on the floor. He got on the sofa. By this time somebody had got through to a doctor who I went to speak to. As I was speaking to this doctor, the ambulance arrived and the ambulance men went in with a stretcher and Eric came out on it. As he passed through the inside lobby of the restaurant, he sort of looked up, saw me on the phone and waved goodbye to me! This was just too comical, like something out of the Marx Brothers!

'He was lying there, lifted his head and said, "Goodbye Nell." And then he lay down again. So I put down the phone and jumped into the ambulance with him. At the hospital, in bed, one doctor came to see him, asked him what was the matter and he said, "Nothing." Then I said, "Well, you know, it's probably because he hasn't had his quota of drink today." The doctor asked him how much he drank and he said, "Not much . . . the occasional brandy." At this, I almost exploded. The doctor really didn't have much patience for husbands and wives arguing. He stalked out. Five minutes later, another doctor

Above: During a Rolling Stones concert in New York in 1975, Eric gets a whisper in the ear from Keith Richard. Ronnie Wood is on the left (*Bob Gruen/Star File*)

From Eric to Willow. A postcard sent to his dog, from Oregon

came in and took his temperature and blood pressure. We had the same argument again. And he was finally released from hospital. Eric hardly remembered any of that scene later, when we got home.'

Next day, Nigel Carroll drove up to Rutland and took Eric and Pattie home. 'Eric carried on drinking,' says Pattie. 'I was so shocked that he didn't realize something had happened.'

The doctor had told Pattie that Eric had had an epileptic fit because alcohol had not reached the blood cells in the brain. 'The doctor said that if someone's drinking that heavily and then stops, this will happen. Usually, a doctor can prescribe a drug to prevent this happening.'

Eric stubbornly refused to accept that he had been ill. Continuing with his old brandy intake, he insisted he had simply fainted: 'I fainted once as a child, it's not that dangerous.' Pattie, horrified, answered: 'No, this wasn't a faint. I'll show you just what happened and you'll see how frightened I was. I thought you were dying and were having a heart attack.' She then simulated Eric's fit. 'I went through all the motions of how he'd collapsed, and I think it got through to him how horrific it was.' For the next two weeks, Pattie woke up, sweating, every night, having a nightmare vision of Eric having that fit. Slowly, it dawned on Eric that he needed medical tests. He pacified her by saying he would go to a hospital, but did nothing about it. His drinking continued. There was no housekeeper at the house. Pattie cooked lunch and dinner most days, 'but his eating habits were erratic'.

Of the worst three years of his drinking, from 1979 until 1982, when Eric was drinking up to two bottles of liquor a day, he says: 'My mind had gone so far that if I didn't have double vision, I was worried. I saw two TV sets all the time, two of everything – and if I didn't, then I'd have to have more drink to perpetuate that double vision, because it was *secure.*'

In his 1979 diary, Eric wrote with astonishing frankness about his relationships and his occasional arguments with his wife. 'Nell and me had a row,' he wrote. 'No, not a row, a quiet game. I don't think she can raise her voice without bursting into tears. That may sound cruel on my part but I believe that if you are angry about something you should shout it out of your system or else it festers and turns from anger into bitterness.' A lighter touch came a month after that entry, when Eric recorded that he had overheard Pattie speaking to a friend on the phone and 'referring to herself as Mrs Clapton. [This was before their marriage.] What next!' Pattie caught sight of Eric's written remark and wrote cryptically in the diary underneath it: 'Well, it could be Miss Boyd, or Ms Harrison, depending on the situation or the first name that comes to mind. I know who I am but I can't always choose a name.' Eric wrote the final words: 'Then I have to choose one for you, doll. Just wait and see.'

Eric's drinking was also rooted in his desperation for a busy social life. Properly reunited with all his old friends from Ripley, he took up residence most nights in the pub in that village, the Ship, with the local people, Johnny H and Scratcher . . . and Guy Pullen, his old schoolfriend with whom he had lost touch during his heroin years. And especially Sid Perrin, a friend of Eric's mother, with whom he was particularly close.

'It was lunacy,' says Pullen. 'We'd spend the night drinking with all the crowd, then go over to Eric's home for snooker. And he'd still drive, full of brandy. On the last righthand bend before reaching his drive, there's a dip and a fifty-foot drop into a car park. One night, we went round a tree on the wrong side of the road, with Eric driving Pattie's Alfa-Romeo, and I thought we'd had it, that moment.'

Pete Townshend and Gary Brooker were regular drinkers with him. 'The booze made Eric the life and soul of the party,' says Guy Pullen. The parties lasted all weekend, with Guy a particularly regular guest at Clapton Towers. 'We'd go for a drink on Friday night and the next thing I'd remember was that it was Monday morning and time for me to drive to work,' says Guy. 'It was one long party.' Snooker and cards were the favourite games, with Eric proving to be an appalling loser – he sulked. But he claims to have been great at arm-wrestling. 'I used to take on anyone, and I was quite good at it, through sheer determination.'

Guy Pullen recalls one Monday morning when he was drinking coffee at 8.30 after two hours of sleep. Eric was sipping his breakfast brandy. 'I was sitting at his kitchen table, staring out across the downs and I found myself saying to him: "Do you know, Rick, I'm pissed again." And he said: "You ought to be. I've just put a treble vodka in that coffee." ' Guy Pullen arrived at work one hour later, drunk.

Running the career of a world-famous guitar hero was a twenty-four hour crisis for Roger Forrester. 'The only certainty,' he says, 'was that Eric would be in a permanent alcoholic haze.' Planning his diary more than a week ahead was a gamble. Forrester, who had himself been down the alcoholic road but was by then a non-drinker, believed that finding new, stimulating aspects of Eric's life might at least keep him interested in work until he stopped drinking.

One such diversion was *Eric Clapton's Rolling Hotel*. In 1979, it was conceived as a documentary film of a rock band on tour in Europe.

The producer, Rex Pyke, thought that the plan by Forrester to tour Europe by train and live on the train would be a perfect backdrop for the film. It was a refreshing change from the normal aeroplane method of transport, and the luxury of *haute cuisine* on the three railway carriages travelling between such cities as Hamburg and Paris would create a stimulating atmosphere.

Rex Pyke was immediately struck with Clapton's acting ability: 'Terrific! He can do perfect imitations. He doesn't do Laurence Olivier doing Richard the Third, but he does Spike Milligan doing Laurence Olivier doing Richard the Third. And I was astonished to find that he could recite from *The Caretaker*, playing all the roles like Donald Pleasance and Robert Shaw.'

Robert Stigwood visited the Clapton show in Paris, and a backstage encounter, which was filmed, showed Eric trying hard to lambast his former manager. Eric grabbed the film camera, aimed it at Stigwood, and said: 'Right, now's the time for some questions . . . There are a lot I haven't dared ask and here they all are.' Confident from his imbibing, Eric went on to assert that Robert had used the money earned from Cream to finance the Bee Gees. Good-naturedly, but with a serious tone underneath, Eric asked where the money earned by Cream had been invested and Robert replied: 'This isn't the right time to speak about this. We should talk about this another time.' But Clapton pressed on: 'Don't go away,' he said to the cameraman and Robert. 'This is my film and I want it in it.'

Like several other items, it was cut from the finished film, which went on to be shown to much praise at London's National Film Theatre. Elton John and George Harrison had been on the train and in the film. But in spite of its creative honesty, it was never shown nationally. Too many moments of tension made the film untenable: like Ben Palmer's insistence that Muddy Waters, who was on the tour, should have the pleasure of being on the train rather than on the band coach, because he was suffering from bronchitis. Ben's compassionate pleas met no response. The concerts filmed showed Eric performing well . . . but his speech was slurred and there was too much evidence of his bad physical condition. *Eric Clapton's Rolling Hotel* gathers dust, a flawed but fascinating, fleeting glimpse of Clapton's weakness and indifference during that year. 'Musically, I was not pleased with anything I came up with,' he says now. 'I was doing the gigs, but just pressing the buttons.'

At Clapton Towers, Pattie's sister Paula had stayed several weekends with her boyfriend, Nigel Carroll. A gradual friendship developed between him and Eric; Roger Forrester completed the trio that drove

my guitars are staring and screaming
'play me, play me' i may be going mad.
i dream about health and death all
the time, lonleyness is so hard to find ~
and the worst fear is: once you
have found it, what do you do with
it? ~ read a book, write a line,
walk in the fresh air, listen to
every sound you can hear, and then
figure it out all over again ~
and put it down to pre nerve tours?
had a nap and i feel a bit more positive ~ later ~ nell came back to
cheer me, well doped up, and daft ~
scotty and his mate martin came
down in the evening and we all
played pool till the early hours of
the next page ~ keith and ronnie
rang up and so did stickboot, fish
and chips, what a give away ~
no word from brian knight yet ~
bye ~ oh yeah, southampton won
against leeds last night knotking them
out of the league cup ~ come on you
baggies

a hundred miles most Saturdays to follow the football fortunes of West Bromwich Albion. Because of his sobriety, Nigel often found himself nominated to drive Eric's Mercedes.

By then, Eric's drinking had definitely become more than an escape route from hard drugs. It had also become a symbol of masculinity. Nigel Carroll, appointed by Eric as his personal assistant, told his boss he had been ordered off drink for a year because he had suffered from hepatitis. 'Oh no!' said Clapton. 'If you don't drink, you're not a *man*! What will I tell the roadies? When we go to the bar, you can't order an orange juice or a Coke. They'll think you're a poofter!' On the football drives to the Midlands, Nigel Carroll packed two bottles of Courvoisier and two bottles of lemonade into a suitcase which was inscribed with the football club's initials. Eric began checking himself into hotels round the world as 'Mr W. B. Albion'. His loyalty to that team was something inherited from his grandparents, who had supported West Bromwich Albion throughout his years of living with them. And, like everything which hooked Eric's attention, it became not merely a hobby, but an obsession. 'On away matches, in real hard parts of the crowd, Roger and I got very worried because Eric would stand there with the WBA scarf on, cheering, and we thought he was inviting trouble because he got so carried away.' In Manchester, after an away match, Eric bought a toy gun before getting on the train back to London. At the barrier, Clapton's party had been joined by a man who challenged him about his team's performance. 'You didn't have a very good day today, did you?' he said, when they all sat down. Eric pulled out the replica gun, put it on the table, and said: 'I've got something here that says we *did*.' The man fled out of the carriage.

Private meetings between Pattie, Roger, Eric's mother Pat, Guy Pullen and Nigel, rather like a committee, pondered what to do about Eric's drinking. But they agreed that he was so stubborn he would have to decide himself. No one could persuade him it was becoming dangerous. Getting Eric to eat, to offset the alcohol, was difficult. Inevitably, the years of hard drinking, erratic sleeping, poor eating, travelling and pressurized work when it came were going to hit him. The thunderbolt happened when Eric and his band were eight dates into a projected forty-five-concert tour of America in 1980.

For months before the tour, and particularly when it began, Eric had had a pain in his back. 'I didn't know what it was and I didn't tell anyone,' he says. When the tour began, it worsened. He stepped up his dose of pain killers to between forty and fifty a day, and together with the brandy consumption of at least a bottle a day, his appetite for food had virtually gone. Nigel Carroll kept the pain killers and became increasingly alarmed at the knocks on his hotel door at four in the morning from a Clapton wanting more tablets. Eric said he thought the pain in his back had come from a very hefty Irishman's slap on the back during Eric's visit a few months earlier to Barberstown Castle, County Kildare, Ireland (the beautiful eleventh-century hotel which Clapton had bought as an investment and visited for hard-drinking weekends).

But Roger Forrester and Nigel decided that, as Eric's knocking on the door for tablets increased to two or three times a night, and a mighty long concert tour lay ahead, they could not risk carrying on without medical help. Before his next show, he needed a pain-killing injection from a doctor.

Eric played the concert at Madison, Wisconsin, and came off stage doubled up in agony. Watching the show from the side of the stage, Forrester sensed it was now very serious, but knew he would have trouble persuading Clapton to go to hospital. On the band's midnight charter Viscount plane to Minneapolis St Paul, Eric was ashen, quiet, not drinking and clearly in trouble. 'I was desperately worried,' says Alphi O'Leary. 'He was just slumped in his seat, out of it.'

Eric had to be helped from the plane into the limousine. Forrester told the driver to go straight to the hospital. Eric sleepily grumbled that he didn't understand why he was suddenly travelling separately from the band. Forrester said: 'This time, you need help. You're having a check-up.' At the United Hospital, Minneapolis, they checked him over and asked him to return later that morning. After some X-rays at the second session, the doctor asked Roger and Nigel to phone them later. By the time they had returned to the Radison Plaza Hotel, the doctor was on the phone: 'Get him back here immediately. He's got an ulcer that's about to explode into his pancreas. We want him back in.'

Forrester's reaction was: 'Well, if it's that serious, we'll fly back to England straightaway.' The doctor chillingly rammed home the urgency: 'I don't think you've got time even to get to the airport. I'll have to lay it on the line to you. We think he could die at any moment.'

Eric had returned to his room. Forrester called Carroll, who had a pass key to Eric's room. A knock went unanswered. They opened the door and saw Eric's jeans lying on the floor – still inside his cowboy boots. 'We could only see the trousers and the boots. It looked like his body was inside them round the corner. We assumed he was lying on the floor, and we went *white*.' They were relieved to find him asleep on the sofa. Forrester woke him and didn't speak a word.

'I'm going in, aren't I?' said Eric. 'Yes,' said his manager. 'Let's go,' said Eric, 'I'm in so much pain.'

Within forty-five minutes, Eric was on an intravenous drip, with a camera confirming the worst suspicions. Eric had five ulcers and one was so big, the size of a mandarin orange, that it was like a time-bomb that could have exploded at any moment. It was so big that at first the doctors thought it was a shadow.

Clapton's dramatic illness, and his four-week stay in the United Hospital, was big news throughout America. Gradually, with drugs, Eric's ulcers were diminished and he returned from the precipice. Pattie flew in from London. Pete Townshend and country singer Don Williams were among the visitors, and more than five thousand cards, flowers and gifts flooded the hospital. Eventually, there were so many that the florists were asked by Eric to divert anything sent to him to other local hospitals and the dozens of teddy bears sent to him went to the children's wards. Eric's nurse, Delia Flynn, had the tough job of coping with Eric's moodiness. As he responded to treatment, Eric went out for two hours each day. By then, he was obsessed with fishing, and he found a local shop where he built up a collection of about twenty-five rods. He used to pretend to cast, with weights on the end, in the hospital corridors, a sight that amused the nursing staff. He became such a local news item that one radio station established a point in the city for people to congregate and sign a get-well card to him each day. 'Eric Clapton's get-well card today will be displayed at the corner of . . . ' And thousands went to sign it.

Eric was allowed out of the hospital quite often during his month there. Once he decided to visit a fishing friend in Seattle, one of his favourite cities. It was part of his therapy. Over dinner, he ordered a glass of milk and then asked the waiter to put brandy in it. Infuriated, Nigel Carroll ordered the waiter not to. He told Eric that because of the drugs he was taking for his ulcers, alcohol was wrong. But Clapton was annoyed at his personal assistant's schoolmaster-like attitude. He asked a girl sitting in the restaurant party to drive him back to his car. Terrified at having Eric Clapton as her passenger, she shot a red light and crashed into a taxi. Eric suffered bruised ribs and a Seattle doctor diagnosed that he had now also developed pleurisy.

He was immediately flown back to Minneapolis. The doctors said that now he had a lung condition, the bottom half of one of his lungs had partially closed. They put a steamer in his room, which finally convinced Eric that he should go home. 'If I've got to sit in a room breathing damp air from steam.' he said, 'I might as well go home to England where the air's *naturally* damp. I can get it by sitting in my

Eric with his manager, Roger Forrester

garden!' He flew back to London next day.

The doctors did not tell him until he was leaving how close he had been to disaster. One estimate said he had forty-five minutes to live if the giant ulcer had not been brought under control in time. 'I had been in agony, but I'd anaesthetized myself so much by booze and pills that I never knew how truly painful it was,' says Eric.

'I never saw the tunnel, never actually visualized myself dying. I just recall feeling very bad on the plane and then recovering in hospital. It's still hard to believe how close I ran to mortality.'

Medical advice on leaving hospital was tough on Eric. He was told to avoid spicy foods, a particular blow because he had a taste for Indian curries, loved Rose's pickled onions and ate a jarful at a time and enjoyed eating lots of raw peppers. But on the question of alcohol, Clapton had skilfully negotiated himself a compromise. Basically, he was told not to drink. But Eric said that a total ban might be too much for him. 'They made deals with me. I said: "Well, if I moderate and cut it down to two or three scotches a day . . . would that be all right?" And they all said yes. They didn't know they were dealing with a completely obsessive alcoholic to whom two or three scotches were just for breakfast.'

The pull of the bottle triumphed over any medical intelligence. 'Within a couple of months of being out of that hospital I was back on a bottle or two bottles a day. And I didn't give a damn about my health.'

For Roger Forrester, the long years of constant worry of whether his friend would be a survivor, began to take their toll. By 1981, with Eric back to heavy drinking, perhaps their most significant conversation took place in Tokyo during Eric's tour of Japan, where the fans adore the depth of his music. 'The day of the Tokyo show, for the very first time ever, Eric had said to me he didn't want to appear on stage. I couldn't believe it.' Despite all the traumas of his young life, Eric had remained steadfastly professional. He knew when he played badly by his own yardstick, but the audience rarely guessed how far he sometimes pushed himself.

'Then that night in Tokyo he showed me what was wrong with him,' says Forrester. 'His whole body was covered in an enormous rash from head to foot, right down to his fingers. Someone said it was food poisoning, but I knew it was alcohol. It was his liver reacting to the booze. Now, I'd been sweating for eight years through literally every number on stage, wondering if he'd get through the show. That night, I had to say something, even though I don't believe in ultimatums. I said we had to do something about this. I said: "I'll cancel all your work, Eric, until we get you together. I don't *think* you drink to *excess*, Eric. I don't think *anything*. I *know* that you're an *alcoholic*." ' It was the first time he'd had the word used on him. ' "You've got a problem," I said.' Eric says he did not believe Roger at first.

'We got back from Japan in December 1981,' says Forrester. 'I insisted that something had to be done.' 'Let me have Christmas at home,' a rational Eric finally replied, 'and if I agree to go into a clinic for treatment, I'll call you. Give me no more than twenty-four hours' notice, and take me away.'

The death in November 1981 of fifty-eight-year-old Sid Perrin who had lived with Eric's mother for the past five years had a profound effect on Eric. Sid was a thoroughbred Ripleyite who worked in the aircraft industry, and endeared himself to Eric by what Clapton calls a 'W. C. Fields-like panache'. He was a raconteur and the best footballer, cricketer and singer in Eric's village. Eric warmed to his sense of humour. They were frequent companions, particularly in the pub, where Sid fuelled Eric's male chauvinism.

'He was a beautiful man, a childhood sweetheart of my mother. But he was also a very hard-drinking man and when he fell ill and couldn't drink, I think he died from a broken heart because he couldn't have a good time any more,' Eric recalls. 'He had a love of life and was something of a hero to me. When he died, Ripley died with him to a certain extent. The good times stopped. It made me determined to stop the boozing. I saw it all as being a dreadful waste of time, and I could end up going the same way as Sid, after stomach disorders.'

After Sid's funeral, with everyone very quiet in Ripley, Eric had too much to drink and became noisy, opening the windows and shouting. In front of many of Eric's friends, Nigel Carroll said to him: 'Cool it.' Eric fired Nigel immediately. 'Fine,' said Carroll. 'Now I can tell you what I really think about you.' He went on to say that Eric's behaviour was disgusting. Moments later, Eric was in tears. 'He wants you to take him home,' Pattie said to Nigel. 'I don't work for him any more,' Nigel replied. He agreed to drive a troubled Eric away. Says Nigel: 'On the way back to his home, Eric made me stop the car for a talk. He was crying. And he said: "Nig, you don't tell me off often, but when you do, it's for the right reasons. Will you come back?" Nigel smiled. "I never thought I'd left!" ' That happened several times; Carroll, now one of Eric's closest friends, never shirks from telling him, straight from the shoulder, when his behaviour is unacceptable.

Christmas 1981 was the worst. By eight o'clock on Christmas morning Eric was 'well on the way to being drunk,' says Pattie. She planned for a house full of both their families and friends, and set about cooking a turkey. By lunchtime she realized that Eric had been missing from the house for hours. He had said he was going off to see the gardener. 'I wandered round the garden looking for a slumped body in the snow. I was in floods of tears because I couldn't find him anywhere. I was furious with all the guests because they'd encouraged him to drink so much, too. I thought he'd passed out. And I found him asleep, absolutely drunk, among the pile of logs in the basement. It was a hideous Christmas.'

A few days earlier, the signs had been equally ominous. Eric and Pattie had become friendly with Phil Collins, who lived nearby. They planned to go to Wembley to see a Genesis concert. Pattie recalls that several doctors had been consulted about him. 'One woman doctor explained that he would have to reach rock bottom and become so ill that he himself would want treatment. She said I was wasting my time saying: "What about poor me?" or "Think of your poor old grandmother." He would have to stop for himself. It was by then getting very worrying: he was going into depressions and saying he didn't want to live any more, life had no meaning. He had sunk so low, mentally and physically, that the only way we could hope for him to come round was for him to acknowledge that he had a *disease* and there was a cure for it.'

Friends persuaded him to go to the Genesis concert. 'He was having a lovely time, jumping up and down, applauding. Within twenty minutes, his face was very hot and flushed and he said. "Let me out, I'm going . . . let me out." So I said, "Oh, what a shame!" And I took off my glasses and he said to me, "Do you know what's the matter with *you*? You'll just do anything I say, won't you?" And I said, "Fine." And I put my glasses back on and wouldn't let him out of his seat. He was trapped because I'd have to move, in order for him to get out. His face started pouring with sweat. He was panicking.

'I had to make him stay there for him to realize that he was ill. I don't normally behave like that. But I'd only been told by this doctor what to do. He had to be pushed to the limit, you see, in order for him to recognize his illness for himself.

'Finally, I think he thought he was going to pass out, he sort of walked across me and grabbed Nigel and said, "Get me out of here." So Nigel took him backstage and sat him down. And that's when Eric said, "Okay, I give in. I think I need help. I need professional help." We'd been waiting for this moment.' Roger Forrester booked the clinic in America. The seventh of January was D Day. 'It was marvellous news,' says Pattie. 'And really, if I hadn't known that, I couldn't have got through that Christmas.'

After Christmas, Forrester asked Clapton if he felt he could undertake treatment, though all the time the clinic had been booked. 'Yeah, I agree, go ahead,' said Eric. But as requested, he was not told until the day before departure that he was on his way. When Pattie told him the flight was only a day off, Eric was livid at the fact that final plans had been made behind his back. He poured himself a large brandy.

On 7 January 1982 Forrester collected a jittery Clapton and drove to Gatwick Airport. Eric had no idea which country he was going to. A North West Orient flight took him to Minneapolis St Paul, scene of his ulcer drama only six months earlier. Immediately on landing, Eric, already full of aeroplane brandy and lemonade and feeling like a condemned man, asked to be taken to a bar near the airport for a final drink before he went for treatment. Forrester refused his request.

Eric was checked into a clinic specializing in the treatment of alcoholics. Forrester stayed in a nearby hotel and was told not to visit Eric for the first two weeks, until he had overcome the worst. He became institutionalized, one of a crowd, and learned to recognize the problems inherent in everybody else's alcoholism as well as his own. It was an intensive four-week treatment which worked. Describing his visit to the Hazelden Foundation, the rehabilitation clinic for alcoholics, Eric says: 'It's quite a way out in the middle of nowhere. It looks like Fort Knox as you approach it, a very forbidding-looking place, low, concrete, government-type buildings, like a top-security prison. Most people arrive there either pissed or dying for a drink, or they've got so much alcohol in their system they need to be detoxified.

'So they put me on a drug called Librium for forty-eight hours. This helps you to come off the alcohol and balances you out. It eases you into the place. You feel very woozy for two or three days. You don't really know who you are, or who these other people are, or what you're doing there.

'I got pissed on the plane on the way there and I was sobering up when I arrived. I was panicking! I'd braved it through up to then and I wanted to go through with it until I saw the place. You sign some papers and start checking in and they put you into one of a number of units into which the place is divided, all named after famous people connected with Alcoholics Anonymous.

'Each unit contains twenty-eight people. All these people have been through the same thing, so their attitude is: here comes a new boy who's bouncing off the ceiling. You get looked after by all the other inmates, for the first three or four days. Then suddenly you're given a schedule of things you've got to do, and details of how you have to contribute to the welfare of your unit. And the unit runs itself, so immediately I had a ton of responsibility which I had not had for years. Mine was obviously to look after myself and make my own bed – which I'd never ever done before! – and then I was given the job of laying the table for my unit every mealtime and tea break. That was quite hard for someone who had never done *anything* domestic.

'Apart from that, I was given projects which involved lots of brain work, thinking and research. There were psychological tests: for example, what would the effect of a certain drug and alcohol be on three members of your unit, as compared with the effect on three other members of the unit. By this method you were supposed to get to know everybody and what their dependence was, and how it compared with what you had been through. So in a very short time you got to know everyone very quickly.

'I thoroughly got my teeth into it all. The one thing that was very hard was not being able to drink and having dreams about drink; waking up feeling drunk when I wasn't, which is an established syndrome among the inmates. I was actually sleeping with four other alcoholics in a billet – it was army-style accommodation.

'On top of that, there's group therapy three or four times a day: prayers, lectures, a thousand things to keep you occupied. At one o'clock in the morning I was still struggling to keep up with the work they'd given me to do during that day. When I got to bed, I passed out from complete mental tiredness. That was great because sleeping was something I had always found difficult to do naturally when I was a drunk – I had to drink to go to sleep. So this was great.

'I was there in January and the temperature was far below freezing, with a very cold wind, which was a bit of a shame because it was too cold to spend much time outdoors. But we did go out for walks a little.

'I came to realize that in many ways alcoholics are some of the best people in the world. Some of the people I met there, and had to muck in with, were fantastic characters who had had amazingly hard lives. And some of them had been into that place four or five times, real hard-liners. Before going into Hazelden, I thought I had had a really tough time and was hard done by. Suddenly I was faced by the rest of my unit of twenty-eight people, many of whom had much worse stories to tell than me.'

Working on integration with the other people in there was just as

In the studio

important as the treatment. 'Every man is expected to pull his weight, and anyone who doesn't is letting the whole team down,' says Eric, 'so it's all integrated. And on top of that I *wanted* to do well. When you see all these other tough guys breaking down and crying, but still making headway, you realize that you're not that badly off.'

Many times Eric felt he could not go through with the full four-week period of treatment. Some patients did leave after coming to the conclusion that they could not cope. 'One bloke, a very wealthy man, had his wife fly a private aeroplane into the nearest field and he left in the middle of the night.'

Some people recognized Eric, but few took much notice of his role as a superstar guitarist. 'The credentials for being there were simply that you were an alcoholic, a drunk. Apart from that, you weren't meant to delve too much into people's lives. Anonymity was the only way you could get on in the place – you couldn't pull any kind of rank.'

Eric underwent many physical and psychological tests. 'There were all kinds of questionnaires which, if you read between the lines, were supposed to spell out whether you were a possible psychotic or whether there was a chance of being one in the outside world. I managed to get through most of those.'

After about three weeks, Eric felt he was coping well with the institutionalization of the place 'but at the same time there was still this rebellious thing coming out. That part of me said I was playing for time, playing the game, but when I got out I would go back to being how I was before.'

But that rebellious streak was finally crushed through a foolproof method used by the clinic authorities: they wrote to the patients' loved ones and asked them to fill out questionnaires. 'They ask questions like: Did your husband ever rape you? What was he like when he was drunk?' says Eric. 'It surprised me then, though it doesn't now, because my wife was suddenly given the opportunity to say something destructive or honest because she knew it would help her husband.

'And when I read out to some of the other clinic inmates what Pattie had said in her questionnaire, how I had treated her without me realizing it – that broke my heart. I was made to understand that I'd behaved like an animal. And that's when I cracked. It was powerful stuff. They judge whether the inmate is fit enough to face it, and then they call you into the head counsellor's office, where it's read out in front of the others. It definitely showed what a bastard I was. They said they'd got a letter from home for me. I went to pick it up and when I read it, it was this questionnaire. I read it out in front of a couple of other inmates. And I broke down. Then I went to see one of the counsellors about it. He said it was a mistake that I'd been given it. But it wasn't a ploy by the counsellors.'

'It was very personal,' Pattie continues. 'The questions were particularly severe, asking what amounted to an intrusion into one's personal life with one's husband. But I decided that the only reason they had asked those questions was to help Eric rather than be intrusive. I knew he was taking the course very seriously, but a part of me I feared I could be letting him down by exposing him to my thoughts because he is a famous person.' She had told nobody of the problems she had had with her husband's behaviour and his drinking problems. It was a difficult decision but she rationalized in favour of telling the whole truth.

Having done so, the next agonizing decision was whether to agree to Eric being shown the questionnaire. 'Finally I decided that he *should* be shown how I felt, because for several years before he went into Hazelden I wasn't able to really talk to him at all. There wasn't one minute, on any day, when he was completely sober, so he had absolutely no idea how I felt. So this wasn't a vicious or vitriolic situation I was making use of; it was a method of getting through to him for me.' Conversely, she knew what she wrote about him would 'hurt him dreadfully' and she felt protective towards him. And it would be part of his therapy.

'Up until then,' Eric goes on, 'at the back of my head I was playing the role of Jack the Lad in there. But when I heard what she'd written, it cracked me. And the people in there wait for that – at some point a man has to give way in a situation. At first, when you go into the clinic, you battle through. You're tough. But that's not the way it's going to work. You're going to have to break. You have to understand what you've done and what you're facing up to.

'And once I'd been broken down I felt a lot better, although it did hurt me very deeply. From that point, though, I started to develop a little bit of a dependency on the place. It suddenly felt like home. It was safe there. The Jack the Lad man was gone. What was left was a very insecure human being, a little bit frightened of the outside world. That was the point where it started to get a little bit worrying. I needed building up again.'

But Eric knew, after that month, that he had at least completed the initial work. 'It isn't all done there. All they do is pick you up and point you in a different direction. I knew they had managed to do that with me, but after that it's up to the person. What to do with life from that point on is your own choice.' He had made several friends there, and has since corresponded with several Americans who went through the course with him. Without a doubt, he says, he could not have conquered his alcoholism without going to Hazelden.

Pattie says she leaned on the bottle, ironically, during her husband's absence because she was 'worried that this new person was going to arrive, a freshly scrubbed baby returning to the nest, and he might not love the person he had previously seen through a haze. I expected him to be back, crystal clear and sharp, and thought I might not go down too well with *him*.'

Her problem was partly solved by therapy for herself. She flew out to the USA and into Hazelden for an intensive five-day course designed to teach relatives, dependants or friends how to cope with people like Eric when they returned home from the 'drying-out' process. 'It was a great relief to mix with other people who had experienced the same problems as I'd had,' says Pattie. 'I had to learn how to live with somebody and not have an automatic reaction to how I *thought* they would behave, as an alcoholic. Which is how I used to live: I'd hear the door open and immediately react to the prospect of a drunk falling or sliding into the house. So I had to *unlearn* all of that ready for Eric's return home.' They saw a little of each other at Hazelden, and she was struck by how 'severely clean' he appeared. 'He was crisp and smart, not at all the person I knew. In fact, he was a bit too clean: he'd been through the dry cleaners a few too many times! He was full of praise for Hazelden and he'd been through an almost religious experience.'

On his return, a rejuvenated Eric craved as much work as Forrester could get him. In his pocket he continually fingered the medallion given to him by the clinic as a sign that he had successfully completed the course. A major factor had been their treatment of Eric's alcoholism as no different from anyone else's, despite his financial ability to buy as much drink as he desired. Now he wanted a quick return to life as a musician. He immediately astonished all around him with his eye-flashing alertness. And he joined Alcoholics Anonymous.

'For the first year, he was nervous of being around people who were drinking too much,' says Pattie. 'I took all the hard liquor out of the house and just kept the wine there, which he didn't mind being left in the wine cellar. He never drank wine anyway. He was very much quieter and he withdrew into himself terribly. He seemed very, very insecure. It showed in the way he became obsessive about buying beautiful and very expensive Italian clothes *every week*.'

During his first year of sobriety, Eric believed work would be one of the greatest therapies. 'It was a rash decision,' he says now. 'The experts always counsel you after you've stopped and say you can

Shorn of his beard, Eric is pictured before two sell-out nights at Madison Square Garden, New York, in December 1983 (*David McGough/Scope, David Hogan/Rex Features*)

expect a good year of completely irrational behaviour, and you shouldn't make any plans or decisions. And they're quite right.

'I felt within three months that I'd changed completely for the better having stopped drinking, and I was ready for work. In fact I wasn't. After five months, I did a tour of America and really didn't understand what I was doing.' But it gave him a great chance to attend a lot of American meetings of Alcoholics Anonymous. One meeting, after a show in Minnesota, proved to be lacking in anonymity. 'It was after I'd done a concert in that town and half the people at the meeting were wearing T-shirts with pictures of me at the AA meeting.' Generally, he found himself recognized more often in the US than in Britain but 'they are all good people who live by what they say. They don't go away saying, "Hey, guess who I saw tonight?" because that would put *their* anonymity in jeopardy.'

Smoking cigarettes has been not merely a habit of Eric's, but a recognized quirk of his stage act: the burning cigarette which sticks in the neck of his guitar has become almost an emblem. In the future, that, too, might vanish as his addiction to nicotine is brought under control. He has smoked at least forty Rothman King Size cigarettes each day for about twenty years, and when under great stress that figure rises to about sixty a day. 'That's the next project – getting that smoking habit under control. I'd like to give it up,' he says. But his friends shudder to contemplate a Clapton who doesn't drink, doesn't smoke, doesn't eat spicy foods and doesn't, above all, *feel* integrated as 'one of the gang' on social occasions, in dressing rooms or on the road. 'Eric needs to join in things with the people around him he likes,' says one of his mates. 'It's hard enough for him to be dry. I can't imagine Eric without a fag.'

6

THE
LOVER

*'I fell in love with her at first sight – and it got
heavier and heavier for me'*

It's late in the evening;
She's wondering what clothes to wear.
She puts on her make-up
And brushes her long blonde hair.
And then she asks me, 'Do I look all right?'
And I say, 'Yes, you look wonderful tonight.'

We go to a party,
And everyone turns to see
This beautiful lady
That's walking around with me.
And then she asks me, 'Do you feel all right?'
And I say, 'Yes, I feel wonderful tonight.'

I feel wonderful because I see the love light in your eyes.
And the wonder of it all
Is that you just don't realize how much I love you.

It's time to go home now,
And I've got an aching head.
So I give her the car keys,
And she helps me to bed.
And then I tell her, as I turn out the light,
I say, 'My darling, you were wonderful tonight.
Oh my darling, you were wonderful tonight.'

Eric Clapton wrote his most eloquent song, 'Wonderful Tonight,' for
Pattie in 1976. He considers it the most perfect love song. They were
not married but living together at Hurtwood Edge. Seven years after

155

he had first fallen in love with her Clapton composed it one night while sitting waiting for her to prepare to go to a party. 'It's all true,' he says. 'It's a good thing I didn't wait to write it till I got home from that party. I was drunk and incapable, again. I was standing outside our bedroom and saying "Come *on*. Are you ready to *go*?" I remember starting to hum, and then within five minutes I was down here, with the guitar, writing the song. It was all over in five or ten minutes.' Unusually, the song stayed exactly as it was, word for word and note for note, when he got into the studios with it for recording on his album *Slowhand* in 1977.

Putting her on a pedestal, writing songs for her, and particularly playing them to her for the first time, have always been part of the sentimental make-up of Eric Clapton. 'When she hears them for the first time, especially in my company, I can sense her tingling feeling mixed with embarrassment; I guess it's hard to live up to being the person who's being written about.'

Yet while 'Wonderful Tonight' is his most popular song, particularly requested by women, Eric names 'Layla' as his most significant, personal favourite of his compositions. 'Because, while "Wonderful Tonight" is a pure love song that can be applied to any couple, and many people do, I wrote "Layla" specifically about Pattie and me. It was my open-heart message that I was in love with her, and she knew it couldn't be about anyone else. I just couldn't visualize a life without her . . . '

The manic intensity of 'Layla', and particularly the opening sweeps of Eric's guitar, still make Pattie melt. 'It pulls at my heart strings,' she says now. But when she first heard the song, when she was married to George Harrison, her emotions were confused. 'I had no idea it would be such an important part of my life . . . or that I'd end up married to the man who wrote it,' she says.

Their route to that idyllic state, one of the most romantic love stories in popular music, could be disregarded as a fable, so unlikely are its ingredients: love at first sight, unrequited; a feverish song to attempt to lure a married woman; the man's years as a recluse with drug addiction; the woman's inquisitiveness and frustration . . . and the astonishing twist that here was a man attempting to attract the wife of one of his best friends, and a musical ally.

When Clapton's yearnings for Pattie began in 1969, the euphoria of Cream was disintegrating and Blind Faith was rumbling along inconclusively. Eric felt loose and free as a musician. He developed a particular rapport with George Harrison, who had co-written with Eric one of Cream's best songs, 'Badge'; George even played rhythm guitar on the record under the pseudonym of L'Angelo Misterioso.

The two men's friendship was strengthened when Eric bought Hurtwood Edge that year, just a few miles from George and Pattie's home at Esher, Surrey. Eric was alone in Hurtwood Edge for nearly a year before Alice moved in; he often went across to see Mr and Mrs Harrison at Esher.

Previously, his girlfriend for three years, during the whole of the Cream period, was Charlotte Martin, a model. He met her at London's fashionable Speakeasy Club when it had just opened and it became one of the hubs of Swinging London's nightlife in the mid-1960s. 'We just hit it off straightaway and she moved into my flat in the Pheasantry and also in Regent's Park,' says Eric. But by 1969, apart from a brief affair with a girl named Cathy James, there was no serious woman in his life as he embarked on a new period as a rich rock star living alone.

'I went to Esher several times,' says Eric, 'and every time I left, after a nice time with George and Pattie, I remember feeling a dreadful emptiness – because I was certain I was never going to meet a woman quite that beautiful for myself. I knew that. I knew I was in love. I fell in love with her at first sight – and it got heavier and heavier for me.'

As Pattie Boyd, one of Britain's top models of the 1960s, she had rocketed into the headlines when she became the girlfriend of George Harrison during the filming of the Beatles' film *A Hard Day's Night* in 1964. Pert, toothy, infectiously smiling and with the flowing blonde hair that was almost mandatory for the models of that era, Pattie married George at Esher Register Office in 1966. Born in Somerset on 17 March 1944, the daughter of a fighter pilot and the eldest of six children, Pattie moved with her family to Kenya from the age of five to ten. Back in Britain, after her boarding school education, she moved to London and took a job training at the Elizabeth Arden hairdressing salon. Her modelling career began almost accidentally from washing the hair of a woman magazine journalist who asked Pattie if she had considered becoming a model. A photographic session followed.

She first achieved a modest degree of fame as the Smith's Crisps girl in television advertisements. The producer of those commercials, Richard Lester, hired her in 1964 to appear in a brief scene in a film he was producing – the Beatles' first movie, *A Hard Day's Night*. Pattie began a romance with Beatle George Harrison and they were married two years later.

By marrying a Beatle, Pattie joined an elite club, a protected species. 'All wives and girlfriends of the four of them were made to feel that we shouldn't leave the family at all,' she says. 'We were all very tightly knit, terribly protected, and none of us were allowed to speak to the press. We mainly went out with each other. John Lennon and Cynthia, Paul McCartney with Jane Asher at that time, Ringo with Maureen. It was just the eight of us and the people involved with the Beatles' company. We were cocooned.'

Pattie recalls an electric moment early in their friendship, when she was married to George but meeting Eric occasionally. 'We went to see a beautiful film called *Kes*. Afterwards we were walking down Oxford Street and Eric suddenly said to me: "Do you like me, then, or are you seeing me because I'm famous?" I answered: "Oh, I thought you were seeing me because *I'm* famous." ' They both laughed, because they both meant what they said. Eric, she believes, has always had problems 'verbalizing his emotions to me', which is why he puts his deepest thoughts into songs. 'He's incredibly romantic, to the point of visualizing his life as a novel.'

She first set eyes on Eric when he played a concert with Cream at London's Saville Theatre. Sitting with George and the other Beatles and their ladies in a box, Pattie recalls thinking Eric 'looked absolutely wonderful and played so beautifully'. Later that night, the owner of the Saville Theatre, Beatles manager Brian Epstein, threw a party at his home at 24 Chapel Street, Belgravia. It was the first time she met Eric, a remote figure but a celebrated musician held in awe by his peers. 'I was surprised by how alone Eric looked at that party,' says Pattie. 'He was terribly reticent, didn't talk to anybody or socialize.' It was that very quietness and his 'rather mysterious' behaviour amid the party babble that intrigued Pattie. 'There was an aura around him which set him apart from the others. Definitely.'

As Eric consolidated his friendship with George, his obsession with Pattie increased. There was no regular girl in his life; in a bizarre method of attracting Pattie's attention, he escorted her eighteen-year-old sister Paula for three months. 'My mother was absolutely furious that Paula at that age was living with this pop star at Hurtwood Edge,' says Pattie. 'I wondered why he'd done it, but it became obvious later.'

Eric tried another ploy. From his home, he telephoned Pattie at Friar Park. 'I asked her if she knew any models that might be on the loose because I didn't have a girl at that time,' says Eric. 'She said she'd think about it.' Pattie remembers: 'I actually did have a girl-friend who wasn't going out with anyone at that time, so I phoned Eric back and said I'd bring her along to the studios the next night.' At London's EMI Recording studios, George Harrison was recording his blockbusting triple album *All Things Must Pass*, and Eric was playing guitar on it.

'Eric was so rude to my girlfriend, I could hardly believe it. She had

Wonderful Tonight. Eric and Pattie Clapton

never met a musician before and she was shocked beyond belief. He ignored her or made fun of her throughout the evening. She just disappeared – I never heard from her again.' Eric's language had offended her; his immature posturing had also irritated Pattie, who was embarrassed for her friend. There was a reason for Eric's uncharacteristic tension.

Next day, Clapton phoned Pattie again. 'Look, I didn't really want you to find me a girlfriend. I mean *you*. I really need to see you. Can I come over and talk to you about it?'

'I was hot and cold all over,' remembers Pattie. 'I said: "Look, I'm married to George, and it's difficult." ' Says Eric: 'Even when I blurted it out on the phone, I could sense she was flattered and pleased.'

'There had been amorous beginnings to it all,' says Eric. 'I went to Friar Park, or she came to parties here at Hurtwood Edge and we made eyes at each other, had a few cuddles and whispered sweet nothings. What I couldn't accept was that she was out of reach. Okay, she was married to George and he was a mate but I had fallen in love and nothing else mattered.' But, musically, there was always complete harmony and an edge of competitiveness between Harrison and Clapton. Only Eric knew that the healthy friendship might be threatened by his love of his friend's wife.

'I'd set myself up to fall,' says Eric. 'It was an impossible situation. Nobody ever steals a Beatle's wife. It's not *on*. They'd become very big Establishment figures, had been awarded medals as Members of the British Empire and here was this rogue banging down the back door. It was an impossible situation for Pattie to cope with, or for me to cope with. I'd actually gone out of my way to find a good enough excuse for me to hit rock bottom.'

Says Pattie: 'I couldn't believe the situation he'd put me in. I thought it wasn't right . . . and after that bad experience with my friend when Eric annoyed us, I thought it was destined to end. Then a letter came, addressed to me at Friar Park. Tiny, scrawly handwriting, unsigned, it said 'I need to see you and I love you.' I showed it to George and told him some nutcase was writing to me; I had no idea who it was from. Next night, Eric phoned me and asked if I'd got his letter.' She stuttered a 'yes', but reaffirmed the complications and problems about doing anything about it. George Harrison was a man of intensity too; he had written the pretty ballad 'Something' about Pattie and it has proved his most popular composition, with more than a hundred and fifty 'cover' versions. She was therefore quite used to being sought after. But Eric decided to increase his own pressure by using one of his strongest assets: an eloquent simplicity in the use of words. His directness, his command of English, has always run parallel with his articulacy as a musician.

Ian Dallas, who had introduced Eric to Alice, took a paternal interest in him and was en route to becoming a Sufi, embracing the Muslim faith. He gave Eric a book which had particularly moved him. It was called *The Story of Layla and Majnun*, by the great Persian writer Nizami.

The sensitivity and intensity of the story made a strong impression on Eric. In Arabic, 'Layl' means night, and Majnun means madman. The man, Majnun, falls hopelessly in love with the unavailable Layla, and this in turn drives him to madness. The story is filled with vivid poetic descriptions of the girl:

> To look at, she was like an Arabian moon, yet when it came to stealing hearts she was a Persian page. Under the dark shadow of her hair, her face was a lamp, or rather a torch, with ravens weaving their wings around it. And who would have thought that such overwhelming sweetness could flow from so small a mouth?
>
> Is it possible then to break whole armies with one small grain of sugar? She really did not need rouge; even the milk she drank turned into the colour of roses on her lips and cheeks . . . and she was equipped with lustrous eyes . . .
>
> The name of this miracle of creation was Layla. Whose heart would not have filled with longing at the sight of this girl? . . . He was drowned in the ocean of love before he knew that there was such a thing. He had already given his heart to Layla before he understood what he was giving away. And Layla? She fared no better. A fire had been lit in both – and each reflected the other.

Clapton identified totally with Majnun. 'I was mucking around, between girlfriends, both Cathy James and Paula,' he says. 'But I started living with Pattie's younger sister Paula because of their similarity in character and in looks. It was like a side route into Pattie, that was my way of thinking.' For his next album, made as Derek and the Dominos, Eric drew several themes from Nizami's book; but nothing equalled the raging song which formed the album's title: *Layla, and Other Assorted Love Songs*. It stands today as one of rock's definitive love songs, and around the world thousands cheer to the spine-tingling opening salvo from Eric's guitar.

LAYLA:

What will you do when you get lonely
With nobody waiting by your side?
You've been running and hiding much too long;
You know, it's just your foolish pride.

Layla, you got me on my knees. Layla,
I'm begging darling please. Layla,
Darling, won't you ease my worried mind?

I tried to give you consolation;
When your old man had let you down.
Like a fool, I fell in love with you;
You turned my whole world upside down.

Layla, you got me on my knees. Layla,
I'm begging darling please. Layla,
darling, won't you ease my worried mind?

Let's make the best of the situation
Before I finally go insane.
Please don't say we'll never find a way
and tell me all my love's in vain.

Layla, you got me on my knees. Layla,
I'm begging darling, please. Layla,
Won't you ease my worried mind?

Layla, you got me on my knees. Layla,
I'm begging darling please. Layla,
Darling, won't you ease my worried mind?

Eric wrote the song at his home. 'The words and the music [percussionist and drummer Jim Gordon helped] came very quickly,' he recalls. He planned and wrote the song with a ruthless, romantic determination that it should reach Pattie and declare, fully, that he needed her.

'I remember writing the song, finishing the album with the Dominos, and then having to go back to record the vocal part of "Layla",' says Eric. 'We'd finished all the other tracks so I invited Pattie's sister Paula to come and hear me sing "Layla" for the first time. When she heard that vocal, she packed her bags and left my home in great distress. Because she realized it was about Pattie and that I'd been using her, I suppose.'

By now, the Dominos were no longer living at Eric's home. The band had moved to a flat in South Kensington. Visiting the theatre in London with Robert Stigwood, to see the play *Oh! Calcutta!*, Eric spotted Pattie across the theatre, and George was not present. Clapton swapped seats with a stranger sitting next to her. 'And after the show, I took her off to the Dominos' flat for the night.'

Clandestine meetings at Eric's home followed. He played her the whole of the *Layla* album and gave her the book which inspired the song. 'When you do that to a woman, their emotions get so confused by your own presence that they hear it but they don't receive it properly. I remember her saying she took it as a great compliment, but who can say what was going through her mind? I've always found that when I've written songs for Pattie, it gets too heavy for her to cope with.'

Pattie remembers: 'He played "Layla" to me two or three times. His intensity was both frightening and fascinating, really. I was taken aback. It was a very powerful record. I hadn't read the book, although I'd also been given it by the same man who had presented it to Eric. I recall Eric telling me that I had to read it because he identified very strongly with the leading character. I was puzzled, flattered, shocked, amazed. I knew his feelings were strong for me, but I had no idea it would run to him writing a song for me.'

It attracted Pattie to him, initially at least. They had an affair, in which Pattie made occasional visits to Eric's house. 'But I felt terrible guilt. He kept insisting I should leave George and go and live with him. I said I couldn't. I got cold feet. I couldn't bear it.'

Pattie became so tense and worried about the situation that she stopped seeing Eric. At what she told him must be their final encounter at Hurtwood Edge, he applied dramatic emotional black-mail. 'I told her that either she came with me, or I hit the deck. I actually presented her with a packet of heroin and said: "If you don't come with me, I'm taking this for the next couple of years." And I did. I put dreadful, dreadful pressure on her but I couldn't help myself. I really could not visualize a life without her. Well, the pressure from me must have been so great that she went back and closed herself back into Friar Park and George.'

Eric says his love of Pattie, and the turbulent frustration at her rejection, was partly responsible for his descent into heroin addiction during the three years from 1971 until 1974. 'Not Pattie herself, as a person, but as an image, she was my excuse. That was the catalyst, a very big part of it. It was a symbol, my perfect reason for embarking on this road which would lead me to the bottom.'

During the three dark years, Pattie telephoned Eric's home a few times. Always, the phone would be answered by Alice; Pattie did not then pursue a conversation with Eric, but hung up the phone. The word was out, anyway, that he was very ill. That both frightened and worried her. Pattie's lifestyle with George was far removed from such abuse of the body. Harrison was deeply involved with meditation and members of the Hare Krishna sect were regular visitors to his home. Pictures of Indian gurus adorned the walls. Pattie sympathized with this philosophy – it was she who originally introduced the Beatles to Transcendental Meditation via the Maharishi Mahesh Yogi, thus beginning an important aspect of the psychedelic period. But the non-stop, daily vibrations on the same theme from George and the endless stream of philosophers tired her.

While Eric says Pattie's non-availability was the catalyst which gave him a good reason to plunge, Pete Townshend has a more positive theory about the heroin period. 'If anything kept Clapton alive throughout that whole period, it was the *possibility* that he might just achieve the impossible. He'd elevated it to a Layla and Majnun relationship, to the level of a spiritual fusion. Here was Pattie, this hopeless target, married to one of the Beatles, endlessly wealthy, snatched out of the world by George into a kind of pop royalty. And for Eric, she was an unachievable. On top of this, he knew and liked George, so it was like falling in love with your wife's sister, or close relative. It wasn't done. And that depth of fantasy was so important to Eric. There was a warm air between George and Eric that could not be breached, particularly in this way. I'm sure the very fact that it was such a *maudlin* desperation got through to Eric's inner psyche, during the heroin period, when nothing else did.'

When Eric came off heroin, the events leading up to his eventual capture of Pattie were as theatrical as the scenarios that had punctuated his four years of unrequited love. He set about renewing contact with her with a streak of determination which surprised everybody except himself. He decided there would be no clandestine relationship this time. Direct action was essential. 'She had become very disillusioned with George. It became clear to me,' Eric continues, 'that if I could somehow arouse her enough, there was a chance I could get her to live with me.'

At a party at Robert Stigwood's home in Stanmore, Eric grasped the initiative. Knowing George and Pattie would be there, Eric went straight up to Harrison and said: 'I'm in love with your wife. What are you going to do about it?' Eric continues: 'George said: "Whatever you like, man. It doesn't worry me." He was being very spiritual about it, and saying everybody should do their own thing. He then said: "You can have her and I'll have your girlfriend," who was Cathy James at that time.

'I couldn't believe this! I thought he was going to chin me. Anyway, Pattie freaked out and ran away and got into her car. Suddenly she was in limbo and I think it was at that point that she became disillusioned with George. So I don't think I stole her,

A year after Pattie went to live with Eric, they are pictured arriving for the premiere of the film *Tommy*, at the Odeon, Leicester Square, London, in 1975; he appeared in the Ken Russell movie as a preacher (*Barry Plummer*)

because I did tell him straightaway.

'Pattie was very upset and it all suddenly became very foreign. I imagine George must have been very upset too. But that's crazy! If he didn't want her to leave him, he shouldn't have let me take her.'

Eric's brutal frankness at least had the redeeming quality of honesty. The party ended amid some tension, George and Pattie driving away, symbolically out of Eric Clapton's life. Or so it seemed.

His next ploy was to lean on his old friend Pete Townshend as a kind of foil. A recording session for the film *Tommy*, in which Eric played the part of a preacher, ended at 11 o'clock one night. Leaving the studios, Eric said to Pete: 'Let's go and see George out at Friar Park.' Townshend declined; he wanted to get home to his wife Karen. But Eric persisted: he had no car and needed a lift. 'Please come with me – I know George really wants to see you.' Townshend said Eric might be stranded out there without a car because he intended to leave soon after taking him there. Clapton said that was okay.

Townshend takes up the story. 'George, Eric and I sat talking for a while. Then Pattie came in and said hello, looking stunning. She was very bright and intelligent. A couple of Indians were walking around the house and George was talking very interestingly to me. It was the first real conversation we'd had and we found a lot of common ground, particularly in the area of mysticism. Anyway, many hours passed, with George and me talking. Eventually we went out and Eric and Pattie were in the big hall, talking. She made us some soup, George went back into the studio he has at the house, and Eric came up to me and said: "I need about another hour." So I said: "What?" He said: "I need about another hour before you go."

'I thought he meant he was just going to fuck her, and maybe this would be the zenith of his cure.

'He'd written this song for her, they'd become Layla and Majnun, he'd become an addict partly because of his emotional desolation at her refusing him, and now he was going to get a quick fuck and then we were going to jump in the car and drive away, out of it for ever.

'Well, I went back and kept George occupied for another hour. Then I thought no more about what they were up to. I got in my car, alone, and drove home. I decided they could all sort this out between them. I later realized that what I'd actually been doing was keeping George busy while Eric talked Pattie into leaving.'

Townshend, hearing of the outcome of that night a few days later, reflected to himself on Eric's iron determination. 'I recall thinking how determined Eric was to face up to what he wanted, and how ruthless he had been in achieving that. I also wished he'd let me into it a bit earlier, what he'd been up to. But I didn't feel used. I felt honoured. He did two remarkable things: he actually straightened himself out from being a junkie, and then he went out and made his fantasy happen.'

Pattie recalls: 'After that night's conversation with me at Friar Park, Eric went on his American tour with the band that had made the album *461 Ocean Boulevard*. Shortly after that, I decided it was all over between George and me; he didn't seem to worry whether I left him or not. So three weeks after Eric's visit, I went to Los Angeles to stay with my sister Jenny who was living with Mick Fleetwood at that time. While I was there, Eric telephoned me and asked me to join him on tour. I joined him in Buffalo.'

That long tour marked the actual union of Eric and Pattie. When it ended, they went to Jamaica to combine recording work with a brief 'honeymoon'. Whilst there, Eric heard from his mother that his half-brother Brian had been killed in a motorcycle accident, so Eric and Pattie flew to the funeral in Canada. For Pattie, it was a difficult and delicate entry into the Clapton family circle.

Back in England, Pattie moved into Hurtwood Edge. Eric warily asked her if she liked the house and its design. 'He was very conscious that Alice had left her stamp on it and was worried what I'd think,' says Pattie. 'But it was fine. I loved the house and being with him. We had a very jolly time setting up the home together. It was not a problem for me despite his worry.'

By the end of 1974, Roger Forrester told Eric that for tax reasons he had to spend a year out of Britain, so Eric and Pattie rented a house on Paradise Island in the Bahamas. 'It was a base for making money,' says Clapton, 'but it was a beautiful spot, and virtually a year's honeymoon for Pattie and me, although I did some work.' From that base, he did an Australian tour. Alone, he went to the US to join his band. Because Pattie had a London conviction for possessing marijuana she was not allowed into America, so had to go from the Bahamas to Australia via London. Changing planes at Anchorage (where she was not allowed beyond the transit lounge), she spotted Eric and ran up behind him, clasping her hands across his eyes. 'Guess who?' said Pattie. Clapton was overjoyed at the sight of her, but was frustrated in his attempts to ensure they flew out from Anchorage together. An even greater irritation followed: once in Australia, Pattie was barred from entering New Zealand because of her drugs bust, so she missed that part of Eric's tour. A furious Clapton vented his views in radio and newspaper interviews.

Life as a Beatle's wife had virtually marooned Pattie. 'Going on tour with Eric was so exciting because that had never been allowed when I was with George. Wives were not allowed to travel with the Beatles because of security. The Beatles were heavily protected. So this sudden new life with Eric and his mad antics was great fun, an absolutely fantastic and completely new world to me.'

Surprisingly, Clapton and Harrison's friendship survived the long episode, and still does. Even in 1971, during a peak of Eric's frustration, George had been able to persuade Eric to go to New York to appear at the Madison Square Garden concert to aid Bangladesh. Eric is full of praise for George's laconic humour, which helped defuse the situation, after his initial pique.

'I think the world of the man,' says Eric. 'His adaptable wisdom for any situation, his wit and his humour are a great source of inspiration for anybody who knows him. That helped us all through the split-up. He managed to laugh it all off when I thought it was getting really hairy. I thought it was tense, he thought it was funny. George, Pattie and I actually sat in the hall of my house and I remember him saying: "Well, I suppose I'd better divorce her." And I said: "Well, if you divorce her, that means I've got to marry her!" In black and white, it sounds and looks horrible. But it was like a Woody Allen situation.' That conversation was in 1975; George and Pattie's marriage was dissolved on 10 June 1977 on the grounds that they had lived apart for more than two years.

Eric's passion for Pattie baffled and intrigued her at first. 'I just couldn't understand his extreme feeling for me, and just why he felt like that. I didn't really know him that well and I couldn't work out how and why he thought he knew *me* so well, to the point of being so in love with me. But through spending a lot of time with him I slowly realized he was a very great person to be with – maddening as well as lovable!'

She demurred on the subject of marriage for several years, despite Eric's persistence. 'I felt we were quite all right as we were,' says Pattie. 'Living together was fine. Marriage was an important step for me, particularly as it had not worked for me the first time and so I was not that eager to take the plunge into it again.' She says that Eric showed her 'in lots of ways' that he loved her very much and wanted to get married. 'But there were also lots of ways in which he behaved like a single person, as this famous musician able to attract any luscious female. So life was pretty precarious for me.

'Maybe he was doing it on purpose to incite my anger or jealousy. But occasionally I took it too seriously. Sometimes I saw it as a game, but other times I didn't, and I wondered what I was doing with him.

nelly saw me pouring myself a double
brandy and lemonade about mid morning
(while she was talking to her mother on
the phone) and gave me the evil eye at
which point i promptly slipped over and
spilt my drink all over fridays page!...
explanation over..... glyn called and has
invited us for a drink at the parrot, could
it be he has heard about john astley coming
to japan to record us?.... we shall see....

Yet there was something magnetic about him.'

For Pattie, changing partners was accompanied by a welcome switch in the tempo and style of her life. 'I felt more earthed at Eric's home than at Friar Park,' she says. 'I felt as if I was losing my identity when I was with George. It was all too exclusive and unreal. I was getting a little lost inside that.'

'Now, with them together, we had one of the greatest really romantic stories of all time!' exclaims Pete Townshend. 'It was quite stunning in its impact on everyone who saw how he had made it happen.' Eric became very protective of Pattie, lying to a journalist who arrived at Hurtwood Edge with the obvious question about her departure from a Beatle. 'I said it was not true, and to get Pattie off the hook with him, I said I was engaged to be married to Alice Ormsby-Gore,' says Eric. 'That's how the story of my so-called engagement got out. It was never true. We were never engaged. I made it up.'

Pattie's love for Eric grew. But she could not have prepared herself for the drunken years that were about to envelop her. 'After the spiritual life with George, within a few weeks of going to live with Eric I seemed to be surrounded with mayhem.' Clapton had hit the bottle. 'I drank like a fish, too,' says Pattie. They were releasing much of the tension of the five years when their future had been uncertain. 'We were leaning on each other,' she says. 'It was jolly good fun but we were quite hopeless for each other a lot of the time.'

Eric denies that taking to drink was a triumphant celebration of achieving his goal of getting Pattie to go and live with him. Within a few months, Courvoisier and lemonade became his regular drink. Pattie says he was not a pretty sight.

'Some of the time I was an accomplice, then I backed out. I thought one of us should be sober some of the time, so I was. I found him very hard to live with. He expected me not to care about his drunken friends lying all over the house. Sometimes he'd even bring drunken strangers back from the pub – tramps, who he insisted should not stay out in the street but should stay the night with us!

'A lot of people were abusing him, encouraging him to drink so they in turn could carry on drinking. And there was another nasty element: some people enjoyed watching Eric get so drunk. They thought it was great to see someone with his reputation, so brilliant with the guitar, behaving in a sloppy, drunken, almost idiotic manner.

'I despised that. And sometimes I didn't even have to be sober to see it.'

Soon after going to live with Eric, Pattie was helping him to design the cover for his 1975 album 'There's One In Every Crowd' (*Keystone Press*)

Five years passed before El and Nell, as they nicknamed each other, were married. It was an erratic period in Eric's life. His career became something of a patchwork quilt, dogged by the uncertainty of his songwriting, his guitar work sometimes set to 'autopilot', and his laziness induced by alcoholism. The albums came out on schedule every year, of course; the concert tours continued as if ordained by some divinity. But Roger Forrester was getting increasingly worried about his condition every night. At home, Pattie found Clapton tetchy.

'Little things annoyed him. He had about two hundred shirts, and he'd go absolutely berserk if I couldn't find the only one he wanted that day. He'd describe it in absolute detail and I'd find him one similar. That wouldn't do.'

He sought comfort in free-spending and amassed loads of clothes. 'He had no idea about money whatsoever and never wanted to know what anything was costing. He adored his huge collection of shoes but treated them badly, scuffed them, which I got cross about. I got worried about his failure to see any value in money. Making money from my career in modelling clothes and shoes has made them more valuable to me.'

The friction between them was not helped by his decision that all women should be banned from concert tours. Clapton agrees that this was part of his chauvinism. But he explains that too many bands suffered from the mere fact that wives and girlfriends did not necessarily get along together. And putting warring women together on planes, in hotels and dressing rooms made no sense. Eric's regular absences on world tours left Pattie feeling lonely and isolated; she, too, leaned increasingly on drink.

'I would always make a point of asking if I could go on tour, knowing that I wouldn't be allowed to,' says Pattie. 'He always said he was working and there were no ladies on the road. So when people asked me, I always turned the phrase into: "I haven't been invited." That sounded much better than "I'm not allowed to go . . . I've been told to stay at home!"'

She regarded Eric as a chauvinist: 'But Roger Forrester is as well . . . and the combination of those two was very strong. They egged each other on.' She did not fight Eric's decision: 'In an argument you do need a leg to stand on . . . and I didn't think that I had one. Because he *was*, after all, working. For me, the travelling would just be something pleasurable to do. He saw me as a potential distraction. There was no point in arguing.' During the whole of his heavy-drinking year of 1979, Eric fastidiously kept a diary in which he wrote, drew cartoons and confessed his innermost thoughts and observations around the world and at home. One of several diary references to his ban on women on the road reads: 'I play better when Pattie is not there to watch me. I wish I could understand that, too.'

Although she accepted the ban, she was hurt by what she considered to be Eric's thoughtless desertion. 'He's not one for using the phone much so he wouldn't ring me, either, while he was away on tour. That was very disturbing for me, when the tours lasted for about six weeks. I'd seen some of the American concerts, and the sight of the candles being lit by the audience at the end was very thrilling on that first tour I went on. Such a different experience from hearing a record. But no, I saw nothing after that 1974 tour when he travelled the world. And I felt very cut off.'

They had little social life even when he was home. 'He doesn't like restaurants. He feels trapped. His idea of eating was to do it as quickly as possible and then leave. Even when we had friends for Sunday lunch, he'd be the first one to leave the table and go and watch television. He couldn't understand the rest of us sitting round the table for another hour after eating, just talking.' Eric's eating habits, including an obsession for eating food while it is burning hot, stem from his childhood. His grandmother produced the food for her husband first, who sat eating in total silence, and then Eric and Rose would sit and eat their meal quietly too. Eating, to Clapton, has remained a functional operation, not a social occasion.

Eric's capriciousness in love, his brandy-for-breakfast routine, and his chauvinism, combined with his provocative treatment of Pattie, led to their surprising first separation just after Christmas 1978. It had been an appalling holiday, Pattie continually berating her lover for being drunk, for not eating, and in one sharp aside to him, she called him 'cold'.

On 7 February he wrote irritably in his diary: 'It's becoming increasingly hard to find anything in this house. We've got so many records, so many tapes, so many photographs, so many books and so on and so on, and none of them are where you'd expect them to be. Everything seems to be in the last possible place you would expect it to be. Madness. I will have to get out of here soon so that the house can get itself straight again. The whole place gets a bad or untidy influence from me whenever I'm here too long . . . [later]: Had a row with Nello and pulled her hair. I stand accused of being cold. My feeling is sometimes too strong to be controlled but that don't make me a cold person. There are a lot of very frayed nerves around here and we've got to beware of pointing fingers at one another. I don't know what is on Nell's mind and my pride prevents me from coaxing it out of her. Not only my pride, but my sense of balance tells me I shouldn't have to, at this time, before a grand-slam tour. I am like a caged animal. Even I don't know what I'm going to do next. How can I expect to know, by instinct alone, what she is up to? Anyway, humble pie is needed all round.'

The next day's entry began: 'Today has started as strained as the day before ended. And you can't go on blaming it on the stars.' After documenting a petty argument with Pattie over who had lost the keys to a window when a cleaner arrived, Eric wrote: 'A definite state of détente exists, and then, just as suddenly, it disappears. I will never understand the female gender. But it's certainly a relief when everything, for no apparent reason, is all right again.' He ended the day's entry euphorically implying that he and Pattie had made up. 'Such a night . . . '

The social butterfly inside Pattie was now finding pursuits outside her home. She had become friends with two young model twins, Jenny and Susie McLean. When Jenny visited Hurtwood Edge one day, Pattie insisted she stayed overnight because it had become so late for her to drive back to her Hampstead home. By the time Pattie got up next day, Eric and Jenny had gone out together, first shopping and then to a pub. Pattie decided to visit her sister.

Returning that afternoon, she found Jenny McLean and Eric sitting 'very closely together on the sofa'. Says Pattie: 'I started to talk to her and then Eric said: "Can't you see . . . I'm in *love* with this girl? Can't you see that I'm talking to her and I'm courting her?" I was so shocked, I couldn't believe it. This was nearly five years after he'd pursued me, and after all that had happened. I was so shocked I carried on talking to her. Then it sank in, so I rushed upstairs, shaking. I thought, how *can* he suddenly change like this? I thought he loved me, that we were having a nice relationship.

'I downed a few Valium which I don't normally do and phoned my sister and she said I should go and stay with her.' By early evening, in the dark and pouring rain Pattie walked, confused and stumbling into bushes, up the Hurtwood Edge drive to be met by her sister – also named Jenny – in her car.

When she phoned Eric two days later, he asked where she was. 'I'm not telling you, but are you still with *her*?' said Pattie. He replied: 'Um . . . yes.' Pattie says: 'I just couldn't bear it.' She phoned some friends in Los Angeles, Rob Fraboni and his wife Myel. Fraboni had been a producer respected by Eric for his work on the seminal album *Music From Big Pink,* by The Band, which made a huge impact on Clapton in 1966; the two men had become firm friends with Fraboni visiting Hurtwood Edge frequently when he was in Britain.

Flying to Los Angeles Pattie was in floods of tears. The stewardess said she would have to move to the rear of the plane to avoid upsetting other passengers. 'I was *so* heartbroken. I didn't know what to do with my life and thought I might start a new life in America. I had no intention of returning to England.'

Meanwhile, Eric had begun a tour of Ireland with his new band. His diary contained several references to his desire for Jenny McLean, 'Sweet Jen', who visited him there. 'The gig was great and sweet Jen flew in to make the day perfect. We talked and talked about our respective wounds.' Noting that Pattie ('Nello') had gone to America, Eric showed some contrition about forgetting her birthday: 'I am a bad man and I think the world better roll on without me for a while, anyway. All in love is fair.'

Three factors played a part in the reunion of Eric and Pattie: first, fate; secondly, Eric's modesty in failing to acknowledge his fame; and thirdly, Roger Forrester's instinct to gamble and determination to win. Between the Irish concerts and the American tour, Clapton visited Roger's home for a game of pool. Casually, the manager said to him: 'You want to be careful with this girl Jenny, Eric. Someone will take a photograph of you and you'll be in the papers.' Eric, often apparently unaware of his value as a news item, replied: 'Don't be silly, who wants to put *my* picture in the paper?'

Forrester insisted that he could ensure that Eric's picture appeared in the national papers next day, if he wished to. Eric, riled anyway because he was losing the pool game, said: 'No way. Ten thousand quid says you can't do that.'

Forrester walked to the phone and called Fleet Street's top gossip columnist, the *Daily Mail*'s Nigel Dempster. Said Forrester: 'Rock star Eric Clapton will marry Pattie Boyd in Tucson, Arizona, next Tuesday.' Eric went home, convinced he had won £10,000; Forrester sat up all night waiting for the paper to slip through the letterbox next morning. To his astonishment the story appeared.

An enraged Clapton hurtled in his Ferrari to Forrester's Mayfair office as soon as he woke to the news of the story. Roger was on the phone, but Eric stormed in, wrapping the cord around his neck and hitting him over the head with the phone. How dare he assume the right to make a personal decision for him? Eric was livid at being put in an impossible situation.

'Really,' said Forrester, calming him down, 'you have to decide whether you want to be with Pattie or not.' By now, his brief affair

i sense a trap, i see the bait and i
knows the method of the hunter, so,
no deal, i cant win at this kind of game,
mainly because im betting against
myself, and i am pretty sure everyone
else is betting against me too, i must
be a very bad man to want to do the
things i want to do, and then not do
them ～ i didnt sleep too well, went
to bed at eight this morning and got
up at twelve, the wind was blowing
up a storm, and that never fails to
freak me out, its still blowing hard
now, and makes all the strangest sounds
you can imagine, too much, for my
overworked ears to battle against-
we called a vocal rehearsal for us
all tonight down here, i hope this wind
dies out soon, it makes me so uneasy ～
● i fell straight into the trap and
confessed that i loved jen, there wasnt
much else to say, but being a little of
a selfish person (thats when im not
really trying) i lost nerve, i asked her
to go away and she left without a word.
i tried to find her, but i dont think she
wants to found me, or something like
that ～ i do love jen and now i know
how much i worry about nell, im sure
she has a reason for disappearing
because she didnt even battle the
idea of letting me go we injured her
very badly this time, and i dont think
she will come back, how can i explain
to anyone that i am in love with a new
woman without having their opinions..
cast that feeling as a rash mistake, ive
been painted black before and im not
about to try and pretend that i was white
to begin with, but i have done a bad
thing today to one person and a good
thing to another person and i only just
now start to realize how much ～
where are you richard ?

no word from nell yet and im shaking
so hard i can hardly hold the pen ~
i am the original fool, i have ~~everyones~~
~~lives into cast~~ thrown everyones lives
into chaos just for a quick glimpse ~~of~~
~~the unknown~~ into the unknown ~
what was to be gained from it, a new found
sense of masculinity? or just a poke in
the eye of conformity? on the other
hand, if nell wanted to be rid of me she
couldnt have a better way of doing it
and at the same time making me the
guilty party, i think she was just testing
me, by leaving me alone with someone
that she knew i fancied, but where do
we go from here, in the fresh and sober
light of day, i have thought about it and
there's no way jenny and i could live with
one another, and how can i ask nell to come
back, like she was a dog, it looks like im stuck
with my own hunger, God what an idiot i
have become, not only that but a sado-
masochistic idiot to boot ~ i know that i
must clear up this mess on my own, but
i have the terrible feeling that i will end
up alone and feeling sorry for myself, it
serves me right if it turns out ~~that~~ way,
so get used to it boyo ~
nell called and sounded okay, she said
she would come over this evening and
help me pack, but she wouldn't say
where she was. she has squarely put
the blame on jen and me and sounds
pretty vengeful towards both of us.
jen called and said she was going mad.
roger called to tell me that wba lost
one nil, and that if i needed any help he
would be available ~ i think this
feels like a crucial time for my sense
of balance to re establish ~~itself~~. this year
has got ~~too down~~ as the worst i can
remember, and its only just started
dear lord, have pity on us all - please.
                                    G

i proposed to nell today and she said
yes, even when i told her that always id
be a bad boy, she said yes, which only
goes to prove that, we are both loonies,
i dont really understand my feelings,
i mean its something i have dreaded all
my life, but, i feel like a dog with
nine tails, im so excited about it that
the town is incidental, so we walk down
the aisle on tuesday in tucson, arizona,
God give us a good start. amen ~

i married well today, hurray,
it was a beautiful wedding. and i had
a really bad case of nerves until i met
the priest, who put me at ease straight
away ~ amazingly must, in fact, all of
what he said to us came straight from
his heart, and then he refered to the
bible, we got married, in the sight of god.
i will tell you more about it later,
when my pen is working. about midday.

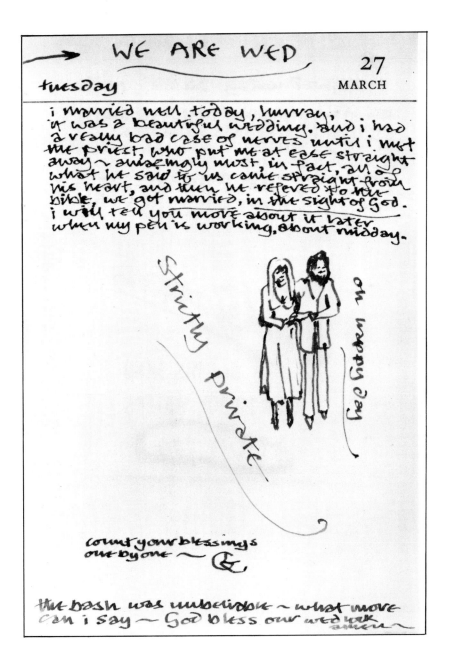

Strictly private

the children

count your blessings
one by one ~ CE

the bash was unbelievable ~ what more
can i say ~ God bless our wedlock
amen ~

the first gig and i feel totally
shagged out, still it went okay, in fact
it was pretty good although i am still
recovering from yesterday ~ later

happy birthday Rose ~

with Jenny McLean had ended and Eric was morose about his messy love life. Forrester told him it was time either to marry Pattie or to make a clean break and be free. Eric was totally confused about his next action; en route to London, he had been congratulated on his imminent marriage by his regular petrol pump attendant and a pub landlord. He was warming to the idea but was furious with Forrester.

'Yeah,' said Eric when his temper subsided. 'I want to be with Pattie but now, because of your stupid behaviour, she's gonna read this story in the paper before I've even proposed to her.'

Not so, said Forrester. Retrieving the phone, he dialled Rob Fraboni's home in Los Angeles. Pattie was not in; she was down in Malibu recovering after a sushi dinner with lots of wine on the beach the night before. Fraboni told Eric he would drive out to see her with any message.

Arriving at Malibu, Fraboni found a tired, hung-over Pattie and walked her out onto the balcony of the house in which she was staying. She was exhausted. She had a nervous rash all over her body and had not yet had her daily trip to the acupuncturist which cleared it.

'Doesn't the ocean look beautiful today?' Fraboni began.

'No, Rob. Nothing looks beautiful with the kind of hangover I've got.'

Fraboni then read out, from the back of an envelope, the telephone message from Eric to Pattie. 'Please marry me next Tuesday in Tucson, Arizona.' Eric's message added that if she refused, 'she was to get on her bike.' Fraboni would be the best man.

Predictably, Pattie's first worry was what had happened to Jenny McLean. She phoned Eric. 'He said she was no longer with him,' says Pattie. 'I asked why it had to be so rushed and Eric explained the bet with Roger and the story in the *Daily Mail*. I said. "How cheap. You should really pay your debts. I can't marry you under these conditions." '

But romance won the day. Finally, with tears of joy, Pattie said yes. Once off the phone, she realized she had only three days to buy a wedding dress, have the blood test for rubella essential for non-residents marrying in America, and get to Arizona.

The day before the wedding, Eric and his party flew in. They checked into the same hotel as Pattie and her girlfriends Myel Fraboni and Chris O'Dell. Pattie was certain there would be a hitch because nothing would persuade Eric to have his blood checked with a needle. He had a horror of injections.

That problem was solved by having a Clapton lookalike, Larry McNeny, from Tulsa who worked with Eric's musicians, going to have Eric's blood test, taking with him Eric's passport. Next, Eric went to the registrar's office to get a licence, and was followed by journalists and an official who stopped him on the steps as he walked away with the licence. 'Exucse me, you have to pay, Mr Clapton.' Eric had no cash with him and his friends found a few dollars to hand over for the licence fee. It was 27 March 1979.

Six local churches had been booked by Roger Forrester, in an attempt to throw the local press off the scent. The wedding took place at Tucson's Apostolic Assembly of Faith in Christ Jesus. Eric and Pattie followed the tradition of not meeting until they reached the altar; in her mind she flashed back to the memory that the last time she had seen him he was snuggled up to another woman. Two identical rings had been bought for the bride and groom by Nigel Carroll. Eric and Pattie were married by the Rev. Daniel Sanchez.

'The service was super,' says Pattie. 'The Mexican preacher was lovely and the roadies and the band looked wonderful in powder blue tuxedos with black piping, some in pink suits, and all with sneakers on.' Rob Fraboni was the best man, Roger Forrester gave Pattie away, Alphi O'Leary and Nigel Carroll were the ushers. Ben Palmer flew in specially for the wedding.

Back at the hotel, the reception satisfied Eric's custard-pie humour by ending in a cake fight. Next night, an elated Clapton began his forty-concert American tour. Appearing with him was one of his greatest musical idols, and a great friend, the legendary blues singer Muddy Waters.

Although Eric was by far the bigger attraction, he felt humble alongside the veteran, and honoured by the fact that Muddy wanted to open the show for him. One night, backstage, someone handed Eric Muddy's guitar to hold for a few moments. Clapton refused to touch it, maintaining that it was no ordinary guitar. Owned by Muddy, it had an aura and demanded special treatment. 'Touching that guitar is absolutely taboo for me,' said Eric.

All seemed sweetness as that tour opened and the newly wed guitarist performed beautifully, kicked along by a great band: Albert Lee, Carl Radle, Dick Sims and Jamie Oldaker. At the Tucson show, Eric insisted on Pattie joining him on stage, so he could sing 'Wonderful Tonight' to her. The crowd loved it as he introduced his wife – but she was crimson with embarrassment. The receptions everywhere were ecstatic. A beaming Pattie stood in the wings as the tour made its way through Albuquerque, El Paso and Dallas. Then Eric's bombshell hit her: he told her he wanted her to go to Los Angeles, collect her baggage, and return to England. 'I was awfully upset,' says Pattie. 'He obviously wanted me to become the little housewife. Anyway, I did as I was told. I wasn't happy because I love New Orleans and was looking forward so much to going with Eric to that city, the next stop.'

There, Jenny McLean checked into the band's hotel and Eric had to quell a near mutiny among his team. Pattie's sister Jenny, then being escorted by Carl Radle, phoned Pattie to break the grim news. Forrester and others threatened to boycott the concert unless Eric ejected her. Pattie was assured by phone that Jenny had stayed alone in her own room before leaving New Orleans the next day.

Back at Hurtwood Edge after a triumphant tour, Eric and Pattie threw a huge wedding party for relatives and friends. It developed into a major occasion for musicians, too, with such notables as Bill Wyman, Mick Jagger, Jeff Beck and Lonnie Donegan attending. Three ex-Beatles – Paul, George and Ringo – joined in the jam-session in the marquee. Informed of the event later, John Lennon told Eric by phone from New York that he would have been there if he'd known about it. Had he done so, that would have been the only time all the Beatles had played together since they split amid such bitterness nine years earlier.

After the firework display and the revelry and the jam-session, there was a sad scene, a commentary on the callousness of all the musicians. Alone among the players, Jack Bruce approached the music of the night with his usual intensity. Playing bass, he improvised with tremendous imagination on old rock 'n' roll songs like 'Johnny B. Goode'. But the rest of the band didn't want to treat the session so seriously. They ostracized Jack. In the early hours of the morning in the chilly tent, Bruce was the lone musician playing.

'The others couldn't take it,' recalls Ben Palmer. 'They treated him *so* badly. He was really playing an advanced form of rock 'n' roll, probably the sort of music Cream would have played if they'd lasted. But they all moved farther and farther away from him leaving him in the marquee. And Jack came off the stage broken. He sat in my lap and cried. He had nothing to say and nowhere to go.' Three hours later, the house was empty and Jack was still there, with a drunken hanger-on. Eric had gone to bed. Ben Palmer persuaded a depressed Jack Bruce to go home.

All the crowd from Ripley were at the party . . . Pat and Rose and Sid and Guy and many others. Eric had put them at ease for the big day, writing a message at the bottom of their invitation cards: 'To the Ripleyites: you don't have to bring a present if you don't want to.' The most original gift came from Guy Pullen on behalf of the villagers: a tin of mock turtle soup. It was an affectionate reminder to

United – Eric and Pattie at their wedding party
Immediately after their wedding, Mr and Mrs Clapton in the traditional limousine
Eric and Pattie arriving at the opening night of the Hippodrome night club in London, in 1983 (*Rex Features*)

Clapton of his roots: 'When he was a kid living with Rose,' says Guy, 'we all remembered him sitting after dinner with a ring round his top lip after drinking mock turtle soup . . . '

To the musicians and other friends and their respective families, Mr and Mrs Eric Clapton epitomized a couple in perfect harmony. Eric had secured the woman of his dreams and Pattie's enjoyment of his music, from a distance, pointed to near perfection in marriage. Their honeymoon was in Kingston, Jamaica, the city whose reggae music Eric so admired. 'They'll last,' said Pete Townshend. 'They'll grow old very graciously together. The country lifestyle suits them, they're good company to be with socially, both very intelligent and percep- tive. I think it could last for ever.'

Eric continued his drinking and his extensive travelling as his career intensified and he sought more and more refuge in work. He wrote another simple love song to Pattie, 'Pretty Girl', and despite the pressures of great periods of separation when he was abroad, he believed all was well.

> Pretty girl you are the light of my life,
> I mean my everything
> You're the one I chose to make my wife,
> That's why you wear my ring.
> And when I'm feeling down and out,
> You're the one who will bail me out
> My love will always guide me home, pretty girl.
>
> Pretty girl don't ever say goodbye, don't ever let me be,
> If you do you know that I would die, You mean that much to me
> And when I'm feeling low and blue,
> You always know just what to do.
> My love will always guide me home, pretty girl.
>
> Pretty girl, hear what I have to say,
> It's something you should know,
> You brought me sunshine on my darkest day,
> That's why I love you so.
> And when my wandering day is through,
> I'll always hurry back home to you.
> My love will always guide me home, pretty girl.

But when he was at home, the obsessive streak that dominated Eric sent him scurrying for hobbies that would take his mind away from alcohol. 'I went strongly for fishing, and that's a very anti-social hobby,' he says. He and Nigel Carroll had become active members of the Ferrari Owners' Club, and of course he and Roger Forrester had become rabid supporters of West Bromwich Albion football team.

Pattie says she felt desperately lonely. Later, when she began drinking too much wine, a now dry Eric insensitively wrote a song to her called 'The Shape You're In'. He may have had good intentions of persuading her not to copy his own destructive behaviour, but to anyone who knew of Pattie's drinking at that time, it was a cruel, humiliating exercise by her husband, exposing her to embarrassment among those who knew Eric wrote the song about her:

I took my baby to see a show,
she was telling me she didn't want to go,
I said come on girl what's the matter with you?
But I could tell by the smell that she'd had a few.
I said hold on girl don't get too tight,
you started early and we've got all night.
You've got to take it easy, take it slow,
we don't want the whole world to know
About the shape you're in.

Well, my little girl really loves that wine,
Wine will do it to her most every time.
If it's red or it's white or it's in between,
She can drink more wine than I've ever seen
I said hold on girl don't get too tight,
You started early and we've got all night.
You've got to take it easy, take it slow,
We don't want the whole world to know
About the shape you're in.

Now I'm not trying to get heavy with you,
I'll mind my own business if you want me to.
But I love you girl, I don't love no one else.
I'm just telling you baby 'cause I've been there myself.
I said hold on girl don't get too tight,
you started early and we've got all night.
You've got to take it easy, take it slow,
We don't want the whole world to know
About the shape you're in.

By mid-1984 rumours were rife around the Clapton camp that all was not well in the marriage. By the autumn, Pattie confirmed it. When Eric returned from his concert tour of Australia and Hong Kong, she had left the house and rented a flat in London's West End, only two hundred yards from Eric's manager's offices.

Eric was distraught. He begged, pleaded and cajoled Pattie to return, even though he, like she, had found a temporary partner. But just as their love affair had blossomed in the least orthodox fashion, this separation was bizarre. They spoke by telephone several times a week, went for lunch together, and Pattie confirmed to Eric that she was still in love with him. Yet, she said, she felt she had to assert her own individuality, away from him, and pursue interests beyond staying at home as a rock star's wife. Eric conceded that perhaps he had been rather chauvinistic and he talked openly to all his friends about his desperation to win back Pattie's total commitment to him. 'I will never love another woman as much as I love Pattie,' Eric told me during the separation.

At home, alone in his mansion, he seemed a sad, lost man. He thought Pattie was making a bad mistake because they were destined to live together; 'But whatever she does during this period away from me, she is still my wife and I have to support her.' Some people close to him advised him to 'play it cool'. It was advice which Clapton utterly rejected. 'No – I'm not that kind of person. She's got to know I *care* and I want her back. I don't feel in the least bit cool about it! Besides, George Harrison played it cool and look what happened . . . '

Despite his ardour, his regular phone calls and his complete belief in their marriage, Pattie proved hard to pin down. They spent Christmas 1984 separately. He remained at Hurtwood Edge and played host to his mother and grandmother and friends; she went to her parents. In January, Pattie flew with some friends to Sri Lanka, telling Eric that she would decide on her return whether to go back to live with him.

Her decision wavered, but by February Eric had persuaded her to go away with him for a ten-day holiday in the sun for some proper conversations. They flew to Eilat, Israel and returned in a positive frame of mind. A week later, Pattie had moved back to Hurtwood Edge, after a six-month absence. They went out together – to the making of a video for Eric's new single, and to the premiere in London of the film *Brazil*. And they held hands and cuddled like two young lovers.

It was a fragile, almost fairy-tale reunion which both delighted and unnerved all Eric and Pattie's friends and well-wishers. Though he was consistent, how could she cause him so much anguish and then return to him with such passion? Pattie explained that she was looking for 'space' during the separation; both said they found it impossible to live without the other. How telling, now, were the songs on Eric's new album. 'Forever Man' took on a new slant, and

Looking more like a city gent than a rock superstar, Eric is with Pattie at Heathrow en route to Los Angeles

the maudlin 'Never Make You Cry' had a powerful message to Pattie which promised a long future together. Eric was certain that the period of separation would mark his life. Physically and mentally, he was at sea during Pattie's absence, and his determination to get her back was another example of his grit in the face of adversity.

Eric's wooing of Pattie had been quixotic. He had bombarded her with red roses during her absence and never eased up in his determination to persuade her to return home. When she eventually did, he relaxed his ban on her joining him on tour. She joined Eric for part of his marathon US tour in 1985, but before she flew out to him, Pattie had to get used to a new tactic by her husband to convince her of his affection. As soon as he reached America, for the start of the tour, Eric telephoned Pattie twice daily. She found the transformation in Eric's attitude somewhat overwhelming – 'but better than the alternative'.

7

THE
INNER MAN

'I think that having money has made me insecure'

Each week, an old-fashioned perforated brown wages envelope is delivered to Eric Clapton at his home. It contains £150 in cash. He does not particularly need the money, but he insists on the 'feeling' of getting a wage packet in his pocket, just like millions of other workers, every week – and he likes the discipline of living within a cash budget. He's gleeful when he underspends and has a few pounds' profit to carry forward seven days.

Typically of people who earn a lot, Clapton spends very freely but is careful with the small change. One of his friends testifies to his largesse, but several people confirm his meanness at the bar: 'He's overgenerous. If a friend admires something in his house, however big, he'll say: "Take it." But in a pub, he often has to be reminded that it's his round. There was even a joke when he got his wallet out. "Look out," said his mates. "That Red Admiral will fly out in a minute!" '

For a period, he compared his salary with those of the people who worked for him, men like Nigel Carroll and Alphi O'Leary. 'How much are you earning, then? Oh, I'm getting twenty quid more than you. Suppose that's right, really. I'm the guitarist!' He was, though, serious about making his salary work on a daily and weekly basis; by Wednesday, during his heavy drinking period, he would say to his friends: 'I can't go out till Friday. I've spent out!' And he meant it.

He has made a very strong, conscious effort to stay in touch with the basic values of the working man. He has been so determined to be 'one of the lads', mixing and drinking daily with the villagers, that some people close to him feared he was distancing himself too far from his natural stardom, and would never get back to work.

He is a stickler for 'playing the game' with money. In cards, he puts

191

his money on the table and refuses to start playing until everyone has done the same; he hates debts or promises that betting money, however small, will be paid later. At a London recording session for an American friend, singer-songwriter Stephen Bishop, Eric was going through a period of feeling exploited. 'No work until you've paid me the £200 in pound notes,' he said to Bishop. The singer peeled off the cash there and then, and the music began. Eric was not joking.

Conversely, Clapton owns four Ferrari cars and drove to Italy just to see his new one being built. He lives in a big, though unostentatious, house with all the trappings of rural splendour, and thinks nothing of flying to Rome, Milan or Florence, on a whim, for a day. He goes specifically to add to his huge collection of Giorgio Armani suits and shoes, and spends about £1000 each time. Yet he is happier with a transport café fry-up or 'thousand on a raft', as he describes baked beans on toast, than with gourmet food in expensive restaurants. That wish to retain contact with reality, and remain unpretentious about his roots and aspirations, has never left him. When his limousine broke down on the way to a gig, Eric enjoyed switching to a hi-jacked fish van.

Eric's attitude to money shows a blissful naïveté that probably comes from having amassed plenty early in his life and never having needed to worry about it, except during his lowest ebb when he had to pawn his guitars to support his habit. But his manager and those around him are still floored by his innocence.

A cheque for several thousand pounds once arrived at his house and he put it in a drawer and forgot about it. He had never paid a cheque into a bank in his life. Weeks later, Roger Forrester asked if he had received the cheque which was due to him. Yes, said Eric, but he didn't realize anything had to *happen* to it. He had no idea about banking systems, credit cards or cheques – and he was amazed when a store refused his cheque for over £50 without a supporting bank card. 'What's a bank card?' asked Eric. Since then, he has been given gold American Express and Visa cards, but does not fully realize they are substitutes for money. In a dressing room once, a band member said: 'Wow, great jacket, Eric. How much did it cost you?' Eric replied, in all seriousness: 'I didn't buy it. It was nothing. I got it on a credit card.'

His pride and joy, a 1957 Tour de France Ferrari, cost him £40,000 but he quickly forgot the price. Twenty grand, he said, when a friend asked him how much it had cost only a few days after he had bought it.

Roger Forrester is able to detect and define Eric Clapton's gullibil-

i have to write this : i am pissed off.
all i see is trouble, and if i cant see
it, i go and look for it. nell is a lazy
selfish woman, but does that have
to be my own distorted illusion ?
or a matter of fact ~ this little heart
of mine says we done wrong but the
same little heart said get out there
and go home ! which heart is telling
me the truth ? ~ dear Lord, please
hold us tight, this tug of war is getting
between us. a pox on princess carpets
and sweet scented sheets, there's
plenty of room for them in other's
lives, save our love from the peril
of obstinacy, and please allow me to
remain a man that she can respect
and forgive, dear nell, whatever you
may think of my love, it is there, all
the time, and sometimes it makes me
do very foolish things, pardon me ....

ity and impulsiveness from wide experience. On a trip to the South of France, Eric caught sight of a speedboat on the water and was immediately enraptured. He asked Roger to buy him one immediately. Forrester agreed. It cost £47,000, but the holiday it was planned for didn't happen; Eric never set foot in it and the vessel did not even leave its original packing crate. Forrester sold it after about a year of Clapton's pointless ownership of it.

After several years of staying there during working trips to Ireland, Eric bought the magnificent Barberstown Castle Hotel in County Kildare. On his visits to Dublin through the years to play some of his greatest concerts anywhere, at the Stadium, Eric found it a marvellous base from which to enjoy fishing. He 'fell in love' with the eleventh-century hotel and bought it as an investment, as well as for his pleasure. But while many local people went to Barberstown hoping to see Eric Clapton as mine host, the staff believe one of the reasons Eric cut Barberstown out of his life was that it reminded him too much of his heavy drinking and he could not face abstaining in his own hotel. But by 1985 Eric returned there, determined to enjoy regular visits.

Eric says he enjoys his money, mostly because he rarely thinks about it. 'Oddly enough, I think that having money has made me insecure. It's distanced me from certain people who don't have so much as me, or from people who know how to handle money and respect it, which are qualities I don't have. My relationships with those sorts of people have become insecure. And I find it impossible to have a relationship with people who have a complete monetary understanding, because to me money is simply something to be used. The value of it is not as important as what it's used for!

'I've been a collector of guitars, then weapons for a short time, then cars, then fishing rods, and no hobby lasts for long. I'm obsessive while it lasts and then it's on to the next. Materially, I've always got more than I ever need, which is quite annoying to me. I'd really like to live in a more spartan fashion but it's hard to keep a rein on my spending. I still buy too many clothes. My wardrobe is always too packed. That enthusiasm for clothes which came early in my life has never left me. I still enjoy seeing what other people wear. I enjoy judging a town, or a country, by the clothes its people have. The spirit of people manifests itself through what they wear. There's perhaps a dormant designer, or art historian, or fashion historian inside my fascination somewhere!'

The intricacies of Eric's personality are strongly connected with feeling free – with people, with money, with material goods. He has an utter horror of locked doors. He trusts everyone whom he meets in the music business, an endearing innocence that has often cost him dearly. He is equally happy playing his guitar to an audience of twenty in a village pub as he is with the glittering 20,000-seater stadiums, because the quality of the people and his standard of performance matter more to him than playing the numbers game.

In contrast, friends say he has been a terrible loser. In games like backgammon, cards, Monopoly or Trivial Pursuit – which incidentally wrongly names his 'comeback' album as *421 Ocean Boulevard* – Eric has sulkily walked away from the table if he was being trounced. But Eric says that was merely part of his make-up during his heavy drinking period. In the snooker room at his home, during the weekend binges, Eric and Guy Pullen would play dozens of frames of snooker against Nigel Carroll and Johnny H from Ripley. And invariably, Eric and Guy lost. When they did, the winning pair taunted them by playing, on the house jukebox, the Hot Chocolate song 'So You Win Again'. At three o'clock one morning, an angry Eric was so bad-tempered at having lost another match that he whipped the record out of the juke box and threw it through the window. 'He's a ratty loser, only interested in competitive games if he thinks he'll win,' says Guy Pullen. His loyalty even to West Bromwich Albion football team faltered when they had a run of defeats.

But typically, when he did support West Bromwich Albion, even his guitar plectrums had to reflect his enthusiasm. They were inscribed: 'Up the Baggies', the team's nickname. Other plectrums bore a bald message for other light-fingered guitarists: 'This is *my* fucking pick. E.C.'

The people around him have become familiar with his idiosyncrasies. He is adamant that, when on tour, there should be no crowds, particularly hangers-on, in the dressing room, and he insists on sharing the room with his band. 'He likes simplicity, but he draws a line,' says Roger Forrester. 'He won't tolerate inferiority. He certainly notices when things are not right.' Clapton does not lose his temper often. He tends to allow a situation that irritates him plenty of time to correct itself before blowing his top. On an American tour, for the first two weeks he contained his irritation that the audience was held back by security men from advancing towards the stage until the final two songs, 'Cocaine' and 'Layla'. 'It was the same scene every night,' says Eric. 'But in the dressing room after a couple of weeks, I did explode to Roger Forrester that it was so artificial that the audience was seen to be released at the same moment in the show every night. It's the only time I can remember really losing my cool. The falseness, the predictability, of every show really got to me.'

Although Eric appears casual before a show, the inner man is tense. Walking towards the stage, he has often told his manager that he didn't feel like playing. 'Oh, I just feel tired . . . ' Forrester, escorting him like a trainer with a boxing champion, knew how to work him up. 'Listen. West Brom just lost, six-nil.' Clapton would get into such a steaming temper, either with the news or with Forrester's ploy, that he would go on stage and play better because of the tension. Only his crew knew the sign, at the end of a show, that Clapton had not enjoyed his performance, or rated the audience as unresponsive. To symbolize a bad gig, Eric holds up his guitar to the audience with the back of the instrument facing them.

After several years, Clapton told Forrester he hated his backstage technique of telling him when it was time to go on stage. It was a corny method: 'That's it, Eric. Let's go on stage . . . ready to *go.*' Finally, Clapton announced to Roger: 'Look, for five or six years, I've *never* liked you walking into the dressing room telling me, it's time to go on stage, Eric. 'Cos I'm waiting for you to walk in through that door and my tension's building up. It's like you're preparing me for the gallows! So don't do it!' Forrester's solution was to arrange, worldwide, for a special coded knock-knock on the door as the signal to *him.* Then, he would say coolly: 'Ready when you are, Eric.'

It's often said that the real man emerges from the drunk. If that is true, then the Clapton of the late 1970s was an aggressive exhibitionist trying to escape from the soft sentimentalist. Many rock musicians revelled then in wild behaviour, destroying hotel furniture and causing mayhem as an immature means of attracting attention. Clapton, enjoying his alcohol but not in the top league of hotel wreckers, was still a hazard for those around him on world tours.The child inside him had a ball.

His most horrific and dangerous moment came one night twenty-six floors up at the Rainbow Hilton Hotel, Waikiki Beach, Honolulu. A drunken Eric, stripped to the waist, and clutching a samurai sword given to him during a Japanese tour, climbed perilously round the balcony into the next-door suite of his drummer Jamie Oldaker, who was in bed. Down below on the street, a woman called the police, petrified at the sight of a man with a sword in his hand, dicing with death. The drummer recognized the drunken Eric but by the time Clapton had walked out of the room into the corridor, there were three Hawaiian policemen moving up to him, with guns aimed straight at his head.

It was like something from an Errol Flynn film. The youngest cop recognized Eric, but the two older policemen hustled him down to

this morning, my throat is even worse and its moved from one side to another not only that, but the gland is swelling pretty rapidly, so ntny is trying to store some tetracyclin, which is a drag 'cause i know how antibiotics can slow me down, and also i wont be able to drink! arrrrgggh! i think i will fly wifey in pretty quick, i am going down fast and who else but her can look after me. i tried to ring her but the line was busy. i finally got through and it was so good to hear her voice, what a selfish bastard i am, what i mean is, if she called me and said she needed me right now, would i be able to drop everything and run to her ? answer; yes i there must never be any doubt in my mind about that, or ~ i am lost — put your skates on darling, i cant hold out too long! to top it all, roger says that i was moved to another room because, people were complaining about the smell coming from my room, i dont smell! do i hell ? just because i dont smother myself in poofdah perfume doesnt mean ive got b.o., bleeding nerve, i am almost tempted to get some stink bombs, and have a bath in them, then they would be a little more appreciative of my natural aroma, diana didnt say anything about me smelling, so there ~ mad gig, i made about a million mistakes, broke about eight strings, but we made the best of it, especially our albert, who had a wale of a time, and he was still steaming on when i went to bed ~ mrs. clapton arrives tomorrow hurray ~ goodnight ~ €

the hotel lobby. 'You can't arrest Eric Clapton,' said the young one. 'Do you want to bet?' asked the angry older cop. Eric put a cigarette in his mouth but they took it from him and snapped it in two. The drama ended after Roger Forrester suggested the police should give Eric a heavy talking to and leave it at that. 'And that's how it finished,' says Forrester. 'The police did say he'd risked certain death. Three people had been killed attempting that balcony walk before. It was a sheer drop. He was very lucky to be alive.'

*

'He was like a little orange on a tree that had started to shrivel,' says Alphi O'Leary, recalling the drunken years. 'And then somebody put a little bit of fertilizer on the tree and the orange became an orange again. If you prick that fresh orange, a lot of zest comes out of it.' Like all the people around Eric during the seven years of hard drinking, O'Leary had seen a totally changed man since 1982. The worst aspect of Eric's drinking was the frightening unpredictability of his moods. 'Tremendous highs, and then terrible depressions,' recalls Roger Forrester. 'But he always did the shows, sometimes to my surprise. They'd be fifty per cent good, fifty per cent bad, but it was so worrying. He could never last all day awake. He'd never be able to get up in the morning and still be awake by the evening for the show. He'd have to sleep the afternoon away.' When Forrester knocked on his door in the early evening to say it was time to get up, he often had problems rousing him. Once, in Dublin, he had to break the door down when there was no reply from a sleeping Clapton. But Eric had amazing powers of recovery when a show was due; not once did his manager have to cancel a show because of his condition.

In Clapton's fertile mind, one of his biggest worries about giving up the bottle was: 'What am I going to do with all that extra *time*?' He realized how many hours of his days and nights had been devoted to actually drinking, then sobering up adequately to face the world before returning to the bottle. 'All the time I'd spent devoted to the bottle, I'd put off doing things that were waiting to be tackled when I returned to real life. Abstract things: emotional problems or family situations. Suddenly, when you're sober again, you have to learn to live with all the problems you've created in your life but which have been cloudy. It doesn't go away.' Eric's membership of Alcoholics Anonymous was crucial: it absorbed his interest as well as helping him practically.

Like everything that makes an impact on his life, Alcoholics Anonymous is something he is still, in his own way, committed to.

He never does anything half-heartedly. He feels that stopping drinking, particularly the quantity he was consuming, would have been impossible without going to group meetings once a week. On tour, anywhere in the world, he attended them, sometimes immediately after a concert when his adrenaline ran high and he needed sympathetic reassurance.

'I'm still active,' Eric said in 1985. 'I'm not such a good member as I could be, mainly because of my travels since I gave up drinking three years ago. My first year off it was good, the second year not so good, because I began to get the urge to drink again. And my third year was disastrous because I stopped going to meetings and gave in to the desire to drink. I did drink earlier this year and carried on for a few months.' He stopped before it took a hold, however. On one plane journey with Roger Forrester, he asked his manager if he minded if he had a beer. No, said Forrester. No attempt would be made to prevent Eric from drinking. Eric has a big guilt complex at being seen to let down those around him who worried about him. So he drank a beer and then stopped totally. But that odd beer was a far, far cry from the days when Eric's personal assistant carried a case with Courvoisier aboard each flight because Eric could not wait for the plane to 'level out' before needing a drink.

Of his AA endorsement, Eric says: 'A lot of people in show business and the music world don't go to AA. They would like to stop drinking and a lot of them do. But some of them have done it on their own, without the help of AA, because they fear being recognized, they fear being treated as a special case. Now for me, because of the way my career has developed overseas, I'm more recognized in America, if I go to a meeting, than I am in Britain. A lot of people in my local group meetings still don't know who I am and it's only after I speak for a little while, they realize that I'm in entertainment. But they have no idea specifically what I do. So now, in England, I'm still pretty anonymous, but in America now, I'm not.

'In America, they've got a slightly better handle on it than in Britain. They're a lot more outspoken and a lot less nervous about it than the British. It still seems to be a bit of a stigma in Britain to be an alcoholic. And the best members of AA in England are always old army types, who have been sober for a long time, or who drank for a long time. They are much tougher, whereas in America it seems to be a younger clan of people, more around my age group and younger, from all walks of life. They don't have that shame and guilt, which a lot of people in Britain still have.'

While he has conquered drink, he is careful not to claim that he will never return to it. He tried a sip of white wine at home in 1984, but hated the taste. 'It's only too often that it happens that people start again. I mean, it's any day! You can be sober for fifteen or twenty years and then one day you'll just put yourself into an impossible position, whereby the only thing you can do is to pick up a drink. It's always premeditated. And God knows what brings it on half the time. You could set yourself up over a period of a year, as I did. I worked myself up to a drink, over a period of six months, at least, just *thinking* about having a drink . . . until I couldn't stand it any longer and I had to find out whether I could take it or not. So you could set yourself up for years and you become very miserable and morose. But it is always possible, no matter how long you've been sober, to drink again. And the thing about AA is that they're always ready for you to come back. If you do drink again, all you've got to do is go back and say, "I've drunk again," and they'll take you in. There are no reprimands, because they all know that it could happen to any one of them, at any time.'

Eric has worked for AA, helping those less experienced than he in withdrawal from alcohol.

'After a couple of years of sobriety, or even just a year, you're invited at some point to give what is called "chair". That's when you sit at the head of the table and tell your life story. You tell how you drank and how you stopped drinking and how you're getting on in your recovery.' He has done several of those sessions. He enjoyed the therapy of that, and would do it again. 'Because I've never got it under control. No alcoholic *ever* has control. He is actually suffering from a killing disease which gets worse. Even if you're not drinking, it's getting worse. So I'm trying, as best I can and that's not very well, to stay sober and to live and learn to live again as a sober human being. And any time that I fall prey to drink, I know that I stand the risk of killing myself within a very short time. And I've no control over that whatsoever, if that happens.

'I see it as being a completely logical chain of events, where when you stop going to AA meetings, there is only one other course of action and that is, if you're an alcoholic, you drink. So it's absolutely necessary if you are doing it properly to go maybe once a week, if not twice a week. Because if you're not there, you'll be in a pub, or you'll be at the bottle.

'So I think anyone who tries to drop alcohol needs this kind of help. If you try to beat it with your own willpower, that always falls down. Because you're just not strong enough on your own.' His doctrine from AA is based on 'one-day-at-a-time'. 'They say, "Do not drink again *today*. Don't worry about tomorrow. You can have a drink tomorrow, if you like. But don't have a drink *today*." Well, it's

Eric as fisherman (*London Features International*)

just based on the fact that you're never actually going to be here tomorrow. So if you don't drink today, you'll be all right.

'It's a struggle at Christmas time! It's always a struggle whenever you're around people who are having fun, or whenever you're having fun. For me, the temptation to drink comes along when I'm most relaxed, or when I'm actually happiest, when things are really going well and I've got no problems. That's when I want to drink. When I'm struggling against adversity, when I'm in a bind, the temptation to drink doesn't cause me any problem, because I know that I have to get through that without any help from the bottle. And then I know for a fact that drink will only make it worse. It's always the times when you're most relaxed and there's nothing to bother you . . . that's when you feel like you could sit back and take it double easy.'

By mid-1985, Eric was 'enjoying a glass of wine or a beer at the right time of day, drinking in moderation. But I do feel that the AA was very instructive and a great deal of help to me when I needed to stop drinking heavily. Now, there's no guarantee that I won't drink heavily again, just as there's no guarantee of anything. So I may have to return to AA at some time in my life. But at the moment, I feel I can drink in moderation. So for the time being, things are a little different.

'What I'm striving for in my life now is establishing a balance – being involved in a little of each of my interests instead of doing one thing to the exclusion of everything else. So when Gary Brooker says I will be a fisherman until the day I die, he's probably right. It's just that I don't need to do it every day or every week.

'I'm constantly striving to be a more consistent human being. I don't want to be predictable but I don't like the idea of people having to wait while I make up my mind about what I'm going to do next.'

Interestingly, Eric sees no connection between the way he ditched drugs and his ending the heavy drinking habit. 'They're totally unrelated,' he says. 'I conquered drugs through my own wish and will to survive, with the help of Meg Patterson and the help of her husband and family, who gave me love. That was the medicine I needed as much as, if not more than, the actual acupuncture which she was practising. It was a totally self-centred way of getting better, for my own benefit really, which is the same in AA. Except that in AA you're thrown in among a lot of other people who are having the same problem, so you have to *give*, whereas with me, coming off drugs, I was just *taking*. When I stopped drinking and came into AA, I'd learned bit by bit and still am learning how to fill the vacuum with a belief in something greater than myself.'

He is a spiritual man: in his wedding photo album, he wrote: 'Dear Lord, Bless our marriage, Amen.' And at the end of every world tour, a Clapton high on emotion always hugs each member of his band and shows tears of joy at the elation of yet another triumph. 'God bless,' he says to them all . . . even though he might be seeing them again the next day.

'I was brought up Church of England with a loose, average religious education,' he says. 'I always did feel there was some kind of destiny preordained for everyone. But I felt, and feel, that the choice and conscience is up to the person. I always felt bad when I knew I was doing something wrong, you know; therefore I believe there is something other than my own momentum in charge. It always felt bad to go against the grain. And I put that down to God.

'But as I grew older that view became a lot more confused and less to the forefront, until quite recently, when I gave up the booze. It was part of the AA doctrine, that you find something to believe in which is a higher power, a power that is greater than yourself, something that you don't necessarily have to put a label on. It doesn't need to be religious, but it just has to be something that you know is in control, rather than you. And that's as strict as I like it to get. I don't really think any religion has got a monopoly over another. They seem to blend into one another quite well. So it's just something that I don't particularly understand or care to analyse too much. But I do know something is actually more powerful than I am. But I can't perceive it as a person, or a tangible thing. I don't think that's within our understanding.'

He is a man of God without practising any religion. In Jerusalem, during his 1979 concert tour, he hardly left his hotel room, despite the enthusiasm of the band to look around the Holy City. 'I'm very aware of where I am,' Eric told them. 'You go. I don't need to be told, shown, or reminded, where I am.' But that night, he had a sharp physical, as well as spiritual, reminder: at the concert, a fan good-naturedly threw a rose on stage and a thorn struck and cut Eric's head. As the man thousands called God, the symbolism of the incident, in Jerusalem, worried him. And Eric has told close friends that he sometimes prays. He carries a small Alcoholics Anonymous book with him most of the time as part of his alcoholism therapy, and reads a little of it on most days.

One of the earliest examples of his songwriting, and the only Clapton song on the Blind Faith album *Presence of the Lord*, manifests his faith:

I have finally found a way to live
Just like I never could before.
I know that I don't have much to give
But I can open any door.
Everybody knows the secret
Everybody knows the score.
I have finally found a way to live
In the colour of the Lord.

I have finally found a place to live
Just like I never could before.
And I know I don't have much to give
But soon I'll open any door.
Everybody knows the secret,
everybody knows the score.
I have finally found a place to live
In the presence of the Lord.

In the presence of the Lord.
In the colour of the Lord.

On another front, he is very superstitious: no shoes are allowed on the table in his house, 'because they bring bad luck', and he never walks under ladders. 'I take my superstitions to ridiculous extremes,' says Eric. 'If I'm waiting for something, I count to thirty and if it hasn't happened by then, something's wrong. On the phone, I let a number ring out a number of times and if they haven't answered by then, it's a bad sign and I hang up.' Palmists and tarot card readers frighten him, though. Superstitions carry over into his work: 'Just as I leave the dressing room, or walk near to the stage, Alphi is always on hand. And he always says the same four words before I walk out: "Have a good one." If he isn't there to say that, well it doesn't throw me completely, but I do wonder . . .'

Eric has lurched from one craze to another. 'I don't think I'll ever level out, until I get very old,' he says. 'I go from one obsession to the next. It's something I'd really like to beat but I don't know if I can. I try in every way I can to do things in moderation – but the impossibility is precisely what made me an alcoholic. We're all obsessive. You know, you can always spot an alcoholic. If you leave a bowl of peanuts on the table, he'll finish the lot. He can't manage with just two or three. I'm like that. And if I decide to paint a room, I have to do it in one day, or until I'm completely knackered'.

So when he stopped drinking and tried to fill all his time, Eric plunged into another hobby, fishing, with an all-consuming zeal.

It began through his friend Gary Brooker. The pianist, who lived a

Holding his trophy after being voted the world's top musician in the 1969 *Melody Maker* pop poll (Barry Wentzell/Melody Maker)

few miles from Eric, often went to the local pub with him, and one day said to Eric: 'I'm going fishing tomorrow.' Clapton replied: 'Ah, I used to go fishing over in Ripley when I was a kid. Caught a perch once.' He was persuaded by Gary that fly fishing was different: it called for a psychological victory over a delicious trout or salmon, rather than coarse fishing which produced carp or perch to be thrown back. Intrigued, Eric saw it as a potentially healthy obsession, one that might contrast with his heavy drinking. Fishing and drinking did not mix well. Brooker, a skilled fisherman, taught Eric to cast, and within weeks it was totally dominating Clapton's life. He bought a place on the River Test in Wiltshire and went trout fishing for days on end – and those absences added to the strain on his marriage as a now bemused Pattie stayed at home. When he returned with trout, she gutted them and prepared them for the deep freezer, but inwardly pondered the new 'fence' that fishing had built between them. Yet it was not without Clapton's dry humour. Once, after a day without a catch, he wanted to impress Pattie with his prowess, so he went, like many another fisherman before him, to MacFisheries and bought some trout in a crazy attempt to fool her.

Eric agrees his days of fishing were 'very selfish' but argues that as an alcoholic coming off the booze, he needed to be selfish. 'It was my *life* and if I hadn't started taking steps to get straight again, I was going to die. Because even if I wasn't drinking, I could have died of misery. You can end up committing suicide while sober. So for me fishing was great contemplation, meditation, and a way of getting physically fit again. For that first year, it was absolutely necessary to have some kind of exercise – with fishing you tend to have to walk a lot. It could have been tennis, squash or golf, but I chose fishing for the first year off booze. The second year, I should have eased off and maybe started setting up a new lifestyle. But I carried on fishing. And that's when it became anti-social. It definitely contributed to a division between Pattie and me.'

The American tours for up to six weeks, the concerts all round the globe, and the recording sessions, all without Pattie, added to the strain on the marriage. Eric's obsessiveness made it difficult for him to contemplate changing his ways. While Pattie nursed her grievances, he in turn felt very aggrieved when, returning home from the airport after a long tour, he found her absent. She often forgot when he was due home.

Roger Forrester, with the world-weary look of one who had observed Eric's fetishes a thousand times, said fishing would not last. Meanwhile, when Eric's concert tours were planned, Forrester was asked to book only hotels near fishing facilities. Eric spent many hours of each day out on lakes, alone, and a new worry loomed: he would be so tired from such a long day in the fresh air that he wouldn't have enough energy for the show.

'We went fishing everywhere,' says Gary Brooker. 'In Japan we had a boat and drifted downriver in the rapids and didn't catch anything at all. But Eric said it was much better than being stuck in the hotel room. And he got so immersed in it that the *last* thing he wanted to do was stop off at a bar for two hours' rest. Booze is not part of the sport, except in America where they load the cooler full of beer as soon as you take the boat.'

Back home after a tour, Pattie's role as a 'trout widow' increased. Eric left at 7.30 in the morning and did not return until late at night from his solitary fishing outings, usually with three or four trout for Pattie to clean and freeze. He collected rods and reels and all the paraphernalia with predictable feverishness. On tour, as soon as the party arrived in a town and he had checked into his hotel suite, Eric was scouring the local phone directory for the name and location of the fishing tackle specialist. The phone would ring in Nigel Carroll's room: 'Right, I've found the shop. Let's go.' He bought dozens of rods and reels, but gave many to his friends.

The intensity of the fishing days and nights surprised even Gary Brooker. Eric went to a lake not far from his home in Surrey, or to his position on the River Test for five-hour sessions at night, or to Scotland, or to one of the four trout lakes run commercially by ex-Who singer Roger Daltrey in Sussex.

'His casting's good and he's sometimes caught fish when I haven't,' says Brooker. 'Once, down at Roger Daltrey's, I caught one and he caught five.' Eric took great delight in boasting of his expertise. 'Did you see what they were feeding on, Hornby?' he said, using his mocking nickname to Brooker. 'It was a pheasant tail nymph,' he said, describing the fly he had chosen.

Clapton enthusiastically told Brooker several times that fishing had replaced alcohol in his life. Gary recalls one outing which emphasized how seriously Eric had immersed himself in the sport. 'There were some fish in the river, and a trout rising underneath a branch. It turned to his fly three or four times. It was difficult to cast the fly to it, too. And Eric chirped up like a little boy: "I've got a real challenge on here, Hornby. I'm not gonna give *this* one up!" Eric loves the confrontation of fishing, as well as encouraging Pattie to cook the trout. Gary Brooker believes he will never completely give it up. But by 1985, Eric's keenness on fishing had gone on to 'hold'.

Everyone involved with a Clapton pursuit has become resigned to the fact that his zest for it might not survive his initial fever. 'I plunge into everything full tilt and then hope to level out,' he says. Eric began his flirtation with the turf as a racehorse owner in 1975, buying Pattie a horse as her Christmas gift. He was going to call it Layla's Song, but at the last moment changed it to Bushbranch. Although she won five races, they were low-category races, but the horse whetted Eric's appetite for more involvement; he had always taken a lively 'punter's interest' in horses. With a prominent trainer, Toby Balding, who runs stables in Hampshire, Eric bought a filly for £500. Named Via Delta by Roger Forrester's secretary, Diana Puplett, the mare was literally a soaraway success: she won twice as a two-year-old, had a fine three-year-old season and finally, in 1979, brought Eric his finest turf hour, winning the Fortnum and Mason trophy at Ascot, with prize-money of £9000. In tweed suit and trilby hat, Eric attended Ascot looking every inch the dapper racehorse tycoon, beaming happily at cameramen recording his surprising entry into the world of racing.

Within two racing seasons, Via Delta was sold because, in the words of Toby Balding, 'we had an offer we couldn't refuse for her to go to the Oman.' After winning Eric about £28,000 in prizemoney, she was sold for £50,000. Toby Balding believed and hoped that the success would encourage Eric to invest in bloodstock. There was even talk of Eric keeping some fillies at his Surrey home. But the idea was dropped when it was realized that staff would be needed to look after the horses.

When Via Delta was sold, Eric turned to his wife for an inspirational name. His next horse, called Nello, won at 25–1 at Leicester. Then came Ripleyite who, in Toby Balding's judgement, 'didn't win us as many races as its ability warranted.' Ripleyite, on which all Eric's friends were persuaded to gamble, won a race at Goodwood as a three-year-old, the Brighton Cup as a four-year-old, and ran second many times. He was eventually sent for sale to America. On the strength of selling him, Eric invested in two young horses, Vague Melody and Shagayle. Balding says he has often 'tried to involve Eric with a fairish capital expenditure.' This was decisively resisted by Clapton, who wrote his trainer a letter:

Dear Toby,
Thanks for your letter. At this rate, I'll be lucky if I cross my own path. Let's race her against good class with a high prize rider up, just for the race. Give me a bell as soon as you can. All my love to you and yours, Eric Clapton.
P.S. Bugger all this long-term investment nonsense. The football season starts in a couple of months.

Pattie and Eric, happily reconciled

Eric immersed himself in the subject of racing. He showed a good grasp of the technicalities of training and ground conditions; he 'picks up things about horses very quickly,' says Toby Balding. 'He absorbed the language and the thinking behind racing and his enthusiasm at the races is enormous. But it's just another interest.' Among the jockeys, there was often competition to ride a Clapton-owned animal. 'He doesn't see enough of the horses to get emotionally involved with them as we do,' says Toby Balding. 'He's businesslike enough to realize that when we get a good financial offer for a horse, it has to be sold. But he obviously enjoys horses and racing, which has a certain poetry for him. He attends races for the atmosphere, the physical thrill of it, and the pleasure of winning. And he loves betting.' Balding says he had hoped for a greater commitment from Eric in the horseracing world, but was thwarted partly by Roger Forrester, who decided it was a bad business enterprise for Eric. To get Roger involved, Eric bought him a horse for Christmas. But Gold Saint did not prove a winner. 'The only real argument I had with Eric's team,' says Balding ruefully, 'was that all the money we got from Via Delta, instead of being spent on yearlings, had gone on buying Eric's smart new Ferrari . . . '

Eric's capriciousness was not always so untroubled.

To many people, particularly musicians and fans, he plummeted to the depths of bad taste and indiscretion when he made a few unrehearsed remarks from the concert stage in Birmingham in 1978.

At that time, the immigration of blacks into England was an explosive topic. Enoch Powell, MP had warned against unrestricted immigration and Birmingham was a particularly sensitive city for Eric to touch on the subject.

Eric called out to his audience: 'Do we have any foreigners in the audience tonight? If so please put up your hand . . . I think we should vote for Enoch Powell.'

It was a highly inflammatory, off-the-cuff remark, particularly as it came from a musician whose inspirational sources were black. The music community was aghast. Partly as a result, a movement called Rock Against Racism was formed in Britain. At the time, Clapton was unrepentant.

'I think Enoch is a prophet. His diplomacy is wrong and he's got no idea how to present things. His ideas are right. You go to Heathrow airport any day and you'll see thousands of Indian people sitting there waiting to know whether or not they can come into the country. And you go to Jamaica and there are adverts on TV saying "Come to lovely England".

'I don't think Enoch Powell is a racist. I don't think he cares about

its a ghastly start to the day when you pick up the paper to read something about whats on the tele or the racing results and Mountbattens face is staring out at you from every page. i have long been a vocal supporter of the rebublic (even though i cant spell it), but i cant equate their professed love of freedom and/or their fight for it, with the murdering of a truly honourable man, and, inevitably, the mass slaughter of their own countrymen. my name isnt patrick for nothing, and i cry for those who will have to suffer as a result of this fucking stupid cruel and pitiless deed, may the bones of the animals who coldly planned and carried out this crime, whether they be catholic, protestant, or church of england, rot in hell before i get down there. as God is my witness.

on the whole a pretty rough day until the chaps came down and we had a good jam which was short but sweet

colour of any kind. His whole idea is for us to stop being unfair to immigrants because it's getting out of order. A husband comes over, lives off the dole to try to save enough to bring his wife and kids over. It's splitting up families. The government is being incredibly unfair to people abroad to lure them to the promised land where there is actually no work. Racist aggravation starts when white guys see immigrants getting jobs and they're not. Yeah, I'm getting a lot of stick for what I said, but so did Enoch. He was the only bloke telling the truth for the good of the country. I believe he is a very religious man and you can't be religious and racist at the same time. The two things are incompatible.'

Today, Eric has few regrets about his remark, for he regards Enoch Powell as having predicted a mounting problem. Recalling the events leading up to it, he says: 'We had travelled up from London, where I think an Arab had made some kind of remark to Pattie in the lobby of the Churchill Hotel. And I was incensed when I looked round and saw all these Arabs and all the signs in Arabic. I began thinking: what the hell is happening to this country? And I was drunk at the time. But though it's a horrible thing to have to admit, I think he's been honest. Every now and then you'll hear a voice that isn't pandering to what people want to hear, uncomfortable for the masses. Then I think you've got to take notice of it. Enoch Powell had a lot to risk by saying these things. He can't have done it for pure gain. But I never believed that I, as a rock musician, had any particular right to make speeches.

'I think rock stars and musicians have got a very good angle on some parts of the sociological ethic, in terms of what is harmonious. But all too often their ideas prove to be based on fantasy.'

Eric is capable of darting in and out of firm old friendships and sustaining them, despite lapses of time or good behaviour. Although he is quick to jettison hangers-on he meets on the road, and also inside the community of music, cherished friends are dear to him. Among them are Chas and Dave. The Cockney singers, who have won great popularity in Britain for their lively singalong music, first saw Clapton when he played with John Mayall's band at Cook's Ferry Inn, a pub in Edmonton, North London, in 1966. But their friendship did not blossom until the mid-1970s, and eventually they opened the concerts on Clapton's British tours.

'He's a genuine, honest geezer and what he likes about our music, and us,' said Chas, 'is that we're unpretentious.' Eric's admiration for Chas and Dave's knockabout, knees-up style surprises some, but their warmth, professionalism and good-natured fun is precisely what Eric likes, and in its simplest form, that's what his music is all about, too. 'He means what he plays, he feels it, and just gets up and does it,' says Chas.

But they had a sharp reminder one night of his competitiveness. Most nights, they had invited guitarist Albert Lee to join them for their finale. After a few nights, Clapton started niggling away at Chas and Dave: 'It's always "Come on, Albert," and never "Come on, Eric," ' he said petulantly. Chas and Dave thought he was joking, but he definitely was not. He thought Albert Lee was getting the more heroic treatment. Chas and Dave had thought Eric, being the star, would not want to join in their spot. 'But he was genuinely choked, and it surprised us,' says Dave. They did bring Clapton into their set . . . and Eric gave Chas a banjo, which he treasures.

'Don't give it away,' Clapton warned him.

'Nah, I wouldn't part with it for Paul McCartney's songwriting royalties,' Chas replied.

The strong bond that links Chas and Dave and Eric is a fundamental love of the blues for its simplicity; Clapton has sung along with them often on the Huddie Ledbetter classic, 'Goodnight Irene'. But Eric's manager hates him doing it, believing it reduces him to the level of a pub singalong. Most times they meet, he tries to bribe Chas and Dave with £5 each not to get Eric involved in the song.

The simple spirit of that old song, and Eric's affinity with such genuine, unaffected characters as Chas and Dave, is important in understanding the man. In matters of hard commercial decisions, when a giant audience or his next album is under consideration, Eric will listen to advice and often accept it. For years, he allowed his concert running order to be devised by his manager, unlikely for such a stubborn man as Eric. His affection for Chas and Dave and their music, reflects one of Clapton's most endearing characteristics: a refusal to believe in the reality of stardom.

This isn't easy. His home is littered with trophies that tell him he is a giant among musicians. While Clapton tries so often to walk away, or submerge, his status, the awards line his studio, the little eight-track which Phil Collins persuaded him to have built at Hurtwood Edge.

There's his hat-trick of awards, for three consecutive years from 1967, as Top Musician in the *Melody Maker* Readers' Poll; the Gallery of the Greats award from *Guitar Player* magazine; three awards from *Playboy* magazine for his guitar work, including a Hall of Fame nomination; the prestigious Best Electric Blues Guitarist award from *Guitar Player*; Britain's Silver Clef award for services to music; even the award as Britain's Best-Dressed Man in 1970. These are only a few of Eric's achievements: the gold and silver discs from around the world are reminders of his record sales – an estimated total of 30 million.

From his years with Cream particularly, Eric had learned how to balance the serious aspects of life on the road with zany interludes. 'Ginger and Jack's humour was vicious but we did have some really funny times and, despite the atmosphere in the band, there was a lot of comedy,' Clapton says. 'Once, we all climbed Ben Nevis together and the hilarious running back down it, chest-high in gorse, will stay in my memory for ever. There were some crazy times as well as hard ones – like going to the office and tearing the place apart, just for a lark.'

Eric's penchant for Monty Pythonesque humour stayed with him when he launched his own band. 'When he came back off the tours, lots of people asked each other for Clapton stories,' says Pattie. 'With great glee, they'd want to know what pranks he'd got up to on the road and how many practical jokes he'd got away with. People eagerly awaited his return from other countries because he was such a source of amusement.' Eric enjoyed the role people had cast for him. 'He enjoyed being the bizarre hero,' says Pattie.

Against the backdrop of superstardom, Clapton believes the best method of surviving the high mortality rate, either personal or professional, among top players, is to refuse to be derailed from fundamental values. He loves to keep contact with other musicians. Few stars of his stature have been such consistent 'sitters-in' on other artists' recording sessions or concerts. For many years, Eric boosted the sales of dozens of other people's records by his presence and his name on the label. But he hated being exploited, or having his friendship used for gain. He eventually decided to surprise some people by asking for a token fee. The 'working man' ethic caused that. And when he occasionally sells some of his guitars, he instructs that they should be sold anonymously so that they cannot fetch inflated prices on resale as 'Eric Clapton's guitars'.

Eric's ability to remain 'one of the blokes' and his easy-going accessibility to genuine Surrey village people were exemplified just after Christmas 1977. The Round Table, an organization which raises money for charity, was wondering what to do for the annual Valentine's Day dance. The 7000 people of Cranleigh enjoyed four events a year in the village hall. They wanted something different from the traditional old-time dancing, raffles, fancy dress or cheese-and-wine parties. When the Tablers were in committee, one member, Roger Swallow, suddenly said: 'What about Eric Clapton?' The

Above: Princess Michael of Kent presented Eric with the Silver Clef award for services to British music, in 1983 (*Richard Young/Rex Features*)
Below: A happy 'Clappers' with drummer Charlie Watts of the Rolling Stones and pianist Georgie Fame, jamming at the wedding of producer, Glyn Johns (*London Features International*)

idea was greeted with howls of derision. Eric Clapton, live, at Cranleigh Village Hall? Forget it! But Swallow thought it was worth a try: he wrote to Eric.

A few days later, the phone rang in Swallow's office. 'Hello, it's Eric here. That dance of yours – I'll do it.' After recovering from the shock and his suspicion of a practical joke, Swallow asked how much he wanted as a fee to appear.

'Nothing, but there's just one thing. It's got to be strictly under the counter,' Eric answered. This puzzled Swallow, 'because in my business, "under the counter" means a hefty back-hander, if you know what I mean. But I quickly discovered that what Eric meant was that he wanted no publicity at all.' Clapton and his manager were so insistent on this that they told Swallow that if a newspaper got advance news, he would not do the show. It went ahead.

Eric even rehearsed at the village hall for two days in the week before the concert; he took a great interest in how much money could be expected, and how it would help re-equip the Cranleigh Cottage Hospital; and he brought an old friend, guitarist Ronnie Lane, formerly of the Faces. The music was laid-back, the hall packed with 350 people, ardent Clapton fans at the front, and soberly suited Round Tablers at the rear. Pattie Clapton and Katy Lane, flouncing around in scarlet and black French dresses and white petticoats, did an impromptu can-can which prompted the locals to dance and Eric to christen the ladies 'The Harlots'. Eric hit his musical peak with a great blues, 'Alberta, Alberta', his stylish instrumental phrases evoking a call-and-response technique between his superb vocal and his guitar. He was in a loose mood for the whole evening, feeling no pressure. The night raised £1000 for the hospital and was described by Eric as a 'good 'un'. The mood of the evening was summed up after Eric and Ronnie Lane had harmonized on 'Goodnight, Irene', like a pair of mates fresh out of the local boozer. The audience joined in. As Eric left the hall, a young fan shouted out: 'Eric, do "Layla" or we won't have you back again!' It was the one song Eric didn't feel like doing that night.

The big arenas around the world are important 'career moves' in pleasing the people, but major artists like Eric always yearn for the intimacy of the clubs that first generated their love of playing. Eric became immersed in blues jam-sessions at Gary Brooker's Parrot Inn. Gary played piano and brought along some distinguished musicians, including saxophonist Mel Collins, violinist Darryl Way and guitarist Mickey Jupp, for evenings which were dedicated to blues music. 'We had a hundred and fifty people in at £1 a head, food included,' says Brooker. 'The amplification was small and Eric sat down behind the pillar and seemed at his happiest. It sounded very similar to what a little Chicago club might have been years ago.' The tunes, too, rekindled Eric's deepest affections: golden oldies by the Coasters and Chuck Berry and Elmore James material.

The Parrot Band, as it has become known, played half a dozen nights at the pub before Eric decided a sense of style was called for. It was just like the scruffy old days with the Yardbirds. He phoned Brooker and asked what uniform they should wear that night to replace the casual look that was gaining too much ground. An air of formality was essential, Eric said, and he would wear a white dinner jacket and a black bow tie. That night, almost in return for their professionalism, they decided that the profits from their work should not go entirely to charity. They each earned £50, and the face of Eric Clapton was alight at the sight of the ready cash.

The Parrot sessions are still alive in the minds of the musicians; Eric and Gary hope to organize at least one each year. It's the camaraderie of pub life, as well as the music, that strikes at Eric's heart. 'Real people,' he says simply. He greatly prefers it to the private-aeroplane-and-limousine life of world tours. On the road in the US, he once became so cynical about the similarity between the journeys, the cities and the halls, that when people asked where the next night's show was he had a set reply: 'Anywhere in America.'

After his world tours of such anonymous, massive stadiums, Eric enjoys the earthiness of the final venue of all his British concerts. This always has to be at the 1500-seater Guildford Civic Hall, a few miles from where he was born and from where he now lives. The Guildford finale is very much a case of the meteor returning to earth, with his mother Pat, grandmother Rose and other local people cheering from the balcony. As a regular appearance for a player of his stature, it is a unique tradition and, with the vibrations of the occasion strong in his mind, Eric often plays his most breathtaking solos.

8

THE
MUSICIAN

*'I worry about the division between art and
entertainment'*

At the last count, Eric Clapton owned a hundred and twenty guitars.
They vary in style, shape and vintage and he says they are needed,
although not in that luxurious quantity, for various roles. 'A Spanish
guitar for a classical melody or a Spanish sound, an acoustic for a
country or folky or even a very old rural blues, and an electric guitar,
depending on the size or quality of the amplifier, if it's country, rock
or blues. And my songwriting can be affected by the guitar that
comes into my hand at the moment I'm composing.'

Of all that mighty collection, an almost valueless guitar which he
made himself occupies a special place as his favourite. Nicknamed
Blackie, it is a 1956 black Fender Stratocaster, a hybrid actually
assembled by Eric from six similar models which he bought for a
mere hundred dollars each in Nashville in 1970. 'It's very tough as a
guitar, with a long, colourful history,' says Eric. 'I picked up these six
Stratocasters at a time when the bottom had dropped out of the
guitar market generally. Les Paul models were ruling the roost for
guitar heroes, but I had a feeling about Stratocasters being somewhat
sturdier. Buddy Holly had been a very big early influence, particularly the way he looked, and I loved the look and sound of his Strats. So
I bought these six and came back to England with them. I gave one to
Steve Winwood, one to Pete Townshend, one to George Harrison,
and I kept three. Out of the three I had left, I made one from the best
ingredients of each guitar, right down to the machine heads or the
volume control.

'That guitar has been with me through all kinds of scrapes. I
remember in Jamaica, rehearsing the band I had for *461 Ocean
Boulevard*, drunk out of my mind, in the middle of the night in this

cinema which we'd rented. We could only get to play in it during the night from twelve o'clock to six o'clock in the morning. I remember ending a Chuck Berry number by falling flat on my face. That was the cue for the drum beat to end the song, and I crushed some parts of my Blackie guitar underneath me. And within half an hour it was playing as good as new, just with a few little running repairs. The body and the neck and everything else were totally gone and I thought: This guitar is my *life*. It can take as much damage as me! And I've never felt quite that secure with any other guitar. I can pick it up, drop it or bounce it off the wall and it will still be in tune and still play with heart and soul. It's irreplaceable.'

On stage, Eric changes guitars to suit a song's style.

'I switch sometimes because of tuning . . . because I use a few different tunings to play slide. But Blackie is the core guitar. Somehow, with that guitar, I can make sounds that are truly me. I can do my total thing, whereas if I use a Gibson, it will sound like a Gibson.'

Understandably, Eric regards Blackie almost as one of his limbs. At the Montserrat recording studios where he was recording his 1985 album *Behind the Sun*, one of the occasional visitors was American musician Stephen Bishop, an old friend of Clapton, who had guested on Bishop's albums.

'After we'd recorded one song, Stephen, as an afterthought, went in to add some electric guitar. He went back into the studio, picked up my special guitar, and began playing it – very brutally.

'This felt, to me, as if someone had taken a dagger and plunged it into my arm and was twisting it. I screamed, ran into the studio and grabbed it off him. Really, it was that bad, a physical feeling, painful. I believe that guitar has got some of me in it. So to see someone else pick it up and abuse it was unbearable.'

After Eric had stopped drinking, he went through a phase of wanting to change all his surroundings – and he planned to spray Blackie a lurid green. His guitar roadie, Lee Dickson, flatly refused to allow him to do it. Though Eric is the owner of the guitar, Lee is its custodian. He ensures that it is treated with enormous care. But on one fact Eric is adamant: it is rarely far from his side, and unlike most of his guitars, is kept at his home. 'What's special about that guitar,' says Eric, summing it up, 'is that it came from a period in my life when I was so conscientious, and it's actually got that feeling in it. My attitude now is much more lax. I could pick up a guitar and if it worked, great and if it didn't I'd put it down again. But the idea of taking three or four guitars and working on them meticulously, as I did, to get one perfect just isn't in me any more. I value Blackie for

Two studies in concentration: Eric on stage at Hammersmith Odeon in May 1976 and 1983 (*Barry Plummer*)

that, too.'

It was remarkable that Pattie knew of Eric's work – it was because of her husband George's fascination with Cream. 'In every way,' says Pattie, 'the Beatles were very exclusive, almost a royalty of the pop world, and we very rarely listened to other musicians' work. The Beatles were totally absorbed with what *they* were producing. So any other band had to be very special before the records were played in the house.' But because George was interested in Cream, Pattie became familiar with the *Fresh Cream* album; it was thus somewhat ironic that Clapton should be the man who fell in love with her, as she happened to know his work quite well.

She has distanced herself from his work but fully understands the psychology of his stance as a musician. 'The *Layla* album affected me deeply,' she says now. 'Just before I completely left George, my sister Jenny and I went for a holiday in Africa and as soon as I put the radio on in Mombasa, 'Layla' started playing. It struck me how incredible it was that this one particular tune had so much depth, and that it was written for me.'

She listens to Eric's music alone, often when driving. 'Living with someone so artistically productive, it is hard to absorb until it is finished, and I need to be on my own to hear it properly. Sometimes, he has asked my opinion of a basic tune and though I've felt honoured to be asked, my musical knowledge is nil and I have no concept of what the end result of his early work is likely to be.'

Asked if she sees Clapton's music as a true reflection of his personality, Pattie answers thoughtfully: 'No, I see him as two separate people. He has a conscious mind working on a day-to-day basis and the other side is the unconscious mind of the artist, with the ability to tap into a different side of himself in the same way that anyone does when they dream. The unconscious mind has a universal consciousness and a natural insight and knowledge, and Eric as an artist can connect with that.

'His day-to-day living is on a conscious level. It's very different from the artistic side. His daily personality is not reflected in any of the songs he writes. And so it's very curious to me to be living with someone who, when he's sitting down quietly, has all sorts of fantastic melodies going through his mind. He taps into a very private source that eventually comes out.'

The qualities in his guitar playing, his singing and his songwriting that have made Eric special – the tearful, emotional and joyful artistry – are not evident on a day-to-day basis, Pattie continues. 'Sometimes I have no idea what he's thinking or feeling but I get the impression that something's wrong, something's troubling him, that he isn't

able to express or can't be bothered to. But if he were to pick up a
guitar he could express it in that way, I'm sure. On a one-to-one
confrontation, as one human being to another, he sometimes can't or
won't express himself without the instrument. How lucky he is to be
able to express himself in that way better than many people can.'

When Eric Clapton talks about his music, words like honesty,
commitment and reality crop up frequently. Twenty years on, he
remains outwardly modest when discussing his work. Inwardly, he
fully realizes his status and his ability. 'I now know I can usually
achieve a certain standard for any gig, any recording session . . . the
challenge is no longer not to fall below that standard but to do
something that I know is special, different. *Better!*'

Although he is revered by his peers, he remains a fan at heart. He
worries about being outclassed by other players: when he went to a
London concert by Dire Straits, he was initially frightened by the
lyrical guitar work of Mark Knopfler but later realized his style was
different from his own. 'I only want respect from the younger guys,'
says Clapton, 'for what I'm doing now. You can't trade on past
glories. If you're a musician, your work has to be evolving as a living
thing.'

The contrariness and the petulance of the man show a different
side to his make-up as a musician. About every three months, he
walks into the office of his manager and says, seriously: 'I'm retiring.
No more tours. I've had enough.' Roger Forrester, used to Clapton's
mercurial moods in his work, wears the resigned look of a man who
had heard it all before. But he can never be certain that Eric is really
not serious. 'Okay, I'll put everything on hold,' Forrester will say.
Next day, Clapton asks for details of his next session or tour.

Apart from his talent, the other quality which has kept Clapton
afloat and thriving for twenty years has been his humility. He knows
he is a fine player, but believes the form of music he has chosen
places him in the role of 'stating a case for the blues', rather than
claiming to be a true original. Because he is able to interpret uniquely
that music, guitarists and singers everywhere recognize his honesty
of purpose. His 1979 tour with Muddy Waters, particularly, struck an
emotional chord in Clapton.

'The very first time I ever got three strings together on my guitar,
when I was a young teenager, and put my fingers on them and
played, it was to copy a Muddy Waters sound. It was a bell-like tone
on the song "Honey Bee". I had no technique, of course, at that age
and I had to copy completely. I spent a long, long time mimicking
without any idea of direction other than knowing that what I was

copying was what I wanted to do. That was blues-based guitar.

'Muddy Waters was the first blues man to get down to me, really into my soul. He has always made me feel this was the end of the road, as good as it could get. I listened later on to B. B. King, or Freddie King, or Buddy Guy and many other great players. There was this element of showmanship, of commerciality, of learning, still going on with those people. When I heard Muddy for the first time, I knew that was *it*. That was the final statement of blues music with no dressing, and that has remained my opinion all my life. No one was better.'

Touring Europe in 1979 alongside his hero was daunting for Clapton. 'It was a treat, but also a severe test of my integrity. He was a man who had stuck to his guns all his life in his music. Every time I went off track during my part of the show, and played a quote from something, something melodic or even classically tinged, I got pangs of guilt. Because I felt that he was watching, and I was being untrue to my art. So at the same time as it being a great privilege and pleasure to be with Muddy, it also made me very self-conscious, in a positive and constructive way'.

Muddy, in many conversations with the young guitarist who, unlike him, had been hero-worshipped by pop and rock fans, set Clapton on a musical course for the rest of his life. 'He kept hammering it home to me that there was nothing wrong with being a blues musician. He said a guitarist didn't have to be *appealing*, to play the biggest halls and sell the most records, to play well. I can never thank Muddy enough, really, for spelling it all out to me, that blues playing is beautiful, because it's from inside yourself.'

Eric first met Muddy in 1966, during his period with John Mayall. The American singer came to do a British tour with Otis Spann. When Mike Vernon of Blue Horizon Records persuaded them to go into the studios in London, Eric was asked along with other players to work as a sideman. 'Muddy paid me a lot of compliments and I took an immediate shine to him as a man. From then on, we kept in touch. Not only as a great musician, but as a person, he was one of the greatest, sweetest. We teamed up for tours and he took me under his wing, told me I was his son, gave me little clues or guidelines about what I should be doing and what he liked to hear me do. He was very instrumental in forming my correct identity as a blues musician.'

Muddy admired Clapton's work, but when the two linked up for a European concert tour, Eric was petrified at being outclassed by Muddy's power of simplicity. Once, when the blues master opened the show, and the crowd was ecstatic, a dejected Clapton gave

All smiles: Eric plays while his friend, hero and mentor Muddy Waters sings at a Chicago concert in 1979 (*Paul Natkin/Star File*)

everyone backstage the feeling that it would be impossible to follow such a performance. Muddy sensed Eric's feelings. Next night and every night after that, he seemed to temper his own show and came off smiling at Eric. 'I've left 'em for you, Eric,' he said smiling. The two men were close in their affection. And what Eric never knew was that on most nights, Muddy stood in the wings watching Clapton's show, saying: 'Whooo, boy, whooo!'

In the early 1970s, when Eric became confused about his direction, Muddy's wisdom prevailed. Eric remembers, 'I was starting to worry about being limited to performing as just a blues player. I started to write more varied material to get out of what I regarded as the trap of being just one kind of guitarist. But Muddy reinspired me, made me realize that to do just one thing well was enough. You see, when I listened to other guitarists, I went through a spell of trying to get flashier, like the younger guys. But I kept coming back to Muddy and the first music I had heard. Always, the maturity of his music got through to me. And although I still struggle to achieve it, that belief in pure blues is now deep rooted in me.'

Muddy Waters, born McKinley Morganfield in Rolling Fork, Mississippi, on 4 April 1915, died in 1983, two years after his second marriage which Eric and Pattie attended in Muddy's Chicago home. Roger Forrester and Ben Palmer also went to the wedding. 'He had a heart condition,' recalls Eric, reflecting on the death of one of his real heroes. 'The road probably did it to him more than anything, as well as worrying about his band. The road, as Robbie Robertson says, is a hell of a way to live.' Eric has a love–hate relationship with 'the road'. He dislikes the lack of reality in the hotel/airport/stage repetitiveness, but as he needs audience recognition, he believes it to be the only real test of his standards.

The discography at the end of this book demonstrates vividly how much Eric enjoys playing with musicians he admires outside his own band. Eric 'jams' simply because he likes to be stimulated by fresh sounds. There is rarely a competitive element.

The Last Waltz, the film featuring The Band, struck a particular chord inside Eric; it touched upon the nerve centres of so many musicians of the 1960s and 1970s who had pioneered a new stance for rock musicianship and the counter-culture. It was The Band whose music had first alerted Eric to the pointlessness of continuing with Cream, for their keyboard-conscious sound was as revolutionary as had been the guitar-led sound of Cream. 'It brings me to the edge of tears,' Clapton wrote in his diary, 'when Robbie Robertson says near the end of *The Last Waltz* that the road is a goddam impossible way of life. It's a heartbreaking reality that very few people have come to

Clapton on stage with Freddie King at Crystal Palace in 1976 (*Barry Plummer*)

terms with . . . One of the few who have, Pete [Townshend], called me later in the evening to congratulate me on scoring Albert [Lee]. He wishes us all well.'

Lee, the spectacular guitarist who toured the world in Eric's band before joining the Everly Brothers for their reunion in 1984, might well have sparked off jealousy from any other bandleader. The crowd's roar when Albert took flight on 'Country Boy' sometimes just about equalled their applause for Clapton. 'But his playing's so different I couldn't consider him a rival,' says Eric. 'He was there to complement my playing and vice versa. I can only feel a slight element of competitiveness when I'm playing with someone who has my style. Then it can get hairy, but it's never dog eat dog. Any time I'm with a good player with a true personality and feeling in his playing, I always find I stretch myself to keep up, and I love that element.

'When Freddie King was alive, we did a tour together and often played side by side. I learned from him, about economy and total commitment to the playing. He was very competitive, but it was tongue in cheek. You couldn't walk off the stage hating the other person or feeling you'd won or lost. At the end of the day, you don't lose or win anything through music.'

Clapton is a cerebral man who, despite appearing casual on stage, is a worrier. Increasingly, as he knows his ability as a guitarist, he considers his future, ponders the possibility of dipping his toes into the world of movies, but above all realizes there is a clash in his roles. Is he an artist or an entertainer?

'I do worry about that division. I do see myself as having to fulfil the role of entertainer a lot of the time and falling short. I also find that my concern about that impinges on my progress as an artist. I am too concerned with popularity or concerned with image, or success – that's the word in which you can wrap it all up: *success.* And that can really be a stumbling block because if you see yourself as having a vocation as an artist, then you must be as pure as you can towards your art.'

But he agrees there's a touch of show business inside him. 'I'm afraid there is! From the very earliest age I was hooked on pleasing people. I remember being very young and singing "I Belong to Glasgow", standing behind the curtain in the front room, and being knocked out by the fact that I could entertain people. So it's a dreadful trap.'

'He's much more emotional than anyone ever sees on the surface. There are tears just behind that poker face. He's actually very, very soft inside, no matter how much we all see him as a strong man,' says pianist Chris Stainton.

The keyboards player in Eric Clapton's band since 1979, Stainton has made a deep study of astrology. He knows Eric purely from being in his band; apart from the expected talk between musicians, they don't have a particularly close relationship. Yet Clapton inspires a fierce personal loyalty among those who go on the road with him or record with him. It's not just his music that commands their admiration. There's something especially unpretentious about him. And yet, he is in no doubt. Everyone, from his wife to the musicians and crew around him, believes Clapton is totally aware of his status and his talent. He tends to push it away, and never 'lets on' that he knows about it or accepts it. That's his form of protection against conceit, and his reason for pushing himself onwards to try to improve his work.

Clapton, born under the sign of Aries, is, according to Chris Stainton: 'direct, forceful, energetic, outgoing, impulsive and loses his temper quickly. He's full of life and energy, a pioneer. But then he has Scorpio rising, which makes him very secretive and poker-faced. You don't know what's going on behind the mask. He might be perfectly sweet on the surface, but somewhere else he might be loading his gun ready to shoot you. He has powerful emotions but they're bottled up . . . and they can only get a release through his music. Hence the intensity of his playing.

'His moon is also in Scorpio, which doubles the effect. This means he has a great need to eliminate things from his life. Drug addiction and alcoholism serve no purpose and he knows that. So he has now eliminated them from his life and they've gone for ever. That's the strange thing about anyone with a strong Scorpio element: he has to undergo a period of trial, a deep and intense test period like Eric underwent. Without that, as just an Aries with the spirit of pioneering and leadership on its own, he wouldn't have the Scorpio spirit of tenacity, the ability to persevere doggedly on. Scorpio in Eric provides him with incredible resistance to setbacks. Nothing will ever put him off. He'll carry on, grinding onwards.

'There's another side to him, really sweet and graceful. He has Venus and Taurus in him, which brings a softness. He is heavily ruled by Mars in Pisces, which means that he's far more liable to break down and is much more emotional than we see on the surface. Pisces figures in Eric because it's the sign of music. That's his outlet for all his emotions. Without that sign figuring in him, I don't know what he'd do. Without music coming out of him, Eric would go berserk. Beneath the gruff exterior, there's gold in that man . . .'

Chris Stainton's reading of Eric comes from one who has returned from the slippery road of drugs himself. As a pianist accompanying such big stars as Joe Cocker and Elkie Brooks, Stainton had by 1979 acquired a reputation as an intuitive, highly melodic rock 'n' rolling pianist.

Clapton hired him when he sought a particularly all-British band. And yet Stainton was a slightly dangerous hiring. Unemployed when Clapton phoned out of the blue to offer him an audition, Stainton was, as a known former drug user, a potential hazard for a 'clean' Clapton.

But the two men have developed a good bond, with the perceptive Stainton observing his boss from the vantage point of amateur psychologist and sideman on stage and in the studio. 'He's a natural bandleader,' says Stainton, contradicting Clapton's own theory of himself as an unnatural leader. 'He always knows what he wants, but maybe he doesn't realize the kind of power, or authority, he has over people. If anyone tries to usurp him, it's all over for that person. He *has* to be in control of all situations, and as long as he is, fantastic things can happen on stage, where Eric is at his best.' But to judge the man takes years of study. 'If a show has gone badly, a certain poker-face comes over him, and you don't go near him. Best to let him alone to suffer in silence.'

When Clapton is sailing away with the right backing from his musicians in a live concert, 'God knows where it comes from, the stuff he plays,' says Stainton, shaking his head. 'He'll hit notes that make me float away. And even Eric says he feels himself lifted two feet off the ground. It's as if the music is coming through him, from somewhere else . . .'

Eric's affinity – as musician and friend – with Bob Dylan, today one of the artists he most respects, has curious origins. When Eric was a Yardbird and Dylan was making his first impact, his genius as a songwriter was touted to Eric by none other than Paul Samwell-Smith. 'That fact put me off,' Eric smiles. But, later, once he had left that band, his Chelsea flatmate Martin Sharp continually played Dylan's seminal album *Blonde on Blonde*. And Clapton was hooked. Dylan and Clapton met several times, in America and in Britain, as members of the rock fraternity, and eventually made guest appearances on each other's albums, Bob on Eric's *No Reason to Cry* and Eric on Bob's *Desire* album.

'We do have a special communication and I think it's because we're both basically shy,' says Clapton. 'In a room full of people, or in a recording studio, we seem always to be the ones who like to remain

One of the earliest pictures of Eric with the Yardbirds during an appearance
at London's Marquee Club in 1964

quiet, so we veer towards each other.' Rather like his bond with Jimi Hendrix, his understanding with Dylan is intuitive rather than spoken. It has resulted in some outstanding open-air festival appearances featuring the two stars together; 250,000 people went to see them at Blackbushe aerodrome in 1978, when Eric jammed with the Dylan band. And in Germany that same year, a similar event was particularly momentous: it was staged in Nuremberg on the field built by Hitler for his rallies and speeches. The heavy irony of the event was not lost on any of the musicians. As Clapton remarked at the time, here was a major Jewish singer and songwriter peacefully entertaining a crowd of 80,000, in sharp contrast with what had happened on the same spot four decades earlier.

The Nuremberg concert was promoted by two men who had a unique connection with Clapton dating back to 1963, when he was in the Yardbirds. Horst Lippmann and Fritz Rau came into rock, like so many promoters during the 1960s, because the jazz musicians they usually worked with flirted with the rhythm-and-blues scene in which Clapton and the Yardbirds were working.

Lippmann was the very first record producer Clapton met. In the Richmond Crawdaddy Club in 1963, he went to record the American blues singer Sonny Boy Williamson, but became particularly impressed by the young man playing lead guitar alongside him. The music was dear to Eric's heart: the raw, compulsive sounds of such blues standards as 'Smokestack Lightnin' ', which he would later convert to his own style. But Lippmann recorded the songs and released them as singles; they sold so poorly in Germany that he was not motivated to continue an interest in the Yardbirds.

With Fritz Rau, Horst's connection with Clapton came much later. They first presented him on tour in Germany with Delaney and Bonnie. Again, they saw Eric as a band member rather than a leader. But as the man's career gathered fresh momentum, his popularity in Germany soared. Interestingly, Eric developed a particularly strong bond with Lippmann and Rau, which they believe is because of their roots in jazz. To many people, including actor John Hurt, Clapton is not a pop or rock star but a modern jazz troubadour. Horst and Fritz say Eric's career in Germany has nowhere near reached its peak. They want him to tour frequently but not as a sideman as he did with Roger Waters around the world in 1984. 'I'm glad the Roger Waters concerts in Germany were cancelled,' says Fritz Rau. 'I never want to see Eric as a sideman again. He is far too big, and people want to see him on his own, playing what my guitar-playing son calls, so beautifully, a *world music*.' Echoing the views of so many, Fritz shakes his head in disbelief at Eric's guitar work: 'One note from him

A rare picture of Eric in April, 1965, at the time when he had just quit the
Yardbirds and was 'in limbo' before joining John Mayall's Bluesbreakers
(*London Features International*)

is worth twelve from anybody else.'

Clapton's work today is a cunning mixture of artist, craftsman and entertainer. He admits that he has sometimes played 'on autopilot', but that was during his drinking excesses. But the smell of alcohol does not, yet, come through vinyl or tape, and Clapton maintains that records and concerts are where he should be judged, rather than by the number of Ferrari cars in his garage. A critical overview of his music is essential to absorb the biography of the man.

Mostly, the Clapton we hear today, on stage and on record, is the natural evolution of the twenty-year-old who played on John Mayall's single, 'I'm Your Witch Doctor', with 'Telephone Blues' on the reverse, back in 1965. His grandmother Rose says she can scarcely listen to it even now without feeling the impact it first made on her. Thousands felt the same spine-tingling sensation that year. In his fur coat and spats on stage with Mayall, Eric was pushing for the limelight soon after leaving the Yardbirds. With 'Telephone Blues' came the first indication on record that he would be a significant musician. The rich 'sustain' of his guitar and the controlled feedback technique on the 'Witch Doctor' track were matched by an expressiveness never heard before 1965 in a young white British player. The influences were obvious: Buddy Guy, Hubert Sumlin and Freddie King's styles were there for anyone who listened carefully. What made Eric Clapton's work with Mayall so special was the depth of his feeling, transmitted through his Gibson Les Paul and Marshall 100-watt stack. *Bluesbreakers*, by John Mayall with Clapton, was the album that helped to put the electric guitar at the forefront of popular music, and it has been there ever since. Eric took the rock guitar away from being an instrument of excitement and used it as a means of serious expression. Knowingly or accidentally, he created *the* guitar sound.

'I had to copy to learn,' reflects Eric, 'and I'm still copying sometimes. I never had a teacher. I just heard a good song on the radio or on a record, and thought the chord changes sounded nice, so I picked up the guitar and copied them. So when I was learning, I had no technique whatsoever, and I never learned a thing properly. I made it my business to copy, to mimic, as much as I could.'

The only direction was towards 'blues-based guitar'. To Eric, it is still, in his words, 'the truest form of rock 'n' roll guitar. I still find it disturbing, sometimes, to hear country-style guitar in a rock framework. I don't like it nearly as much as the biting blues, seventh-note kind of playing.' He enjoys country music in itself – but not when it is fused with rock 'n' roll.

Even on his album with Mayall, Eric's influences, black blues musicians, stood out: Otis Rush (on the track 'All Your Love'), Freddie King (hear 'Hideaway') and Robert Johnson ('Ramblin' on My Mind'). Interestingly, Clapton never sought at that time to emulate Robert Johnson's exceptional slide guitar playing, choosing only his songs. This last track marked the introduction of Eric's voice which would later blossom into an instrument almost equal to his guitar work.

In 1966, rock music was becoming an art form and Eric Clapton one of its innovators. The guitar playing on *Bluesbreakers* was unrivalled for creativity, emotion, taste and subtle humour (listen to the Ray Charles classic 'What I'd Say', in which Eric suddenly bursts into a 'Day Tripper' riff). And on the track 'Have You Heard' Eric's playing was devastating.

The *Bluesbreakers* album spawned a new breed of guitarists, earned Eric the dubious tag of 'God', and the influence of it is still evident twenty years later. Gibson and Les Paul were to become household names and Eric the first guitar hero.

If Mayall's band was the laboratory, Cream was the sales point, the launching pad. At the band's major concert debut at Windsor, an Eric Clapton, resplendent in a Cecil Gee smoking jacket, introduced a hybrid crowd to the world of progressive rock, or 'commercial jazz' as it was so deftly described by their manager Robert Stigwood. The ten-minute solo, the drum solo, the bluesy vocals, everything that would be taken for granted in the next decade was here in its formative setting.

Cream turned the world of music round on its axis. Eric rose from being a blues-influenced guitarist to being the most progressive musician in modern music. Suddenly, too, the word 'rock' overtook 'pop' in the fans' vocabulary. It came to mean a contemporary form of jazz, carrying articulate instrumental work allied to meaningful lyrics, a huge distance from the watery 'company music' that Eric found so empty.

Inside Cream, his improvisation were lessons in inspirational creativity. He formulated a unique style, a feel for the blues in a modern-day framework. And the Mods still couldn't dance to it.

Cream initially released a single, 'Wrapping Paper', which unfortunately sounded more like the sound of the Lovin' Spoonful than what we came to recognize as music from Eric, Jack and Ginger. But there wasn't long to wait before their next salvo. 'I Feel Free' pointed the way to the band's original style, with the guitar way out in front. The solo was a typical Clapton masterpiece, starting with a warm bassy tone (later to be christened the 'woman tone' by Eric) ending in a quick flick to the old treble pick-up with his nimble fingers way up the fingerboard. It wasn't just a solo; it was a statement.

About that time, a series of EP records were released by Pye-International in Britain demonstrating the talents of the black blues artists who recorded mainly at the Chess Studios in Chicago. One featured 'Spoonful' by Howlin' Wolf. Cream's version bore little resemblance to the original, and contained one of Eric's epic solos.

Fresh Cream, the band's debut album, was awaited by musicians and fans with equal anticipation. 'Spoonful' had progressed from a simple Willie Dixon tune into a powerhouse of improvisation, with Jack Bruce's wordly-wise vocals and Ginger's percussive feel taunting the licks from Eric's Les Paul.

Now Eric was singing more. He and Jack had developed their own style of vocal interplay, heavy on the vibrato, with Eric's voice perhaps a little sweeter. On tunes like 'NSU', 'I Feel Free' and 'I'm So Glad', they harmonized like brothers, but when Jack spat out 'Spoonful', he gave it everything he had. The man's pungent personality came through.

Eric's songwriting talent did not really blossom in Cream. 'I wrote a few arrangements and riffs but I wasn't composing at all,' says Eric. 'But when it came to the time to make an album, Jack saved our lives. He'd come up with enough songs for the album, which meant that we were just about getting by. Ginger would kick up a fuss even at that. He'd argue that it was a cooperative band and we'd have to do two or three of his songs, as a kind of obligation. We did them to be fair to Ginger, but it was no way to keep a healthy atmosphere in the band.'

The massed limbs of Ginger Baker were in evidence on 'Toad', together with another instrumental, 'Cat's Squirrel'. Cream had by now shown us what virtuosity could do to a set of blues-orientated tunes. Next they would demonstrate what progression was all about.

The Yardbirds, with Jeff Beck in Eric's old role, had been involved in some earlier attempts at 'progressive rock', but that had come to a halt rather quickly when Beck left the group. Jeff's own style was never comparable to Clapton's, though they both shared a love for the blues. Eric retained the earthiness; Beck was flashier.

Once in Cream, Eric changed his chosen guitar from his familiar Gibson Les Paul to a Gibson SG Standard, a guitar with similar pick-ups to a Les Paul but with a thinner, lighter body. His sound became more refined, a little less raunchy, but continued to have his cutting edge.

Disraeli Gears was the first 'real' Cream album: the band had become aware of their musical progression and Jack Bruce realized their capabilities in the studio. 'Sunshine of Your Love' was the

Easy Now. For once Clapton is seated (*Michael Putland*)

ultimate example of the band's ability to produce its own sound and create a song that stands as a classic in the history of rock. It was revolutionary at the time, featuring heavy guitar and bass riffs plus an economical, powerful drum pattern coupled with an intense yet sparing guitar solo. Eric's 'woman tone' had arrived. Cream broke away from traditional approaches to rock and took full advantage of the artistic freedom then so prevalent, not just in music but in entire attitudes. Jimi Hendrix, taking the same stance to his music, projected himself on a more personal level. He was an experience, while Cream were a unit, but the similarity in ideals was certainly there, and Hendrix was also the leader of a trio.

'Strange Brew', in contrast with 'Sunshine of Your Love', found Cream paying homage to a blues master, Albert King. Along with Freddie King, he'd given authentic blues guitar playing a bit of 'beef', and Eric had obviously noticed. The inspiration from Albert's 'Crosscut Saw' was evident – Eric's actual cover version came much later. There were a couple of weird tracks on *Disraeli Gears*, such as 'World of Pain' which deals basically with the inherent sadness of a tree outside someone's window. But then these were strange days. Eric shone through anew on 'Outside Woman Blues' and 'Tales of Brave Ulysses'.

Wheels of Fire, released in 1968, was probably the most representative of Cream's music. It showed the band at its best, both in the studio and in concert. Tracks like 'White Room' and 'Politician' were fine examples of their ability on a creative and recording level, while every other live recording showed off their individual talent as virtuosos. There was a light touch, too, with three of our most respected musicians singing about 'Pressed Rat and Warthog'.

Eric reached the pinnacle of his creative talents on *Wheels of Fire*. He played like a demon, not only as a soloist but as an accompanist. On 'Sitting On Top of the World', he took us to where he had left off in the Bluesbreakers. 'Spoonful' was an outrageous sixteen minutes and forty-four seconds of one of the best performances from any late sixties progressive rock outfit.

The front cover design of *Goodbye*, the farewell album from Cream, showed just how Eric had viewed the band: as a *tour de force*. There they were, looking happy in grey silk suits and matching grey shoes, bowler hats and canes, and the music inside was a fitting farewell. There, too, was Eric's songwriting partnership with George Harrison on the spirited 'Badge'.

In a surprisingly short spurt of less than three years, Cream had given some of the most stunning performances, through the exceptional chemistry of three musicians who came together at the right time. The reverse was the case with Blind Faith, for the partnership was doomed from the start. On their only album, just two songs, 'Had to Cry Today' and 'Presence of the Lord', had anything to offer guitar enthusiasts. But while their tour of America was designed to pull in the dollars at the risk of the music and the band's future, it had an important effect on Clapton. He met Delaney and Bonnie Bramlett. Delaney and Bonnie's brand of funky rhythm-and-blues was attractive to musicians because it was loose and enjoyable to play. There were fewer strictures than in the more conventional bands; the formula allowed players to stretch out without getting in each other's way.

Eric looks back on that period now with circumspection. When Blind Faith collapsed, he purposely ambled into a less organized lifestyle, he says. His direction through Delaney and Bonnie and Derek and the Dominos was not particularly fruitful for his career. But it was an essential diversion for his life. As a musician, he wanted to merge with others rather than command the limelight. This contradictory diffidence has been a recurring theme in his life. But fate did not allow that change of route to happen for long.

The cover of the 1970 *Eric Clapton* album, his first solo outing, portrayed a serious-looking young man lounging on a chair, a Fender Stratocaster nestling between his legs with a few rolls of carpet and a couple of apples nearby.

The Fender Strat sound was something never associated with Clapton. He had always been a Gibson man, apart from a brief flirtation with Fender Telecasters and the odd Gretsch in the Yardbirds days. Moving to a Stratocaster now affected his music considerably: there was less emphasis on the heavy, block-chord, riffy solo playing we'd known Eric for in Cream days. Here was a tighter, more restrained and melodic approach. Crucially, here was a definite American influence.

'Slunky' opened the album. And it cooked! A rocking instrumental with saxophones, it begged the question: is this an all-instrumental album? But no, it was a collection of songs sung and played by Clapton complemented by a bunch of great session musicians and giving us the first example on record of the direction to which Eric has remained faithful. This freshly found guitar/vocal role was to establish him as a solo artist in his own right.

'Slunky' sounded at first like one of those familiar King Curtis-type jam-sessions until Eric burst forth with a cascade of repeat-echo and a *different* sound. The Strat had not so much affected his playing as his *attitude* to his playing. He got stuck into singing on this album

Blind Faith at the free concert they gave in Hyde Park for 150,000 fans in the summer of 1969; from left, Rick Grech, Ginger Baker, Eric Clapton and Steve Winwood (*Barry Wentzell/Melody Maker*)

and developed his guitar sound to complement the vocal work. Technically, he didn't use many effects, just a little 'wah-wah'. This foot-operated pedal helped give a crying sound to the solo work, and was used to greater extremes by Jimi Hendrix. Clapton had first used the wah-wah on some of Cream's albums, on 'White Room' and 'Tales of Brave Ulysses'. But in the new, freer surroundings of his first solo album, he employed the technique differently.

He also showed his fondness for the acoustic guitar. He realized there was much more to guitar playing than having to rely on electricity to transmit his feelings. Stephen Stills was involved in these Clapton sessions, and his tasteful acoustic work had impressed Eric on the album *Déjà Vu*, by Crosby, Stills, Nash and Young.

Three songs particularly have endured from that debut solo album. 'Blues Power', which remains one of Clapton's favourites, was the perfect vehicle at that time for Eric's solo experiment, and Leon Russell's influence was very evident. 'Bottle of Red Wine' showed us that Eric had not forgotten how to play a shuffle, and 'Let It Rain', today an enormously popular song with concert audiences round the world, developed into an epic performance, vocally and in-strumentally. 'After Midnight' was, for many people, an introduction by Eric into the world of J. J. Cale, and survived for many years as a driving opener to Eric's concerts. Delaney Bramlett's contribution was considerable: as well as producing, he co-wrote eight of the eleven tracks.

If Eric had scaled a peak on *Wheels of Fire* with Cream, then the title of virtuoso was claimed when he metamorphosed into Derek and the Dominos and produced 'Layla'. Fired by the unrequited love of Pattie, and induced by the wafts of dope that permeated the music scene of the late 1960s, the album *Layla, and Other Assorted Love Songs* brought back the elongated guitar solos from Eric, missing since Cream days, coupled with a fabulous collection of original material and a couple of blues classics. His performance had an especially emotive quality, and the album still sounds masterful, inspired.

Clapton had retained the same rhythm section used on the *Eric Clapton* album, christened them the Dominos, renamed himself Derek and added the spectacular guitarist and slide specialist Duane Allman, who had made such an impact with the album *Idlewild South* (although it wasn't until *Live at the Fillmore* by the Allmans that Duane's full genius could be appreciated). He showed off his original slide guitar style on 'Nobody Knows You (When You're Down and Out)' on the *Layla* album. It complemented Eric's solo playing, never getting in the way, while adding a rich colour to this old blues standard.

On stage during an American tour in 1975 (*David S. Melhado/Star File*)

'Bell Bottom Blues' oozes emotion from the heartfelt lyrics to the beautifully sensitive solo in which Eric slips in a few chime-like harmonics, a technique that The Band's Robbie Robertson had started to perfect. The Clapton–Robertson appreciation society had begun. So had the one with Duane Allman, and for a while the two men's names were linked inextricably.

Duane was a Clapton fan who had developed his own distinctive guitar style in an incredibly short period. Like Eric, he was a naturally inventive player, with a blues feeling. There's a track on the Duane Allman 'anthology' album, released after his death on a motorcycle in 1971, called 'Mean Old World'. It came from the *Layla* sessions and features Allman and Clapton duetting on acoustic slide guitars. This was Eric's first embrace of the slide technique, and Duane was partly responsible.

'Key to the Highway', which has remained in Eric's repertoire, was live, loose and lovely. Overdubbing throughout the album was kept to a minimum, and there was not a synthesizer in sight. The title track, 'Layla', is still considered by many to be rock's perfect love song, a fascinating combination of soliloquy and *cri de coeur*. Almost overnight, the power and delivery of the song transformed Eric Clapton from the guitar-hero syndrome into a singer-guitarist-songwriter of world stature. Eric has told me that this performance of 'Layla', performed in the studio under the influence of various substances, was the only time he believes drugs to have allowed him to free himself of all inhibitions and produce a piece of work superior to that which might have come from him without drugs. But then, the subject of 'Layla' was a drug in itself, and the message in his mind transcended the music anyway.

Coming in at seven minutes and ten seconds, 'Layla' was probably the most produced track on the album, Eric's scorching guitars weaving a compelling pattern that vied for urgency with his tortured vocals. With Duane's heavenly slide playing on top, the tune seems to find peace with itself just as the listener feels it's all over. Bobby Whitlock's piano leads into a lamentful finale with Eric and Duane crying out to each other through their instruments.

Partly because of the inspirational title and also because of the company he kept, Eric's playing on the *Layla* album was incredibly eloquent. Some inner force, together with the talents of Allman, Jim Gordon, Carl Radle and Bobby Whitlock, set a new musical standard for the 1970s. 'Why Does Love Got to be So Sad?' steams in with Duane exercising his fingers without the aid of a slide, and 'Little Wing' was a celebratory tribute to Jimi Hendrix. Eric duets with Bobby Whitlock, who had a hand in writing six of the tunes. The density and soaraway vocal by Clapton on 'Have You Ever Loved a Woman?' helped make *Layla* one of the greatest rock/blues albums ever recorded.

*

It was difficult to follow. The hardest problem in any performer's career, once he has reached a high level, is to stay there. The pressures are great. It's tough enough for a conceited, confident artist. For a sensitive man like Clapton, it was especially challenging, and remains so. It could have been this pressure, as well as his love for Pattie, which exacerbated his heroin addiction and seclusion for three years. Whatever the reason, there was no record until *Derek and the Dominos – Live in Concert* was released in 1973. The record company covered his absence by releasing compilation albums, *History of Eric Clapton* and *Eric Clapton At His Best*. In the autumn of the same year came the album from the momentous Rainbow comeback concert. It was a qualified success, important more for its spirit than for the quality of the music. It was, though, crucial in Eric's story.

What followed was Eric's biggest-selling album ever. *461 Ocean Boulevard* was a landmark in so many respects that it stands as the definitive Clapton album. It was his return to the studio from his three-year heroin addiction; it featured majestic music in which Eric's voice assumed a richness and poignancy derived from the physical experiences he had just endured; and the songs plus the musicians merged in an exceptional chemistry. It was not all rock 'n' roll, but the glorious ballads, 'Let It Grow', 'Please Be With Me' and 'Give Me Strength', were handled in a manner that only a rock 'n' roll musician could have conceived. 'Give Me Strength', one of the first songs Eric had written after receiving treatment from Meg Patterson, carried its own pathos. It begins with Eric playing a sensitive slide figure on Dobro (an acoustic guitar with a built-in resonating speaker hidden behind a metal plate). The soul-searching vocal indicates quite starkly the torment he has just been through, and with the bittersweet sound of the Dobro, it is a very special lyric and music.

Apart from the bass player Carl Radle, Eric was working with a completely new band: guitarist George Terry from Florida and, from Oklahoma, Dick Sims (keyboards) and Jamie Oldaker (drums). Together with Albhy Galuten on keyboards and an exceptionally well-suited duetting vocalist, Yvonne Elliman, Eric seemed, with *461 Ocean Boulevard*, to have found what he was searching for. The atmosphere at the studios in Miami was perfect for him at that time; the energy level shows it – but not in the predictable sense. The guitar work has become very laid back and his expressive vocals a more dominant force in his work. There is more evidence of his slide playing in 'I Can't Hold Out Much Longer', an Elmore James classic which was an old favourite of Eric's, and there is the first hint of Eric's love of the music of Bob Marley with his jaunty version of the reggae king's 'I Shot the Sheriff'. The song became a big hit for Clapton, and a particular stage favourite.

Gone, now, was the raw intensity of Derek and the Dominos, the experiment of Cream, the blues purist of John Mayall's band and the unwilling puppet of the Yardbirds. With *461 Ocean Boulevard* came the music – and particularly the warm voice – of a man who had come of age artistically. As a 'return' album, it was stunning. Eric had grown up.

His extremities once again shone through. Contrasting with 'Give Me Strength', there was Johnny Otis's 'Willie and the Hand Jive', a rhythm-and-blues shuffle from the late fifties with an infectious Bo Diddley beat. While the Fender Stratocaster was his main instrument, the slide Dobro comes shining through on 'Please Be With Me', where Eric's almost tearful vocal work is at its most endearing. Coincidentally, the original recording of this beautiful song, by Charles Scott Boyer, had featured Duane Allman playing slide Dobro. Eric's electric slide work was great on 'Motherless Children', where, for students of the guitar, Eric was using an 'open A' tuning, as opposed to 'open E' on 'I Can't Hold Out Much Longer'. Eric's regular Dobro tuning is 'open E'.

While he was musically growing, Clapton never forgot his roots, his earliest, simplest inspirations. It was refreshing, on such an adventurous record, to find Eric's arrangement of the song 'Steady Rollin' Man', by Robert Johnson, whose work had touched so many of the serious musicians who shone through in British and American rock during the 1970s. *461 Ocean Boulevard* contains a transparent honesty which made for magic. It stands as one of Eric's finest hours.

There's One In Every Crowd was a natural progression. It featured the same line-up, and the band's abilities, together with Eric's newfound confidence, permeated the record. Clapton had returned to the land of the Gibson guitars for most of the album. The back cover confirmed it: he is pictured strapped to an old Explorer model, which gave him a meatier sound than the Strat.

The album starts with 'We've Been Told (Jesus Coming Soon)', a gospel-tinged tune sung by Eric, and introduced by a solitary acoustic guitar giving way to the man's now familiar Dobro playing,

Duetting with Yvonne Elliman, and displaying his usual sartorial style, in Philadelphia, 1974 (*London Features International*)

the instrument now shifting to G tuning for a change. The girl singers take over at the end, Marcy Levy – who was to become a long-term vocal supporter of Eric – joining Yvonne Elliman. 'Swing Low Sweet Chariot' continues in the same vein with a hint of reggae and a wah-wah slide break. The album shows signs of being a touch too religious when Eric lets rip with 'Little Rachel'. But while his vocal is tasty, his guitar work is too laid-back for comfort. The influence of Bob Marley on Eric is evident on 'Don't Blame Me' and his penchant for the slide guitar is demonstrated in 'The Sky Is Crying', a laid-back blues with a neat, subtle key-change.

Touring is the best way to bring a band closer together, both artistically and on a personal level. The playing and singing on 'Singin' the Blues' and 'Better Make It Through Today' proves this happened; but while the record was strong enough on performance, Eric needed to take more chances with his music.

E.C. Was Here which followed was a live album with the now familiar line-up of musicians, produced by Tom Dowd. Clapton the live performer is a totally different animal from the rather tense studio artist, and this album was the first proof of this. Here was the same intensity he had shown on the John Mayall *Bluesbreakers* album, and on the *Layla* LP. *E.C. Was Here*, with all its flaws of a live record, features a very special version of 'Ramblin' On My Mind', the blues at its best.

The albums were now coming thick and fast, but with a solid quality. *No Reason to Cry* was a continuation of the easy-going studio style which Clapton had successfully adopted. There were a number of guests including Bob Dylan, who duetted with Eric on 'Sign Language', which featured some of Robbie Robertson's manic guitar playing. Other members of The Band also contributed to the recording, as well as a few more friends, such as Ronnie Wood and Billy Preston.

The Band's influence on so many musicians during the late 1960s and early 1970s was enormous. Their effortless output of great songs, played with nonchalant ease, helped create a style of playing that demanded subtlety. Eric cites The Band's album *Music From Big Pink* as one of his most powerful influences; their joining him on this album was a compliment to his own stature. They returned the gesture by featuring him in their film, *The Last Waltz*, in which he performed 'Further On Up the Road'.

No Reason to Cry was not, though, a Clapton/Band album. The blues undertone rang out on 'Double Trouble', a track originally recorded by Otis Rush and 'County Jail Blues', which sports both Dobro and electric slide guitars. The Dobro again features on Dylan's

'Sign Language' and 'Innocent Times', which is sung by Marcy Levy. Eric's performance, inspired by the presence of such big names, was tasteful but generally laid-back. It was a hugely musicianly album, but his least accessible as far as fans were concerned.

But *Slowhand* sparkled the following year, 1977. Perhaps it was the introduction of a fresh producer, Glyn Johns, who helped to remotivate Eric. It could also have been the mood of the time, before video, the battalions of heavy-metal headbangers, punks and the New Depression dragged down most sensitive people in the West. Whatever, *Slowhand* had a firm direction, and with his favourite Blackie Fender Stratocaster firmly in his hand to the exclusion of most other instruments, Clapton reached a very big audience with this album.

There is vibrant feeling of rejuvenation and optimism on most tracks, so many of which have passed into Clapton folklore and touch audiences deeply. 'Lay Down Sally', 'Cocaine', 'Wonderful Tonight' all have a magnificent swing, whatever their individual tempo. It was a very difficult album to top.

But *Backless* at least equalled *Slowhand*, with totally different qualities. It had a nice warm glow about it, with the Tulsa influence still strong through his musicians from that part of America, now nicknamed by Eric the Tulsa Tops. The Dylan influence was still there with 'Walk Out in the Rain', and Eric's voice had now the resonant masculinity upon which he has built since that period. 'Watch Out For Lucy', 'Tell Me That You Love Me' and a knockout duet with the driving Marcy Levy on 'Roll It' carried the more predictable Clapton textures. The surprises came with two refreshing tracks, 'Promises' – which brought him a wide radio public – and 'Golden Ring'. Both had a slight country-and-western touch, both oozed sentimentality, and both were unerringly right for a rather new Eric who wasn't afraid to project his feelings as a vocalist as well as a guitar virtuoso. The song 'Tulsa Time', which went on to become the opening song on so many of his concerts, had an insistence and drama of its own. *Backless*, as an album, crossed a certain frontier. Its curious title was a subtle, but affectionate, send-up of Bob Dylan. Eric remarked to several musicians that the master evidently had eyes in the back of his head, so knowledgeable was he about what each musician was doing all around him. Hence, 'Backless'. The album's handsome sleeve carried a neat touch of Eric's own fanmanship in the picture of him on a settee: draped at the far end of the sofa is his West Bromwich Albion football club scarf.

The 1970s had provided a turbulent but rich harvest for Clapton the musician. But at the end of the decade, his survival instinct told him there was a need for change. He said goodbye to the American musicians and replaced them with some of Britain's most respected players: session men Henry Spinetti (drums) and Dave Markee (bass), Gary Brooker on keyboards, and Chris Stainton (keyboards).

The new band's formation coincided with Eric's hard-drinking period but even through his bleariest alcoholic haze, Clapton knew that while he liked all the men individually, and they deserved no individual criticism, they rarely united with him to form a 'happening' band. And as a complement for his own work, they were bereft of blues feeling.

The first 'British' album was the live *Just One Night*, recorded at the famous Budokan in Tokyo. The sound of thousands of young Japanese chanting Eric's name made for a great atmosphere, and the sort of welcome Eric has grown to love from that country. 'Lay Down Sally' was as contagious as ever, with Eric's playing carrying stacks of gusto, and Albert Lee broke out on 'If I Don't Be There By Morning', along with some great keyboard work from Stainton on 'Worried Life Blues'. A devastating solo by Eric on 'Blues Power', one of his most descriptive songs, was followed by 'Ramblin' On My Mind', a tremendous version of 'Cocaine', with the crowd chanting the chorus, and 'Further On Up the Road'. By now, Eric's voice had matured into a rich, bluesy and natural instrument: his rendition of Sleepy John Estes's 'Floating Bridge' on the follow-up album, *Another Ticket*, was exceptional, as was most of his vocal work from then on. This was the first and, as it turned out, the only studio album from the all-British band. It was competent but disappointing: 'I Can't Stand It' and the meaningful title track were strong enough, and Eric excelled on a Muddy Waters song, 'Blow Wind Blow'. It was a craftsmanlike album but lacked personality. Deep personal change was imminent for Eric; *Another Ticket* as a title was a tongue-in-cheek jibe at a friend who was constantly asking for 'another ticket' for his concerts. As a pointer to Eric's future, the phrase was just as ominous.

While he has nurtured a successful career as a guitarist, singer and songwriter, the quality of leadership has been elusive. Running a successful band, even as a subtle disciplinarian, is still the hardest role for Clapton; he still leads by his ability, his example and people's respect for who he is rather than as a benevolent dictator, which is the hallmark of the best leaders. It's enough, of course, that Eric plays and inspires people with what he does. But the inability to grapple with handling people has been one of his regrets.

Yet the massive change in demeanour that swept over Eric in the

mingus lives ~ wot ~

roger came round to talk about
working and suggested that if another
guitar player was needed albert he
would be (maybe) available, that would
be good (maybe), ginger and his harem
arrived shortly after so it all got a bit
lost ~ well went to bed early and i
stayed to find that charles mingus
had crossed over ~ wot ~

later ~ getting back to the
subject of having another guitarist
in the band, if he was tasteful and yet
powerful, i would dig it, but i know
that the other fellas will need some
convincing, what they have to come to
terms with is that there are certain songs
that i am committed to perform for the
audience sake, namely layla and badge
and a few others, where dickie and i
alone cant hold down the fullness of the
sound, they actually need two guitars ~
so, if albert was interested, he would be
ideal ~ as to the subject of work, we
start in february, (about half way through)
in ireland as a dry run, take two weeks
off, and then america, what it all depends
on, needless to say, is the attitude of the
tulsa tops towards having another guitar
player up front, i should mention here
that albert is also a fine singer ~
wait and see ~ later ~

first year of his sobriety, 1982, brought with it a new, more determined, decisive leader of the band. Eric had gone to Compass Point studios in the Bahamas to record the album which became *Money and Cigarettes*. He had spent several weeks in Wales, hibernating in a rented cottage to write the songs, and was pleased with them. The producer was again Tom Dowd. Sober and pouring himself into work, Clapton arrived at the studios with the band that had seen him through his drunken years. Eric had been running through songs with them for two weeks when he, like Tom Dowd, realized that things were not sparking properly. The musicians were also playing far too much tennis and not enough music.

Eric's previous album, *Another Ticket*, had been successful but had somehow 'marked time'. He agreed with many friends that it lacked a blues feeling. Without that, Clapton was directionless. There was a feeling throughout the Clapton camp that new energy was essential . . . and it took a sober Eric and a wise producer like Dowd to realize it – and act. Dowd's pedigree was impeccable, and Eric respected him; his production experience dated back to the days of the famed Stax label which produced legendary names like Otis Redding, Sam and Dave, Booker T and the MGs and Aretha Franklin. He had produced the Allman Brothers and knew all about blues feeling.

Eric decided for the first time in his life to fire virtually the entire band on the spot. Chris Stainton, Gary Brooker, Henry Spinetti and Dave Markee were on their bikes. Only the star guitarist Albert Lee remained, partly because his style complemented Clapton's work – and also because having such a lauded player in the band was quite a coup for Eric. 'I'd always used the old maxim of giving people enough rope and letting them cook themselves,' says Eric, 'rather than calling a halt to it at an early stage. But down at Nassau, we'd tried every method there was to record a couple of songs. It wasn't happening.' After two weeks they had hardly got one track complete. 'I said nothing to the musicians. In the old days, I used to let people make mistakes because I hadn't got the guts to say: "This is wrong." '

Advice given by counsellors at the American clinic where Eric had dried out played a key part in his decision to fire the band. 'They had kept telling me that if something bugged me, I should be assertive about it. If I wasn't happy with situations, I should say so rather than bottle it deep inside, or moan about it, or resent it. So firing the band was partly me exercising that advice purely for the sake of it, being decisive for the first time in my life.'

He amazed himself with the ferocity of the decision.

'I gathered them all together in one of the little chalets near the

At the ARMS concerts in 1983. *Above:* on stage with Jeff Beck, *below:* Eric relaxing with a cigarette with Bill Wyman (*Bob Gruen/Vinnie Zuffante–Star File*)

studio. I told them there was nothing personal, they were a great band for touring with and going on stage with, and nice people to be around. But because I'd been out of the studio for so long, and this album we were preparing was so important as a result, I said I didn't think they were up to the standard required. I said I'd have to bring in some professional studio people, so there was no point in them being there any more. They'd have to go home. I added that I'd give it some time before thinking whether or not I would bring them back into the working situation on tour.'

For Clapton, who treasures friendships, it was the most momentous decision allied to his career since he had kicked heroin. 'It was a terrible thing to have to do, and it was probably over the top,' he reflects. But it was the right move for him at the time. 'They were my mates. They'd been working for me through my years of drunkenness, and they'd seen a very sloppy individual who was almost incapable of making any rational decision whatsoever. And here I was, making a decision which concerned their working lives. They must have thought that I was actually flipping out.' Dave Markee and Gary Brooker took it particularly badly, but Clapton's friendship with his old fishing companion Brooker continued.

Chris Stainton went back to London and sent Eric a postcard to Nassau. 'I think you've done the right thing,' Stainton wrote wryly, 'and it was a bloody long audition.' As a result of that postcard, says Eric, Stainton was immediately rehired. 'He forgave me immediately and saw the whole thing for what it was. There was no doubt about that band being lethargic. It would have been very difficult to get the album done in the time required. I'm a blues guitarist, and that just wasn't a good blues band.'

The firing of the British musicians was at least as important psychologically to Eric as it was as a musical decision. 'With those guys, I'd been trying to get a *band* together with that unique British feeling. I'd be able to hide and continue losing myself within it – just a band of mates, doing pub gigs and village halls as well as the bigger concerts. I was after a *feeling*. But when I remembered what they'd told me in the clinic, about being assertive, I realized I was fooling myself to carry on. Firing the whole band, it left me back on my own. I'd employ musicians who suited me. It was the restart of my solo career, really.' Significantly, when Roger Forrester flew into Nassau to be told of the firing plan, he asked Clapton if he wanted him to deal with the practical problem of telling the band. Forrester had become accustomed to pulling Eric out of awkward situations: the gullible guitarist was always committing himself to ideas and projects that needed Forrester's veto and action at the eleventh hour.

'No, I'll deal with it,' Eric said. There was a stunned silence when he broke the news to them. 'They were all very, very shocked.' For Clapton, that moment emphasized a dominating part of his character: come drugs or drink or shyness, he could usually apply a streak of ruthlessness when it meant survival.

Who would replace them? Tom Dowd mentioned some possibilities to Eric: what about Duck Dunn, the unique house bassist at the Stax label during the mid-sixties? Dowd knew that Eric held him in high esteem for his work with Otis Redding, Booker T and many other giants of soul music. How about drummer Roger Hawkins, the man Eric had once played alongside on an Aretha Franklin album, and who was known for his robust work as one of the regulars at the Muscle Shoals studios? Maybe Ry Cooder could be persuaded to guest, Dowd added.

Clapton laughed off the ideas with genuine modesty. 'You'll never get people of *that* level here. Why should they come and be on my album?' Dowd assured him that his reputation was bigger than he thought; a few phone calls later, and despite other work, two of those three top musicians virtually left their homes at once for Compass Point. The electricity between the new band worked well. Duck Dunn and Eric struck up such a firm rapport, and the bassist's work proved so intuitively right for Eric's music, that he went on to tour the world with Eric's band from 1983 onwards.

When Dowd said the maestro of slide guitar Ry Cooder might also drop in, Eric laughed again. 'Don't tempt me with these names! If it's not possible to get them I don't want to be frustrated by good-sounding impossibilities!' But Cooder was elated when he heard that a new Clapton album was under way and jumped at the invitation to drop in on the record. Suddenly, there was a new dialogue when Ry arrived, different again from the excellent relationship that had been struck up between Eric, Duck and Roger. Cooder's roots, like Eric's, skirted jazz, and the communication between the two men, musically as well as out of the studio, was firm. As a master stroke, the talent of Albert Lee was deployed to the concert piano, while Roger Hawkins spent a complete day buying a new set of skins for his drums to achieve a very special sound which Eric required.

Money and Cigarettes had its moments of triumph, with Eric's voice ruggedly mature. There was massive radio play around the world for the lilting '(I've Got a) Rock 'n' Roll Heart', while purists loved the old Albert King favourite, 'Crosscut Saw', and the Sleepy John Estes classic, 'Everybody Oughta Make a Change'. For the Johnny Otis song, 'Crazy Country Hop', Otis was excitedly on the phone to

Clapton to remind him of the lyrics during Eric's recording session. The maudlin songwriter inside Eric shone through with 'Man in Love' and 'Pretty Girl', another unashamedly tearful song to his wife. The album contained his cutting message to her about alcohol, 'The Shape You're In', which presaged their matrimonial strife. Conversely, Eric made his own vital statement on his renunciation of dope and drink with a song which received little attention. 'Ain't Going Down', with breakneck guitar runs and splendidly bluesy vocals, laid bare the dangers he had survived in his thirty-seven years, and set forth his determination to carry on living:

It ain't no big deal, we're all lucky to be alive,
I myself don't believe in luck, or taking chances I will survive
Every move I make, every twist every turn,
You scandalize and humble me, I may be slow but I will learn

'Cause I ain't going down anymore
'Cause I ain't going down anymore
'Cause I ain't going down anymore
'Cause I ain't going down anymore

If I had my way, I would probably just sit and stare.
Watch the TV or read a book, I'd have no reason to be aware,
But I ain't got time, I just could not live that way.
I've got to step outside myself, I've still got something left to say.

'Cause I ain't going down anymore
'Cause I ain't going down anymore
'Cause I ain't going down anymore
'Cause I ain't going down anymore

Channelled in my groove, part of another space and time.
Please allow me to introduce another good friend of mine.
Some call him fear, some call him righteousness.
I myself ain't clear, and you can't force me to make a guess.

It was not a great album, but a solid, important one. It marked a turn in his confidence. Tom Dowd, who worked so closely with Eric before 1975 and helped to mastermind the changed stance on *Money and Cigarettes*, says: 'I have never found him easy to handle. He's not the kind of person of whom you can predict that if he gets up one morning and takes two steps one way, that's the direction he's going for the whole day – or even for the next couple of hours! He can tire of any route very quickly. He changes on a whim. So people who play with him, or work with him as I do, have to go with his beat or give

Eric, contemplative and replete with beads and long hair (*Barry Wentzell/ Melody Maker*)

up. I think Eric thinks spherically rather than in straight lines. And so it's difficult to achieve a balance of judging when he is re-entering the planetary system. But then, he's an artist, and it's essential never to curb his energy. I try to direct it carefully, the way he instinctively thinks it's going.'

Eric's friendship with Roger Waters of Pink Floyd dates back many years. When Waters was planning his solo album and tour, *The Pros and Cons of Hitch-Hiking*, in 1984, he persuaded Eric to guest on the record and go on a world tour with him. Such was Eric's hunger for work, and his loyalty to an old friend, that he agreed. It was probably the weakest career move he made. The decision was against the advice of his fuming manager, Roger Forrester. Clapton was far too established to play what amounted to second fiddle around the world on a project with which neither he nor his music had anything in common. But he loyally followed through, and did European and American dates, having told Waters he would.

Clapton originally liked the idea because it gave him the chance to submerge himself within a band led by someone else; he fancied a world ticket with no responsibilities; the musical company, including Andy Newmark (drums) and Mel Collins (saxophones), sounded interesting. But once on the road, he quickly tired of what he regarded as a pretentious atmosphere. It was more like a travelling five-star hotel, with a mental distance between the players, a sharp contrast with the camaraderie he enjoyed in his own band. Tensions developed. Eric felt lonely, exposed. Once, in Stockholm, at an after-the-show dinner hosted by Waters's record company at a luxury restaurant, a hungry Clapton grew tired of waiting ages for food from obsequious waiters. He said to Nigel Carroll: 'I could do with a Big Mac and French Fries.' Carroll left and returned with the fast food fifteen minutes later. Eric enjoyed watching the expressions on the faces of the dinner guests as he tucked into his burger at the table while they still waited for their culinary delights.

Musically, as well as socially, Clapton was utterly unsuited to the Waters show. By far the finest musician on the stage, he had no natural place in the theatricality and posturing of it all. For many thousands of genuine music enthusiasts, the show came to life only when Eric played. But he looked uncomfortable, bored, and smoked endlessly to relieve what he saw as the dreariness of the stage show. Fed up from the start, he could hardly wait for the tour to end. The icy coldness of the music and the bad vibes of the touring entourage depressed him.

A far greater, and more appropriate, tour for Eric had been his reason for agreeing to the Roger Waters tour. In 1983 his old friend

Ronnie Lane, suffering from multiple sclerosis, helped to organize a series of gala concerts in aid of ARMS (Action Research into Multiple Sclerosis). The producer of the concerts, in London's Royal Albert Hall, and then in New York, Los Angeles and San Francisco, was Glyn Johns, whose record collaboration with Eric goes back many years. Major stars rallied to the cause, to raise many thousands of pounds for the charity, and the concerts became majestic celebrations of the careers of such luminaries as guitarists Jimmy Page and Jeff Beck, singers Joe Cocker and Andy Fairweather-Low, Rolling Stones Bill Wyman and Charlie Watts, and Clapton's great friend Steve Winwood. Amid feverish excitement, particularly in the USA, where they filled 20,000-seater arenas, the all-star band rekindled the fire of their long careers which each ran to twenty years or more.

'There was a special atmosphere for those ARMS concerts,' says Clapton. 'Although all of us had been around for all those years, we were playing together for the first time. I don't think we'd ever have done it for money. There would have been too much aggravation. But because it was for multiple sclerosis and Ronnie Lane, it seemed right. We all put down our egos and got on with it. It was a circus, and great entertainment.'

Back in London after the Roger Waters tour, a relieved Eric planned his 1985 album and songs. It was time for a change. 'My career,' he says, 'is nothing more than a collection of sounds in my head. I am faced, and always have been, with some notes in my head and the question of how I get them to sound the best I can, through those fingers, on the guitar. That's my whole ambition, and my entire career. The songs have to have simplicity and emotion. I can sing other people's songs if they do that to me. Or I can write them, if I'm feeling secure enough – or insecure enough!'

His confidence, though, was strong for his 1985 tour, and the ticket touts outside Wembley Arena in March, asking and getting £100 for a ticket, confirmed his increasing popularity. Inside, his refreshed band received a thunderous reception. This year, too, he embarked on his first video to help promote his album *Behind the Sun*. And significantly, on stage, he added a dash of presentation hitherto missing throughout his career. Instead of almost ambling on stage with the musicians, as 'one of the crowd', Eric sometimes let them all take up their positions before making his own entrance. It was part of the coming to terms with himself.

9

THE
LAST CHORUS

*'Whatever strength I've got can only function in
adversity'*

The mood of the man is always mirrored in his music. In Montserrat,
during the recording of his 1985 album *Behind the Sun*, Eric tore into
one song with an angst none of the musicians had seen before.
Playing and singing his own personal favourite on the record, 'Same
Old Blues', Clapton was full of fire in his guitar power and in his
raging, but still mellow, vocal work. So impulsively fierce was Eric's
playing and singing that the 'guide vocal' was impossible to improve
upon; it went on to the final album unvarnished.

The true reason for Clapton's fury on that performance was a
reflection of his pride and character. Around the studio, he had heard
that people surrounding his band and crew were enjoying themselves, indulging in excesses of drink. But nobody had told him in
advance of these sessions; he only heard about them later,
accidentally. He disliked the fact that he wasn't told about the
'action' and given at least the option to join in.

'He got this feeling that everyone was holding out on him,
unnecessarily protecting him from getting close to anything like
drink or drugs, because he wasn't considered sensible or moderate
enough to know better,' recalls the album producer, Phil Collins. 'He
was very, very annoyed. Everyone was denying it. I was oblivious to
it all, and didn't even know he was angry when we went in to record
"Same Old Blues". It was great! He played and sang really aggressively and we stayed with that first take.'

Next day, Clapton called Collins aside. 'Come here,' he said,
reprovingly. 'Why are you holding out on me?'

'What are you talking about?' said a bemused Collins.

Clapton was furious with him, and with the whole company, for

260

not allowing him to know what revelry was going on when he was out of the way. He strongly resented people treating him with kid gloves and excluding him from everything that was happening around him. He felt he was being mollycoddled. Having taken full control of his drugs and drink problems during the previous ten years, he disliked any whispering campaign that spread rumours implying he might be 'fragile' when addictions and indulgences were being discussed.

'Somebody's been holding out on me,' Eric finally told the assembled musicians. 'Now you guys, listen, I'm not a kid. I want to know everything that's going on.' This was no posture. It was an angry man who convinced everyone that in the future everything should be 'out in the open'.

For Phil Collins, who has been friendly with Clapton since 1978, it was an eye-opener. He was used to the complexities of the man but was treading with difficulty in combining comradeship with his first production role on an album by one of his heroes. While Eric knew little of Genesis and Collins's musical history, Phil had been weaned on the music of Cream and was in awe of the guitar work. In the sunshine of the West Indies, Collins was charged with the tough job of refreshing Clapton's music: Phil felt Eric had sounded jaded on *Money and Cigarettes*. Although he had not touted for the album, Phil Collins had been suggested as the kind of contemporary 'ear' to give a new production edge to what would be a vital record.

Living a few miles from each other in the Surrey countryside, Clapton and Collins had become great mates, visiting each other's homes; on one visit, Eric played guitar quietly in the background in Phil's home studio during the recording of 'If Leaving Me Is Easy,', which appeared on Collins's *Face Value* album. But their friendship went far deeper than musical compatibility. It had its magnet in Clapton's deepest values, the strongest of which are honesty and unpretentiousness. Like Clapton, Phil Collins loathes phoney show-business preening, and the two men are very close, despite Eric's ignorance of Genesis's music. Money does not impress either Eric or Phil, another major factor they have in common.

By 1985, the man renowned for his devotion to the sound of the guitar was warily coming to terms with the modern effects of the synthesizer. Eric bought a Roland guitar synthesizer and featured it a little on his *Behind the Sun* album. 'The coming of the synthesizer took a long time for me to pick up on,' he says. 'It crept up on me through the use of keyboards, which came about through my working with Phil Collins. When he came in as producer, my recording sound changed, and what happens on stage follows suit to a certain extent. When I do the older stuff, it stays pretty much the same, and my actual songwriting is motivated by the same things. It's hard for me to see, from where I am, what's going on musically because I feel I'm basically doing the same thing all the time. I was lucky in working with Phil, not just because he's a good friend, but because he wanted to produce an album that would show lots of different sides that hadn't been seen or heard before. It really didn't matter to him whether it was commercial or not, as long as it was true. Working with Phil was like falling off a log.' Clapton likes fast action. 'We finished recording in a month and mixed it in a month, and by today's standards that's quick.'

Although the two men are firm friends, Collins surprised Eric by admonishing him in the studio. 'After a month, when it was almost finished, I started getting a bit loose, mucking about, and Phil gave me a bollocking that I'll never forget, in front of everybody. Almost nobody had ever talked to me like that. It was unbelievable. But it straightened me out and I was very grateful for it. The only other person who's ever done that to me was Pete Townshend. Both he and Phil are professionals of the old school. Admirable stuff!'

Despite the nonchalant vibrations which he sometimes sends out, Eric Clapton is today keener than ever on preserving his status. He tends to look forward rather than over his shoulder: 'I only expect to be recognized by the public, and other musicians, for what I produce *now*.'

But he is penetrating in his self-analysis of his past. 'By giving in to drugs and booze, I wasted a good seven years of creative life. It had a stultifying effect on my work and when I finally realized that, I was very upset and shocked at the time I'd lost. My personal happiness was gone, too.'

Nor does he feel stronger for having overcome two big hurdles. 'No, my strength, whatever strength I've got, is the kind of strength which can only function in adversity. My strength in 'peacetime', if you like, is almost negligible. My strength, as a human being able to live happily in a peaceful situation, is not there. I'm only strong if I'm in a bind. Now that isn't good.' That weakness, he admits, is a result of having had to fight his vices. 'If I hadn't gone down that road, I might have learned to be strong as a happy human being.

'Until those years spent indulging in the sins of the flesh, I had a pretty positive idea of what I wanted to do. Of course it was ruled more by what I *didn't* want to be or do. But towards my late twenties, I got a bit confused: the Blind Faith thing, Delaney and Bonnie, Derek and the Dominos. With the benefit of hindsight, I can see I was getting a little bit unsure of myself. I was an Englishman playing

Eric with his producer and close friend Phil Collins in Montserrat during the
recording of 'Behind The Sun'

American music, the blues. My direction got a bit stifled, unsure, and that let the door open for anything in terms of distraction.

'Looking back on it, what a terrible waste! Instead of giving in to those things, I could have actually come to grips with something even stronger. By now, I would actually have been a lot more towards the goal I should have. And so now, I still find myself at a crossroads quite a lot of the time. I'm back to where I was, doing what's musically right for me, but I should have been here earlier.' But then, if he had gone the more orthodox route, concentrating on his career at the start of 1970 instead of opting out, '*this* might be the time I would have chosen to start taking drugs and drinking'. That, in view of his age, would have been extremely serious.

On the subject of fitness and drugs and drink today, Eric is succinct and positive: 'I don't believe in any kind of excesses any more. I don't want to do it because I don't like the after-effects. Drinking and taking dope . . . I've done all that and I'm lucky to be alive. I regret those years because they were wasted and I can never get them back. And now I feel that life is much better when it's lived in a real way, without any kind of crutch other than the emotional ones which we've all got. I'm very happy, and very grateful, to still be here. And I think that if I blow it now, I'd be a fool.'

On popularity today, Eric is clear-thinking: 'I would find it very hard to go on without it at this stage in my life. Earlier on, I didn't give a damn. I was so self-confident that it didn't matter if I played to one person who didn't clap, or a hundred people who didn't clap, or a hundred who did clap. But now, I feel I *need* an audience. I don't like it if people don't respond positively to my performance.' His earlier independent stance was born of 'the flame of arrogance', he continues. 'I'm afraid that's gone now. I now rely on the crutch of being popular – walking on stage, and maintaining a stance while I'm there.' He is genuinely pleased and flattered when asked for autographs and never refuses a request.

On showmanship, he's terse: 'I gave up trying years ago. The only time I came anywhere near it was when I was drunk and falling around. I could never sit down and consciously work out what I'm going to do on stage. The only thing we work out is a running order and a lighting plot.' He takes only a mild interest in the visual planning of the concerts. 'It wouldn't be fair to the people involved if I cast more than an approving eye. I can only give the technicians an idea of what I do or don't like. Then it's up to them. They're artists, too.' Yet he's aware that, walking on to big concert platforms, he has to compete with other artists for the attention of fans who pay to see him. 'I know I have to compete in terms of material and visuality, but

I don't feel there's much chance of winning!' He adds that he makes 'a token gesture' to visual appeal, and then hopes his work will pull him through.

When Eric stopped drinking, his wife told him she found him so tense that he was intimidating. To her amazement he replied that he was behaving in that way quite deliberately. 'He said he didn't want anyone to get close to him,' says Pattie. His insularity worried her. 'I felt I couldn't get through to him and I didn't like the fact that I wasn't making him happy enough to relax. Then I told myself that he was probably worked up because he resented not being able to do the one thing he enjoyed: drink.'

Since Eric has learned to control his drinking habit, he has immersed himself in work almost as obsessively as he did twenty years ago. 'Almost all the time, I haven't been pleased enough with my performance,' he says. And while the concert halls and giant arenas continue to be sell-outs, his career more solid and his voice and guitar richer than ever, Clapton thrives on putting himself through the hoop. 'Life's like a razor blade,' he once said to a close friend. 'I'll always walk along its edge.'

He inspires passionate loyalty from the team around him; the safety valve for them all used to be the backstage banter, and the winding up on their journeys used to be the practical jokes. Like the night on an American concert when one of the crew tied string to the base of Eric's microphone and pulled it into the wings of the stage while he was singing, eyes closed, oblivious to the prank. Walking out to a concert, Eric sometimes asked his manager which city he was in, because after a day of travelling and in the middle of a tour he'd forgotten. 'Cleveland,' said Forrester once, taunting him. 'It's great to be in Cleveland tonight!' Clapton walked out and told the Detroit audience. Eric liked those wind-ups for years, then abruptly told Forrester to stop: he enjoyed the fun but could not detect when he was joking or when he was serious. He always smiled wryly at Roger Forrester's references to 'Eric's three-year day off with the flu'. That kind of jokiness remains in the camp, but less so as Eric and his musicians have grown up.

The Clapton of 1982 onwards refers to his entourage as 'the most boring rock 'n' roll band in the world . . . concert, back to hotel, game of cards, sleep, airport, shopping, hotel, concert . . . what do you expect from old men?'

*

'I don't lead the band very well,' says Clapton. 'There are very, very few occasions when I am totally and utterly satisfied with what I've done. This is strange in itself: I can look back on those occasions, hear the tapes and be surprised by how good they sound. So it's at the *time* of the concert that I'm never a hundred per cent happy.

'And because of that, I suppose, I don't lead properly. I only lead by example. I don't have any idea about instruction, or how to keep a band on the road happy. I choose the players I've got because I like the way they play and I just hope that they'll carry on playing like that with me, adding an ingredient to what I can offer. The only way they can look up to me as a bandleader is in knowing that I'm *easy*. They probably feel there's not enough push in me.' On subjects like this, when he is unsure, Eric sounds lke an inexperienced guitarist forming his first band.

That is the fundamental modesty of the man talking. But since 1979, when he had the leadership problem of hiring and firing the all-British line-up, Eric has been that rarity among superstars: one shy of his own stature. His contradictions loom all the time: he wants recognition, success and all the material pleasures that brings, but would rather achieve it by being 'a musician in the band' than through the burden of leadership. Yet he loves applause.

'If anyone's the boss in my band in 1985,' says Eric, 'then musically it's my bass player Duck Dunn. I chose him as a surrogate band-leader. The bass, to me, is actually the core of what's going on in the band. It has to be solid, so the most solid *person* in the band has to be the bass player. In terms of philosophy I would look towards him. That's Duck at this time. From the point of view of motivation, he's the leader of the band.'

He equivocates on the subject of firing musicians. 'In my twenties and early thirties it seemed to me that if I fired a musician, or left a band myself, it was a very light-hearted decision. Chances were that you'd run into one another again. It didn't matter much. I might even rehire them – and that happened in the case of my drummer, Jamie Oldaker, who I fired and then rehired a couple of years later. I realized that what he gave my band, a cockiness, a spikiness, a toughness, was something nobody else had. And whatever draw-backs there are to his personality, and there are hardly any, they're worth putting up with to make sure I keep him around. Same with Chris Stainton and Duck Dunn – they've all got quirks but they're all great players, and for me to change now I'd have to have a damned good reason.

'In the past, I've fired people too lightly and regretted it. I've had to grow older to realize that if you're happy up to a point with what

Above: Clapton and friend relax in the sun.
Below: Mr and Mrs Clapton relax with a tape

you've got, then it's blind stupidity to get rid of it on a gamble, *hoping* it could be better with someone else.'

But he is capable of ruthless decisions that wound. In Montserrat, recording his album *Behind the Sun,* one of his oldest musician friends telephoned to ask producer Phil Collins if he could come out and guest on the album. Collins passed on the request but Eric would neither phone him back nor agree to his request.

Pete Townshend has good reasons for reflecting on his relationship with Eric, which has seen peaks and troughs. 'In 1982, when I'd come away from Meg Patterson's treatment myself, I did an interview with *Rolling Stone* magazine in which I had a little crack at Eric. I said then what I know as a former heroin addict to be true: that you *do* change permanently. It could be a change for the better, but you *do* change. And I think that unfortunately it does reduce you slightly, because I think it denies you the true experience of the years that you spend as an addict.

'For me, mercifully, that was a short time. For Eric, it was two and a half years or something. I mentioned that he'd lost two and a half years and maybe they were precious years and no one will ever know what might have happened had Eric not done that. It wasn't meant to be a criticism. But Eric was extremely hurt that I should talk in public about him in any way that was critical, or that I could abuse a friendship.' Townshend says he wrote to Clapton to apologize – 'but also to defend what I felt was the case. It's strange. Show-business friendships are built on so much fatuousness . . . this is the real world and you know what makes it go round: gossip, success, scandal and controversy! That's what makes life worth living, and if you don't feed the machine occasionally, nothing happens. In a relationship like I have with Eric, or similarly with Paul McCartney, they should be strong enough to take it occasionally. Maybe it's a bit romantic, a bit stupid to think that we're all members of a great clan and we can knock one another in public. But we should know that behind the scenes we're still friends. With Eric, perhaps that isn't true now.'

Eric's response to Townshend is succinct: 'He thought I was very shallow because he believed I was upset that I didn't win a Best Guitar Player award. This wasn't actually true. He had heard that second-hand. I wrote to him to say that it wasn't true, but even if it was there was nothing wrong with wanting to be the best guitar player in the world. It was that very idea that had kept me going through all my hardship. So I ticked him off and said that if he felt that way about me, why didn't he tell me face to face, or on the phone instead of blabbing to the papers? I felt strongly that if people like Pete were going to comment on what they *heard* people were saying, it was dangerous because it was second-hand. It was Pete's supposition of what I felt that I objected to.'

But Townshend has enormous admiration, and even a little envy, for the way in which Eric has marshalled his art. 'What he's doing is what I've desperately wanted to do, which is to age with dignity in this business. It's partly because he still maintains he's a blues performer. But it's greater than that: people like Muddy Waters and B. B. King aged with fantastic dignity. Eric has a trace of that but his dignity has come from allowing his inner spirit *freedom* as he plays. That is the biggest step any musician can take. So few people have ever done it. Charlie Parker, John Coltrane and Jimi Hendrix did it, and now Eric has done it. And once free, it can never be contained. This flower has blossomed. Eric's life has been the most fantastic romance.

'What is ironic is that in the years he was going through the motions of playing the blues, he had nothing to say. He was a purist, very much an apologist. Now he's risen above that. He might use the same keys on the typewriter, but he's speaking from a difference within. With something really important to communicate – a feeling of real human aspiration, of the real qualities of dignity and openness, "take me, warts and all", Eric had it at his fingertips, from his original sources, to communicate that. And now he's doing it.' In late 1984, after seeing Eric 'change the colour of the atmosphere' by his playing at the bleak Roger Waters concert, Townshend went up to Eric and said: 'Well, it's true, after all these years, Clapton is God.'

Pete felt stunned at the fact that he'd said it, but he stands by it. 'This was Eric making communication from heart to heart. It was divine.'

Townshend believes that one of the reasons for the poetry of Clapton's guitar playing and vocals is that: 'He doesn't do *anything* else. He just plays. He doesn't make speeches, have a band to struggle against, have children – music is all to Eric. So in a way, Eric's like royalty. He's always very polite, considerate, upright, dignified, moral overall, but he survives on being, above all, not strong but a gentleman.'

Clapton has great respect for Townshend's intelligence although he has sometimes had reason to resent Pete's tactlessness in dealing with his sensibilities. 'Pete's an important influence on the life of anyone who's ever met him or heard him,' says Eric. 'Once you've got him as a friend, he's there. That's *it*. He's probably the kind of friend that you sometimes really don't want to have, because he's the most honest man you'll ever meet and he'll tell you stuff you don't want to hear. But in the long run, it's good for you. So you have to value it.'

Says John Hurt: 'Eric has got a theatricality about his thinking as well as his music. It's very much as if he does it for his audience – I don't think he's wasting time doing it for himself, yet he's not pandering to the audience in any sense, which is as it should be for any performer. He doesn't have that unpleasant arrogance of quite a lot of young musicians: "Well, I'm playing what I'm playing, and fuck the audience." I've always known that if he felt it wasn't working, he'd go straight back to the drawing board.'

Eric has written two film themes, one for a John Hurt film called *The Hit*, and another for the Michael Caine film, *Water*. 'I'd love him to do more,' says Hurt. 'He has a tremendous dramatic understanding. He sees a film and it strikes him deeply somewhere . . . it reminds me of what Ben Palmer said to me when we went to see him appear with John Mayall in 1966: "He plays one note to everybody else's fifty and it's such a perceptive note that it makes me feel I might as well not have bothered to go to the piano." '

On the inevitability of advancing years and the future, Eric is quietly philosophical: 'As I get older, I get stiffer. My fingers take a little bit of time to get loose. I'm still doing exactly the same thing, except that it's becoming a little bit more refined or polished. I pace it a little slower but it all feels the same to me. And I do enjoy it.

'I've gone through periods of thinking I'm retiring, and others wondering if I'll continue making records and touring until the day I die. I'm constantly changing my mind about it. I think I'll carry on until I can't do it any more – because something will stop me, like arthritis or fatigue. Aside from that, I can't see myself doing anything else. What else is there? Grand Prix driving, maybe? I don't know. It would have to be that exciting because I'm used to such a buzz, a thrill, playing on stage in front of an audience. You can't get that from writing film scores. So I think this is my destiny.' He says he now *needs* audience applause as part of his life. 'I've worked towards making that integral to my whole being,' he says. 'It's not just being successful by making hit records, but being true to myself as a musician. Knowing I get applause for that is very satisfying.'

Shortly after he had stopped drinking, Eric went to visit Ben Palmer in Wales. Clapton gave Ben a book on the peregrine falcon, and Ben became absorbed by the characteristics of the bird. It has astonishing eyesight – it can see for about twenty miles – and hunts by a dive-bomb action. When Eric had left and Ben absorbed the book, he pondered the analogy between birds of prey and Clapton's own style. 'There's a tension that a hawk at a thousand feet high will feel from the wind. The bird's mathematical certainty, drive, strength – it's something very similar to Eric's movements which have followed his life.'

Palmer ruminates on a conversation with Eric in 1963, during a Roosters rehearsal. The two men were talking about the importance of money. Eric conceded that it was essential if a person was to behave like a star and adopt the necessary style. 'But what would you do,' asked Ben, 'if you were down to your last sixpence, Clappers?' Clapton's reply was: 'I'd buy a Mars bar.' And, says Ben: 'That's how he saw it then and that's how he sees life still.'

*

By the spring of 1984, when Eric went to Montserrat to record *Behind the Sun*, his marriage to Pattie was creaking. He had written most of the songs during two weeks of solitary confinement in a cottage in Wales. 'I've written most of the songs of my life here, the lounge of my home,' he says. 'But this time, I couldn't. The home situation was sticky. I felt exposed. But when I got to Wales I had no idea what I was writing about. All my messages in the songs seemed abstract until the events of the next few months unfolded and my marriage ran into trouble.' It was as if he had a vision of the storms ahead. 'One of the heartbreaking things about being an artist is not knowing what the hell you're creating until you've finished it . . . and then it may be too late. Other people can see what you're saying. But the artist can't.'

The melancholia of the album was unconsciously caught by Eric in his title. *Behind the Sun* was inspired by Eric's great hero, Muddy Waters. One of his most celebrated songs, 'Louisiana Blues', starts with the words: 'I'm going to New Orleans, baby, behind the sun. . .'

'I suppose Muddy means he's going to follow the sun down, and I always loved that phrase. It's been used several other times in a blues context,' says Eric. As the months passed, and Eric and Pattie's relationship flickered, Eric thought the phrase aptly summarized the state of his marriage. The other songs were much more direct, written as if he had a vision that his marriage, but not his love of Pattie, was foundering. 'Never Make You Cry', the slow love ballad of the album, has Eric's sensitive voice and coaxing lyrics set against his guitar at its most whining and eloquent. When the musicians played it back in the studio, there were tears at the realization that here was yet another sentimental song by Eric for Pattie, at a critical time in their relationship. 'I think it replaces "Wonderful Tonight" as the ultimate love song I've written,' says Eric. Phil Collins collabo rated with him on the lyrics. When Pattie heard the song, she says she knew that Eric had written yet another special poem, but such was the state of their relationship that her emotions were mixed.

The album marked a subtle, but positive, change in Clapton's recording career. His voice resumed the robust air of *461 Ocean Boulevard*, and with two girl singers back with him, Marcy Levy and Shaun Murphy, there was a vigour and buoyancy that had been missing from his last two records. The songs, though, carried titles and messages to his wife that amounted to a soundtrack to his troubled marriage: 'She's Waiting (for another love)', 'Tangled in Love', the heavy sarcasm of 'It All Depends', the optimism of 'Forever Man' and the desperation of the dirge 'Just Like a Prisoner', which Eric says is how he felt about his life at home at the time.

While the feeling of the album lacked raunch, the songs carried a personal commitment that must have come from deep inside Eric's subconscious. 'They're mostly songs of unrequited love, from me, but there are plenty of positive thoughts as well,' he says. 'Even "Knock On Wood", though I didn't write it, is about Pattie. "Same Old Blues" is about me and her and my relationship with the road, and one of my favourite songs of my own to date. It tells the story of a guy who's leaving, he's out there on the road, and he's coming back one day. It's very simple, but it actually says a lot of the really deep feelings I have about the road. Musically, it's very satisfying for me, too. "She's Waiting" is about her predicament and how I blew it, except that I hadn't blown it when I wrote the bloody song!'

As he worked to resolve his marriage, Eric was acutely conscious of the pressure the album songs would place on Pattie. 'Difficult to know what she really feels when she hears them,' says Eric. 'I can see she always gets a tingling feeling, but the problem is that she feels obligated to live up to the person who's being written about. That may be why she comes back at me with the reflection that she isn't strong enough as an individual or doesn't feel a good enough person to be with me – because of the pedestal I've often put her on.'

And so, by 1985, the inner torment, the wailing guitar tone, the fragility, the romanticism, the soul, the ability to present complete honesty in his work were confronted by the greatest emotional test. He sang autobiographically about his marriage while hardly realiz ing it. These were feelings of the blues that he would rather not have experienced. They tested to the full his obsessiveness, his determina tion and his artistry.

Eric at the ARMS concerts in America to aid multiple sclerosis victims, in the autumn of 1983. On stage at New York's Madison Square Garden, from left: Jimmy Page, Eric, Ronnie Wood, Bill Wyman and Joe Cocker (*Bob Leafe/Star File*). *Below:* Jimmy Page and Jeff Beck on stage with Eric (*London Features International*)

For all that he is a natural musician, Eric moves about purposefully while exuding the air of a casual artist. He rehearses methodically, in exactly timed four-hour sessions, only when he needs to, and does not walk around strumming. The first time he sees his ready-tuned guitar before any concert is when it is handed to him as he steps on to that stage. 'When I pick up that guitar, it's to actually try to get something out of it,' he says. 'It's a means of communication, yeah, but it's also my job. I'm just lucky, I suppose, that so many people actually like what I consider my work.'

The baffling, fascinating dichotomy remains, all the time he stands at centre stage. He appears unconcerned, supercool about his audience. Inside he cares deeply. If people drift out of the hall, it worries him and unnerves his performance. In perhaps his most revealing admission, Eric says he spends a lot of time, when he's on stage, 'watching those Exit signs . . .'

THE ROOSTERS March 63 to Oct 63
- BEN PALMER — piano
- TERRY BRENNAN — vocals
- ROBIN MASON — drums
- TOM McGUINNESS — bass
- ERIC CLAPTON — guitar

THE YARDBIRDS #1 May 63 to Oct 63
- TOP TOPHAM — guitar
- KEITH RELF — vocals
- JIM McCARTY — drums
- CHRIS DREJA — guitar
- PAUL SAMWELL — bass

THE YARDBIRDS #2 Oct 63 to Mar 65
- ERIC CLAPTON — guitar
- KEITH RELF — vocals
- JIM McCARTY — drums
- CHRIS DREJA — guitar
- PAUL SAMWELL — bass

THE YARDBIRDS #3 Mar 65 to Jun 66
- JEFF BECK — guitar
- KEITH RELF — vocals
- JIM McCARTY — drums
- CHRIS DREJA — guitar
- PAUL SAMWELL — bass

THE GLANDS Aug 65 to Oct 65
- BEN PALMER — piano
- JAKE MILTON — drums
- BERNIE GREENWOOD — sax
- JOHN BAILEY — vocals
- ERIC CLAPTON — guitar

CASEY JONES & THE ENGINEERS Oct 63 only
- ERIC CLAPTON — guitar
- BRIAN CASSER — vocals
- RAY STOCK — drums
- DAVE McGUMSKY — guitar
- TOM McGUINNESS — bass

MANFRED MANN #1 May 63 to Jan 64
- PAUL JONES — vocals
- MANFRED MANN — organ
- MIKE HUGG — drums
- MIKE VICKERS — guitar
- DAVE RICHMOND — bass

MANFRED MANN #2 Jan 64 to Oct 65
- PAUL JONES — vocals
- MANFRED MANN — keybds
- MIKE HUGG — drums
- MIKE VICKERS — guitar
- TOM McGUINNESS — bass

MANFRED MANN #3 dec 65 to July 66
- PAUL JONES — vocals
- MANFRED MANN — keybds
- MIKE HUGG — drums
- TOM McGUINNESS — guitar

MANFRED MANN #4 July 66 to Jun 69
- MIKE D'ABO — vocals
- MANFRED MANN — keybds
- MIKE HUGG — drums
- TOM McGUINNESS — guitar
- KLAUS VOORMANN — bass

GRAHAM BOND ORGANISATION 1963 to 1965
- GRAHAM BOND — keybd/voc
- DICK HECKSTALL — sax
- JACK BRUCE — bass
- JACK BRUCE — bass/voc
- GINGER BAKER — drums

JOHN MAYALL'S BLUESBREAKERS #5 July 65 to Apr 65
- ROGER rep DEAN — guitar
- BERNIE WATSON — guitar
- JOHN MAYALL — keybd/voc
- HUGHIE FLINT — drums
- JOHN McVIE — bass
- TOM McGUINNESS — bass

BLUESBREAKERS #6 Apr 65 to Aug 65
- ERIC CLAPTON — gtr/voc
- JOHN MAYALL — keybd/voc
- HUGHIE FLINT — drums
- JOHN McVIE — bass

BLUESBREAKERS #7 Aug 65 to Nov 65
- VARIOUS SUBSTITUTES — guitar
- JOHN MAYALL — keybd/voc
- HUGHIE FLINT — drums
- JOHN McVIE — bass
- JACK BRUCE — bass

BLUESBREAKERS #8 Nov 65 to July 66
- ERIC CLAPTON — gtr/voc
- JOHN MAYALL — keybd/voc
- HUGHIE FLINT — drums
- JOHN McVIE — bass

BLUESBREAKERS #9 July 66 to Sep 66
- PETER GREEN — gtr/voc
- JOHN MAYALL — keybd/voc
- HUGHIE FLINT — drums
- JOHN McVIE — bass

CREAM July 66 to Jan 70
- ERIC CLAPTON — gtr/voc
- JACK BRUCE — bass/voc
- GINGER BAKER — drums

BLIND FAITH Feb 69 to Jan 70
- ERIC CLAPTON — gtr/voc
- STEVE WINWOOD — keybd/voc
- RIC GRECH — bass
- GINGER BAKER — drums

DELANEY & BONNIE & FRIENDS Dec 69 to Mar 70
- ERIC CLAPTON — guitar
- BOBBY WHITLOCK — keybds
- CARL RADLE — bass
- JIM GORDON — drums
- DELANEY BRAMLETT — vocals
- BONNIE BRAMLETT — vocals
- GEORGE HARRISON — guitar
- RITA COOLIDGE — vocals
- HORN SECTION — brass
- DAVE MASON — guitar

DEREK & THE DOMINOS May 70 to Apr 71
- ERIC CLAPTON — guitar
- BOBBY WHITLOCK — keybds
- CARL RADLE — bass
- JIM GORDON — drums
- DAVE MASON — guitar
- DUANE ALLMAN — guitar

FAMILY 1967 to Feb 69
- ROGER CHAPMAN — vocals
- CHARLIE WHITNEY — guitar
- JIM KING — sax
- ROB TOWNSEND — drums
- RIC GRECH — bass

TRAFFIC #1 Apr 67 to Jan 69
- CHRIS WOOD — sax
- DAVE MASON — gtr/voc
- STEVE WINWOOD — keybd/voc
- JIM CAPALDI — drums

WOODEN FROG Jan 69 to Mar 69
- CHRIS WOOD — sax
- MICK WEAVER — keybd/voc
- DAVE MASON — gtr/voc
- JIM CAPALDI — drums

TRAFFIC #2 Feb 70 to May 71
- CHRIS WOOD — sax
- STEVE WINWOOD — keybd/voc
- RIC GRECH — bass
- JIM CAPALDI — drums

TRAFFIC #3 May 71 to Dec 71
- JIM GORDON drums
- CHRIS WOOD sax
- STEVE WINWOOD keybd/voc
- JIM CAPALDI vocals
- RIC GRECH bass
- DAVE MASON guitar
- REE BOP percussion

ERIC CLAPTON'S RAINBOW CONCERT Jan 73
- STEVE WINWOOD keybd/voc
- JIM CAPALDI drums
- REE BOP percussion
- RIC GRECH bass
- PETE TOWNSHEND gtr/voc
- ERIC CLAPTON guitar
- RON WOOD guitar
- JIMMY KARSTEIN drums

TRAFFIC #4 Jan 72 to Sept 73
- ROGER HAWKINS drums
- STEVE WINWOOD keybd/voc
- CHRIS WOOD sax
- JIM CAPALDI vocals
- REE BOP percussion
- DAVID HOOD bass

EMMYLOU HARRIS & THE HOT BAND Feb 76 to Feb 78
- EMMYLOU HARRIS gtr/voc
- JOHN WARE drums
- EMORY GORDY bass
- HANK DE VITO pedal steel
- GLEN D HARDIN piano
- RICKY SKAGGS mand/voc
- ALBERT LEE gtr/voc

PROCOL HARUM April 67 to May 77
- B.J. WILSON drums
- ROBIN TROWER guitar
- CHRIS COPPING bass/organ
- MICK GRABHAM guitar
- GARY BROOKER piano/voc
- SEVERAL OTHERS various

BOOKER T & THE MGs 1960 to 1972
- BOOKER T JONES keybds
- STEVE CROPPER guitar
- AL JACKSON drums
- DUCK DUNN bass

JEFF BECK GROUP late 70s
- JEFF BECK gtr/voc
- TONY HYMAS keybds
- SIMON PHILLIPS drums

ARMS BENEFIT CONCERT GROUP Sept 83 to Dec 83
- STEVE WINWOOD keybd/voc
- JEFF BECK guitar
- TONY HYMAS keybds
- SIMON PHILLIPS drums
- ERIC CLAPTON gtr/voc
- CHRIS STAINTON keybds
- ALBERT LEE gtr/piano
- HENRY SPINETTI drums
- GARY BROOKER piano/voc
- CHARLIE WATTS drums
- JIMMY PAGE guitar
- RONNIE LANE vocals
- ANDY FAIRWEATHER LOWE gtr/voc
- BILL WYMAN bass

ROGER WATERS & HIS BAND May 84 to July 84
- ROGER WATERS bass/voc
- TIM RENWICK guitar
- MICHAEL KAMEN keybds
- ANDY NEWMARK drums
- ERIC CLAPTON gtr/voc
- CHRIS STAINTON keybds
- MEL COLLINS sax
- DOREEN CHANTER back voc
- KATIE KISSOON back voc

GEORGE HARRISON'S BANGLA DESH CONCERT GROUP Aug 71
- ERIC CLAPTON guitar
- RINGO STARR drums
- LEON RUSSELL piano
- JIM KELTNER drums
- GEORGE HARRISON guitar
- BILLY PRESTON organ
- JESSE ED DAVIS guitar
- HORNS SINGERS etc
- KLAUS VOORMANN bass

BOB SEGER & HIS BAND 1973 to Mar 74
- DICK SIMS keybds
- CARL RADLE bass
- JAMIE OLDAKER drums
- TOM CARTMELL sax
- BOB SEGER gtr/voc

QUATERMASS Sept 69 to Apr 71
- PETER ROBINSON keybds
- JOHN GUSTAFSON bass/voc
- MICK UNDERWOOD drums

ERIC CLAPTON & HIS BAND #1 Apr 74 to Aug 78
- ERIC CLAPTON gtr/voc
- DICK SIMS keybds
- CARL RADLE bass
- JAMIE OLDAKER drums
- MARCY LEVY back voc
- GEORGE TERRY guitar
- YVONNE ELLIMAN back voc
- SERGIO PASTORA percussion

ERIC CLAPTON & HIS BAND #2 Aug 78 to Jan 79
- ERIC CLAPTON gtr/voc
- DICK SIMS keybds
- CARL RADLE bass
- JAMIE OLDAKER drums
- MARCY LEVY back voc

ERIC CLAPTON & HIS BAND #3 Jan 79 to Aug 79
- ERIC CLAPTON gtr/voc
- DICK SIMS keybds
- CARL RADLE bass
- JAMIE OLDAKER drums

ERIC CLAPTON & HIS BAND #4 Sept 79 to Oct 82
- ERIC CLAPTON gtr/voc
- ALBERT LEE gtr/voc
- CARL RADLE bass
- DAVE MARKEE bass
- CHRIS STAINTON keybds
- HENRY SPINETTI drums
- GARY BROOKER piano/voc

ERIC CLAPTON & HIS BAND #5 Oct 82 to Feb 84
- ERIC CLAPTON gtr/voc
- ALBERT LEE gtr/piano
- ROGER HAWKINS rep by JAMIE OLDAKER drums
- DUCK DUNN bass
- CHRIS STAINTON keybds
- KENNEY JONES drums
- JOE COCKER vocals

ERIC CLAPTON & HIS BAND #6 Mar 84 to Dec 84
- ERIC CLAPTON gtr/voc
- CHRIS STAINTON keybds
- JAMIE OLDAKER drums
- DUCK DUNN bass
- MARCY LEVY back voc
- SHAUN MURPHY back voc
- PETER ROBINSON synthesizer

Pete Frame © December 1984

ERIC CLAPTON
DISCOGRAPHY
1964–85

This definitive discography, unlike any other, is the first complete documentation of Eric Clapton's work prepared in conjunction with the artist. Eric's recollections of his extraordinary recording career eliminate several previously accepted rumours and include some facts published here for the first time. The result is a detailed, chronological look at the work of probably the most industrious recording artist in rock music.

Every track ever committed to vinyl on which Eric Clapton can be found is included here. The discography sets out to reflect his recording career as *he* planned it. So it does not include promotional discs, twelve-inch singles, re-packages, re-releases or compilation albums except where they contain particularly sought-after collectors' material gathered together in one place for the first time, or where they contain previously unissued tracks. The list does not include picture discs or any other gimmicks released for marketing purposes.

In both sections – the main discography, and the listing of Guest Appearances/Session Work – only the first, intentional release of a track is detailed. Subsequent re-releases or compilations or singles lifted from albums are not included.

The detailed listing, together with all release dates in Eric's twenty-one-year career until 1985, refer to British record releases except where stated; foreign discs are only included where they contain material otherwise unreleased in Britain.

Songs either completely written or co-written by Eric or songs described as 'traditional' but with a new arrangement by him are printed in capital letters. The exceptions are two songs which Eric did not write but whose titles consist, stylistically, of capitals: 'NSU' and 'SWLABR'.

SINGLES

June 1964	'I Wish You Would'/'A Certain Girl' (*The Yardbirds*)
October 1964	'Good Morning Little Schoolgirl'/'I Ain't Got You' (*The Yardbirds*)
March 1965	'For Your Love'/'GOT TO HURRY' (*The Yardbirds*)
October 1965	'I'm Your Witch Doctor'/'Telephone Blues' (*John Mayall*) [with the Bluesbreakers]
August 1966	'Lonely Years'/'Bernard Jenkins' (*John Mayall and Eric Clapton*)
September 1966	'Parchman Farm'†/'Key to Love' (*John Mayall and the Bluesbreakers*)
October 1966	'Wrapping Paper'/'Cat's Squirrel' (*Cream*)
December 1966	'I Feel Free'/'NSU' (*Cream*)
June 1967	'STRANGE BREW'/'TALES OF BRAVE ULYSSES' (*Cream*)
May 1968	'ANYONE FOR TENNIS'/'Pressed Rat and Warthog' (*Cream*)
September 1968	'SUNSHINE OF YOUR LOVE'/'SWLABR' (*Cream*)
January 1969	'White Room'/'Those Were the Days' (*Cream*)
April 1969	'BADGE'/'What a Bringdown' (*Cream*)
October 1970	'After Midnight'/'EASY NOW' (*Eric Clapton*)
July 1972	'LAYLA'/'BELL BOTTOM BLUES' (*Derek and the Dominos*)
April 1973	'WHY DOES LOVE GOT TO BE SO SAD?'/'PRESENCE OF THE LORD' (*Derek and the Dominos*)
July 1974	'I Shot the Sheriff'/'GIVE ME STRENGTH' (*Eric Clapton*)
October 1974	'Willie and the Hand Jive'/'Mainline Florida' (*Eric Clapton*)
April 1975	'SWING LOW SWEET CHARIOT'/'PRETTY BLUE EYES' (*Eric Clapton*)
August 1975	'Knockin' On Heaven's Door'/'Someone Like You' (*Eric Clapton*)
October 1976	'HELLO OLD FRIEND'/'ALL OUR PAST TIMES' (*Eric Clapton*)
February 1977	'CARNIVAL'/'Hungry' (*Eric Clapton*)
November 1977	'LAY DOWN SALLY'/'Cocaine' (*Eric Clapton*)
March 1978	'WONDERFUL TONIGHT'/'PEACHES AND

September 1978   'Promises'/'WATCH OUT FOR LUCY' *(Eric Clapton)*

February 1979   'If I Don't Be There by Morning'/'Tulsa Time' *(Eric Clapton and His Band)*

February 1981   'I CAN'T STAND IT'/'Black Rose' *(Eric Clapton and His Band)*

April 1981   'ANOTHER TICKET'/'RITA MAE' *(Eric Clapton and His Band)*

January 1983   '(I've Got a) Rock 'n' Roll Heart'/'MAN IN LOVE' *(Eric Clapton)*

March 1983   'THE SHAPE YOU'RE IN'/'Crosscut Saw' *(Eric Clapton)*

May 1983   'SLOW DOWN LINDA'/'Crazy Country Hop' *(Eric Clapton)*

February 1985   'Forever Man'/'TOO BAD' *(Eric Clapton)*

ALBUMS

December 1964   **Five Live Yardbirds**
'Too Much Monkey Business'; 'I Got Love if You Want It'; 'Smokestack Lightnin''; 'Good Morning Little Schoolgirl'; 'Respectable'. 'Five Long Years'; 'Pretty Girl'; 'Louise'; 'I'm a Man'; 'Here 'Tis'.

(The Yardbirds)

December 1965   **Sonny Boy Williamson and the Yardbirds**
'Bye Bye Bird'; 'Mister Downchild'; '23 Hours Too Long'; 'Out On the Water Coast'; 'Baby Don't Worry'*. 'Pontiac Blues'; 'Take It Easy Baby'; 'I Don't Care No More'*; 'Do the Weston'. (This final track a.k.a. 'Western Arizona'.)

(Sonny Boy Williamson and the Yardbirds)

July 1966   **Blues Breakers**
'All Your Love'; 'Hideaway'; 'Little Girl'; 'Another Man'; 'DOUBLE CROSSIN' TIME'; 'What I'd Say'. 'Key to Love'; 'Parchman Farm'†; 'Have You Heard'; 'Ramblin' On My Mind'; 'Steppin' Out'; 'It Ain't Right'.

(John Mayall with Eric Clapton) [with the Bluesbreakers]

December 1966   **Fresh Cream**
'NSU'; 'Sleepy Time Time'; 'Dreaming'; 'Sweet Wine'; 'Spoonful'. 'Cat's Squirrel'; 'Four Until Late'; 'Rollin' and Tumblin''; 'I'm So Glad'; 'Toad'.

(Cream)

* Williamson solo

† Eric is known not to have played on this.

November 1967   **Disraeli Gears**
'STRANGE BREW'; 'SUNSHINE OF YOUR LOVE'; 'World of Pain';
'Dance the Night Away'; 'Blue Condition'. 'TALES OF BRAVE
ULYSSES'; 'SWLABR'; 'We're Going Wrong'; 'OUTSIDE WOMAN
BLUES'; 'Take It Back'; 'MOTHER'S LAMENT'.

(Cream)

August 1968   **Wheels of Fire**
'White Room'; 'Sitting On Top of the World'; 'Passing the Time'; 'As
You Said'. 'Pressed Rat and Warthog'; 'Politician'; 'Those Were the
Days'; 'Born Under a Bad Sign'; 'Deserted Cities of the Heart'.
'Crossroads'; 'Spoonful'. 'Traintime'; 'Toad'.

(Cream)

March 1969   **Goodbye**
'I'm So Glad'; 'Politician'. 'Sitting On Top of the World'; 'BADGE';
'Doing That Scrapyard Thing'; 'What a Bringdown'.

(Cream)

August 1969   **Blind Faith**
'Had To Cry Today'; 'Can't Find My Way Home'; 'Well All Right';
'PRESENCE OF THE LORD'. 'Sea of Joy'; 'Do What You Like'.

(Blind Faith)

June 1970   **Live Cream**
'NSU'; 'Sleepy Time Time'; 'LAWDY MAMA'. 'Sweet Wine'; 'Rollin'
and Tumblin''.

(Cream)

August 1970   **Eric Clapton**
'SLUNKY'; 'BAD BOY'; 'Told You for the Last Time'; 'After Mid-
night'; 'EASY NOW'; 'BLUES POWER'. 'BOTTLE OF RED WINE';
'LOVIN' YOU LOVIN' ME'; 'Lonesome and a Long Way From
Home'; 'DON'T KNOW WHY'; 'LET IT RAIN'.

(Eric Clapton)

December 1970   **Layla, and Other Assorted Love Songs**
'I LOOKED AWAY'; 'BELL BOTTOM BLUES'; 'KEEP ON GROW-
ING'; 'Nobody Knows You (When You're Down and Out)'. 'I AM
YOURS'; 'ANYDAY'; 'Key to the Highway'. 'TELL THE TRUTH';
'WHY DOES LOVE GOT TO BE SO SAD?'; 'Have You Ever Loved a
Woman?'. 'Little Wing'; 'It's Too Late'; 'LAYLA'; 'Thorn Tree in the
Garden'.

(Derek and the Dominos)

June 1972   **Live Cream Volume 2**
'Deserted Cities of the Heart'; 'White Room'; 'Politician'; 'TALES OF
BRAVE ULYSSES'. 'SUNSHINE OF YOUR LOVE'; 'Steppin' Out'.

(Cream)

March 1973   **Derek and the Dominos – Live in Concert**
'WHY DOES LOVE GOT TO BE SO SAD?'; 'GOT TO GET BETTER
IN A LITTLE WHILE'. 'LET IT RAIN'; 'PRESENCE OF THE LORD'.
'TELL THE TRUTH'; 'BOTTLE OF RED WINE'. 'ROLL IT OVER';
'BLUES POWER'; 'Have You Ever Loved a Woman?'

(Derek and the Dominos)

September 1973   **Eric Clapton's Rainbow Concert**
'BADGE'; 'ROLL IT OVER'; 'PRESENCE OF THE LORD'. 'Pearly
Queen'; 'After Midnight'; 'Little Wing'.

(Eric Clapton)

August 1974   **461 Ocean Boulevard**
'MOTHERLESS CHILDREN'; 'GIVE ME STRENGTH'; 'Willie and
the Hand Jive'; 'GET READY'; 'I Shot the Sheriff'. 'I Can't Hold Out
Much Longer'; 'Please Be With Me'; 'LET IT GROW'; 'STEADY
ROLLIN' MAN'; 'Mainline Florida'.

(Eric Clapton)

April 1975   **There's One in Every Crowd**
'WE'VE BEEN TOLD (JESUS COMING SOON)'; 'SWING LOW
SWEET CHARIOT'; 'Little Rachel'; 'DON'T BLAME ME'; 'The Sky Is
Crying'. 'Singin' the Blues'; 'BETTER MAKE IT THROUGH TODAY';
'PRETTY BLUE EYES'; 'HIGH'; 'OPPOSITES'.

(Eric Clapton)

September 1975   **E.C. Was Here**
'Have You Ever Loved a Woman?'; 'PRESENCE OF THE LORD';
'Drifting Blues'. 'Can't Find My Way Home'; 'RAMBLIN' ON MY
MIND'; 'Further On Up the Road'.

(Eric Clapton)

August 1976   **No Reason to Cry**
'Beautiful Thing'; 'CARNIVAL'; 'Sign Language'; 'COUNTY JAIL
BLUES'; 'ALL OUR PAST TIMES'. 'HELLO OLD FRIEND'; 'DOUBLE
TROUBLE'; 'INNOCENT TIMES'; 'Hungry'; 'BLACK SUMMER
RAIN'.

(Eric Clapton)

November 1977 **Slowhand**
'Cocaine'; 'WONDERFUL TONIGHT'; 'LAY DOWN SALLY'; 'NEXT TIME YOU SEE HER'; 'We're All the Way'. 'THE CORE'; 'May You Never'; 'MEAN OLD FRISCO'; 'PEACHES AND DIESEL'.

(Eric Clapton)

November 1978 **Backless**
'Walk Out in the Rain'; 'WATCH OUT FOR LUCY'; 'I'll Make Love to You Anytime'; 'ROLL IT'; 'TELL ME THAT YOU LOVE ME'. 'If I Don't Be There by Morning'; 'EARLY IN THE MORNING'; 'Promises'; 'GOLDEN RING'; 'Tulsa Time'.

(Eric Clapton and His Band)

May 1980 **Just One Night**
'Tulsa Time'; 'EARLY IN THE MORNING'; 'LAY DOWN SALLY'; 'WONDERFUL TONIGHT'. 'If I Don't Be There by Morning'; 'Worried Life Blues'; 'ALL OUR PAST TIMES'; 'After Midnight'. 'Double Trouble'; 'Setting Me Up'; 'BLUES POWER'. 'RAMBLIN' ON MY MIND'; 'Cocaine'; 'Further On Up the Road'.

(Eric Clapton)

February 1981 **Another Ticket**
'SOMETHING SPECIAL'; 'Black Rose'; 'Blow Wind Blow'; 'ANOTHER TICKET'; 'I CAN'T STAND IT'. 'HOLD ME LORD'; 'Floating Bridge'; 'CATCH ME IF YOU CAN'; 'RITA MAE'.

(Eric Clapton and His Band)

February 1983 **Money and Cigarettes**
'Everybody Oughta Make a Change'; 'THE SHAPE YOU'RE IN'; 'AIN'T GOING DOWN'; '(I've Got a) Rock 'n' Roll Heart'; 'MAN OVERBOARD'. 'PRETTY GIRL'; 'MAN IN LOVE'; 'Crosscut Saw'; 'SLOW DOWN LINDA'; 'Crazy Country Hop'.

(Eric Clapton)

March 1985 **Behind the Sun**
'SHE'S WAITING'; 'See What Love Can Do'; 'SAME OLD BLUES'; 'Knock On Wood'; 'Something's Happening'. 'Forever Man'; 'IT ALL DEPENDS'; 'Tangled In Love'; 'NEVER MAKE YOU CRY'; 'JUST LIKE A PRISONER'; 'BEHIND THE SUN'.

(Eric Clapton)

MISCELLANEOUS

Blind Faith
June 1969   **Promotional record (single)**
Instead of issuing cards to notify the press of their change of address
in London, Island Records sent out a special single, limited to 500
copies, featuring Blind Faith performing an untitled instrumental
jam, commercially unreleased before or since. The new address was
printed on the record label.

Eric Clapton with miscellaneous musicians
June 1966   **What's Shakin'? (LP)**
A various artists' compilation containing three tracks by a one-off
studio band, Eric Clapton and the Powerhouse: Eric Clapton (guitar);
Jack Bruce (bass); Paul Jones (harmonica); Steve Winwood
(keyboards); Pete York (drums). They perform three songs: 'I Want to
Know'; 'Crossroads'; 'Steppin' Out'.

April 1968   **Blues Anytime Vol.1 (LP)**
An Immediate label compilation featuring three of the seven tracks
recorded in 1966 by Eric Clapton (guitar) with Jimmy Page (guitar),
Mick Jagger (harmonica), Bill Wyman (bass), Ian Stewart (piano) and
Chris Winters (drums). The tracks are 'SNAKE DRIVE'; 'TRIBUTE
TO ELMORE'; 'WEST COAST IDEA'. (Note: This album also con-
tains both sides of the John Mayall [and the Bluesbreakers] October
1965 single 'I'm Your Witch Doctor'/'Telephone Blues' *(qv).)*

May 1968   **Blues Anytime Vol.2 (LP)**
A second compilation, containing three more tracks from the above-
detailed 1966 session: 'DRAGGIN' MY TAIL'; 'FREIGHT LOADER';
'CHOKER', plus a previously unreleased John Mayall and the Bluesbreakers track featuring Eric Clapton *(qv)*.

November 1968   **Blues Anytime Vol.3 (LP)**
The third and final compilation, apart from the plethora of subsequent reissues and repackaging, contains the seventh and last all-star
track: 'MILES ROAD'.

May 1975   **Prime Cuts (10" maxi-single disc)**
An unusual sampler disc, more like a mini-album, commercially
released by RSO Records and featuring tracks by artists on the label's
roster. A previously unissued live recording of 'SMILE' by Eric
Clapton is included.

May 1982   **(12″ single)**
The 12″ pressing of a single featuring two rereleased tracks, 'I Shot
the Sheriff' and 'Cocaine', contains a previously unreleased bonus
live version of 'Knockin' On Heaven's Door', recorded in Tokyo in
December 1979 but left off the *Just One Night* double album.

Cream
March 1975   **Cream (LP)**
A re-release, with a new title, of the *Fresh Cream* album *(qv)*, but also
containing two bonus tracks, 'Wrapping Paper' and 'The Coffee
Song', the second of which had only previously been available in
France.

Derek and the Dominos
September 1970   **'TELL THE TRUTH'/'ROLL IT OVER' (single)**
This first offering from Derek and the Dominos, produced by Phil
Spector, was withdrawn just days after release. 'TELL THE TRUTH'
eventually resurfaced on the double-album compilation *History of
Eric Clapton (qv)*, while 'ROLL IT OVER' remains unreleased,
although a different version of the song, recorded live, appears on
the album *Derek and the Dominos – Live in Concert (qv)*.

July 1972   **History of Eric Clapton (LP)**
A double-album compilation which also includes two previously
unreleased Derek and the Dominos tracks: 'TELL THE TRUTH',
produced by Phil Spector (see above) and 'TELL THE TRUTH–JAM'.

John Mayall
May 1968   **Blues Anytime Vol.2 (LP)**
This Immediate label compilation (see p.210) also includes a John
Mayall and the Bluesbreakers track, 'On Top of the World', recorded
at the sessions which produced the October 1965 single 'I'm Your
Witch Doctor'/'Telephone Blues' *(qv)* but which had been previously
unreleased.

September 1969   **Looking Back (LP)**
A John Mayall compilation, including one previously unreleased
track which features Eric Clapton on guitar: 'They Call It Stormy
Monday'.

April 1983   **Primal Solos (LP)**
Another John Mayall compilation, Side One of which comprises a
live recording, previously unissued, from the Flamingo Club, London, dated April 1966, with Mayall (piano), Eric Clapton (guitar), Jack

Bruce (bass) and Hughie Flint (drums). The tracks are: 'Maudie'; 'It Hurts to Be In Love'; 'Have You Ever Loved a Woman?'; 'Bye Bye Bird'; 'I'm Your Hoochie Coochie Man'. (Note: This album was released in the USA in September 1977.)

The Yardbirds
September 1965   **Heart Full of Soul (LP)**
This Capitol of Canada Yardbirds album contains an alternative version of 'A Certain Girl', unissued elsewhere.

June 1971   **Remember . . . (LP)**
A Yardbirds compilation which contains an alternative version of 'I Wish You Would', otherwise unreleased in Britain.

May 1972   **Rock Generation – Volume 5 (LP)**
A various artists' compilation, released only in France, containing three further Yardbirds tracks, unissued elsewhere, which feature Eric on guitar: 'Slow Walk'; 'Yardbirds Beat'; 'My Little Cabin'.

March 1974   **History of British Blues (LP)**
A various artists' compilation, released only in the USA, including an otherwise unavailable recording of the Yardbirds, with Eric Clapton, playing 'Baby What's Wrong'.

November 1984   **The Yardbirds – Shapes of Things (7-LP box set)**
An attempt to house, in one collection, most of the myriad alternative versions, unreleased and erratically released Yardbirds material spanning both the Eric Clapton line-up (1963–65) and some of the band's later work (1965 and 1966). Instead of having to scrabble around for obscure and multifarious French and West German albums, each containing one or two rarities, this boxed set presents collectors with almost every Yardbirds track from these years released anywhere in the world (the only exceptions are those listed above), plus previously unissued material. In addition to the regularly released Eric Clapton-period Yardbirds material detailed elsewhere in this discography, this box set contains the following other tracks/alternative versions which feature Eric on guitar: 'Smokestack Lightnin'' (live); 'You Can't Judge a Book by the Cover' (live); 'I'm Talking About You' (studio); 'Let It Rock' (live); 'I Wish You Would' (live); 'Boom Boom' (studio); 'Honey in Your Hips' (two versions: one studio, one live); 'Who Do You Love' (live); 'The River Rhine' (live); 'A Lost Care' (live); 'Putty (in Your Hands)' (studio); 'Sweet Music' (studio); 'Good Morning Little Schoolgirl' (two more different studio takes); 'GOT TO HURRY' (two more different studio takes).

GUEST APPEARANCES/SESSION WORK

Duane Allman
An Anthology, released December 1972. Eric plays on 'Mean Old World'. (Note: Derek and the Dominos' 'Layla' is also included on this album by virtue of Allman's guest role on guitar.)

Ashton, Gardner and Dyke
The Worst of Ashton, Gardner and Dyke, released February 1971. (Issued in the USA September 1970 as **Ashton, Gardner and Dyke**.) Eric plays on 'I'm Your Spiritual Breadman'.

The Band and Friends
The Last Waltz, released April 1978. Eric plays on 'Further On Up the Road', 'I Shall Be Released' and an untitled 1 minute 29 seconds jam at the end of Side Five of this triple album.

The Beatles
The Beatles, released November 1968. Eric plays on 'While My Guitar Gently Weeps'.

Marc Benno
Lost in Austin, released June 1979. Eric plays on 'Hotfoot Blues'; 'Chasin' Rainbows'; 'Me and a Friend of Mine'; 'New Romance'; 'Last Train'; 'Lost in Austin'; 'Splish Splash'; 'Monterey Pen'; 'The Drifter'; 'Hey There Senorita'.

Stephen Bishop
Careless, released December 1976. Eric plays on 'Sinking in an Ocean of Tears'; 'Save It for a Rainy Day'.
Red Cab to Manhattan, released October 1980. Eric plays on 'Little Moon'; 'Sex Kittens Go to College'.

Gary Brooker
Eric plays on 'Leave the Candle', the A-side of a single released April 1980.
Lead Me to the Water, released March 1982. Eric plays on the title track, 'Lead Me to the Water'.

Joe Cocker
Stingray, released June 1976. Eric plays on 'Worrier'.

Phil Collins
Face Value, released February 1981. Eric plays on 'If Leving Me Is Easy'.

Corey Hart
Corey Hart, released June 1984 (USA only). Eric plays on 'Jenny Fey'.

The Crickets
Rockin' 50's Rock 'n' Roll, released February 1971. Eric plays on 'Rockin' 50's Rock 'n' Roll'; 'That'll Be the Day'.

Roger Daltrey
One of the Boys, released May 1977. Although Eric is credited on the album's inner sleeve under the 'Special Thanks To . . .' section and not under the 'Musicians' credits, he remembers playing on the sessions, but not the title of any particular song. The full track line-up is as follows: 'Parade'; 'Single Man's Dilemma'; 'Avenging Annie'; 'The Prisoner'; 'Leon'. 'One of the Boys'; 'Giddy'; 'Say It Ain't So, Joe'; 'Satin and Lace'; 'Doing It All Again'.

Rick Danko
Rick Danko, released January 1978. Eric plays on 'New Mexicoe'.

Jesse Davis
Jesse Davis, released April 1971. Eric plays on 'Reno Street Incident'; 'Tulsa County'; 'Washita Love Child'; 'Every Night is Saturday Night'; 'You Bella Donna You'; 'Rock and Roll Gypsies'; 'Golden Sun Goddess'; 'Crazy Love'.

Delaney & Bonnie
Eric plays on the studio single 'COMIN' HOME'/'Groupie (Superstar)', released December 1969.
Delaney & Bonnie on Tour with Eric Clapton, released June 1970. Eric plays on all tracks. 'Things Get Better'; 'Poor Elijah/Tribute to Robert Johnson'; 'Only You Know and I Know'; 'I Don't Want to Discuss It'. 'That's What My Man Is For'; 'Where There's a Will There's a Way'; 'COMIN' HOME'; 'Long Tall Sally/Jenny Jenny/The Girl Can't Help It/Tutti Frutti'.

Danny Douma
Night Eyes, released August 1979 (USA only). Eric plays on 'Hate You'.

Dr John [The Night Tripper]
The Sun, Moon and Herbs, released November 1971. Eric plays on 'Black John the Conqueror'; 'Where Ya at Mule?'; 'Craney Crow'; 'Pots On Fiyo (File Gumbo)/Who I Got to Fall On (If the Pot Get Heavy)?'; 'Zu Zu Mamou'; 'Familiar Reality (Reprise)'.
Hollywood Be Thy Name, released November 1975. Eric plays congas on 'Reggae Doctor'.

Champion Jack Dupree
From New Orleans to Chicago, released April 1966. Eric plays on 'Third Degree'; 'Shim-Sham-Shimmy'.
Raw Blues, a various artists' compilation album, released January 1967, contains another Dupree track on which Eric plays, 'Calcutta Blues'. (Note: This album also contains 'Pretty Girls Everywhere' by Otis Spann (*qv*) and both sides of the August 1966 single by John Mayall and Eric Clapton, 'Lonely Years'/'Bernard Jenkins' (*qv*)).

Bob Dylan
Desire, released January 1976. Eric plays on 'Romance in Durango'.

Aretha Franklin
Lady Soul, released April 1968. Eric plays on 'Good To Me As I Am To You'.

Kinky Friedman
Lasso from El Paso, released February 1977. (November 1976 in USA). Eric plays on 'Kinky'; 'Ol' Ben Lucas'.

Buddy Guy & Junior Wells
Play the Blues, released July 1971. Eric plays on 'A Man of Many Words'; 'My Baby She Left Me (She Left Me a Mule to Ride)'; 'Come On In This House'; 'Have Mercy Baby'; 'T-Bone Shuffle'; 'A Poor Man's Plea'; 'Messin' with the Kid'; 'I Don't Know'; 'Bad Bad Whiskey'.

George Harrison
Wonderwall Music by George Harrison, released November 1968. Although unnamed in the long list of musician credits, Eric remembers playing on the sessions for this soundtrack album, but not any particular tracks. The full track line-up, only a few of which feature Western instruments, is as follows: 'Microbes'; 'Red Lady Too'; 'Tabla and Pakavaj'; 'In the Park'; 'Drilling a Home'; 'Guru Vandana'; 'Greasy Legs'; 'Ski-ing'; 'Gat Kirwani'; 'Dream Scene'. 'Party Seacombe'; 'Love Scene'; 'Crying'; 'Cowboy Music'; 'Fantasy Sequins'; 'On the Bed'; 'Glass Box'; 'Wonderwall to Be Here'; 'Singing Om'.
All Things Must Pass, released November 1970. Eric plays on nine of the twenty-three tracks on this triple album: 'Wah-Wah'; 'Isn't It a Pity (Version One)'; 'What Is Life'; 'Run of the Mill'; 'Beware of Darkness'; 'Awaiting On You All'; 'Plug Me In'; 'I Remember Jeep'; 'Thanks for the Pepperoni'.
George Harrison, released February 1979. Eric plays on 'Love Comes to Everyone'.

Howlin' Wolf
The London Howlin' Wolf Sessions, released August 1971. Eric plays on 'Rockin' Daddy'; 'I Ain't Superstitious'; 'Sittin' On Top of the World'; 'Worried About My Baby'; 'What a Woman'; 'Poor Boy'; 'Built for Comfort'; 'Who's Been Talking?'; 'The Red Rooster'; 'Do the Do'; 'Highway 49'; 'Wang-Dang-Doodle'.
London Revisited, released October 1974 (USA only). (Album credited to Muddy Waters and Howlin' Wolf although each artists' songs are entirely separate.) Eric plays on Howlin' Wolf's 'Going Down Slow'; 'The Killing Floor'; 'I Want to Have a Word with You'.

I Jah Man
Haile I Hymn (Chapter One), released May 1978. Although the guitar credits for this album are obscure Eric remembers playing at the sessions. The album contains four tracks: 'Jah Heavy Load'; 'Jah Is No Secret'. 'Zion Hut'; 'I'm a Levi'.

Jonathan Kelly
Eric plays on 'Don't You Believe It?', the A-side of a single released June 1970.

Bobby Keys
Bobby Keys, released July 1972. Eric plays on 'Steal from a King'; 'Bootleg'; 'Command Performance'; 'Crispy Duck'.

King Curtis & Friends
Eric plays on 'Teasin'', the A-side of a single released July 1970.

Freddie King
Burglar, released November 1974. Eric plays on 'Sugar Sweet'.
Freddie King (1934–1976), released October 1977. Posthumous collection of King's work, including 'Sugar Sweet' (see above), plus other tracks on which Eric plays: 'TV Mama'; 'Gambling Woman Blues'; 'Further On Up the Road'.

Alexis Korner
The Party Album, released March 1980 (West Germany only). Eric plays on 'Hey, Pretty Mama'; 'Hi-Heel Sneakers'; 'They Call It Stormy Monday'.

Corky Laing
Makin' It On the Street, released May 1977. Eric plays on 'On My Way (by the River)'.

Ronnie Lane (see also Pete Townshend/Ronnie Lane)
See Me, released July 1980. Eric plays on 'Lad's Got Money'; 'BARCELONA'; 'Way Up Yonder'.

Brenda Lee
Eric plays on the A-side of the single 'Is It True', released August 1964.

Jackie Lomax
Is This What You Want?, released March 1969. Eric plays on 'Sour Milk Sea'.
Eric also plays on the A-side of the single 'New Day', released May 1969.

Arthur Louis
Eric plays on both sides of the August 1975 single 'Knockin' On Heaven's Door'/'Plum'.
Eric plays on both sides of the June 1978 single 'Knockin' On Heaven's Door'*/'The Dealer'.
Eric plays on both sides of the July 1981 single 'Still It Feels Good'/'Come On and Love Me'.
Arthur Louis' First Album, released August 1975 (Japan only), contains all the tracks from the above UK singles, plus two others on which Eric plays, 'Train 444'; 'Go and Make It Happen'.

Christine McVie
Christine McVie, released February 1984. Eric plays on 'The Challenge'.

John Martyn
Glorious Fool, released September 1981. Eric plays on 'Couldn't Love You More'.

John Mayall
Back to the Roots, released June 1971. Eric plays on 'Prisons On the Road'; 'Accidental Suicide'; 'Home Again'; 'Looking at Tomorrow'; 'Force of Nature'; 'Goodbye December'.

The Mothers of Invention (see also Francis Vincent [Frank] Zappa)
We're Only in It for the Money, released June 1968. Eric's spoken voice can be heard on two tracks, 'Are You Hung Up'; 'Nasal Retentive Caliope Music'.

Shawn Phillips
Contribution, released June 1970. Eric plays on 'Man Whole Covered Wagon'.

Plastic Ono Band
Eric plays on the studio versions of 'Cold Turkey' and 'Don't Worry Kyoko (Mummy's Only Looking for Her Hand in the Snow)', released as a single October 1969.

* Same version as the August 1975 single.

Live Peace in Toronto 1969, released December 1969. Eric plays on all tracks. 'Blue Suede Shoes'; 'Money (That's What I Want)'; 'Dizzy Miss Lizzy'; 'Yer Blues'; 'Cold Turkey'; 'Give Peace a Chance'. 'Don't Worry Kyoko (Mummy's Only Looking for Her Hand in the Snow)'; 'John John (Let's Hope for Peace)'.

Some Time in New York City, released September 1972 (June 1972 in USA). Eric plays on Side Three of this double album, recorded live in London on 15 December 1969. 'Cold Turkey'; 'Don't Worry Kyoko (Mummy's Only Looking for Her Hand in the Snow)'.

Billy Preston
That's the Way God Planned It, released August 1969. Eric plays on 'That's the Way God Planned It (Parts 1 & 2)'. (Note: A substantially edited version of this song was trailered as a single in June 1969.)
Encouraging Words, released September 1970. Eric plays on 'Right Now'; 'Encouraging Words'.

Leon Russell
Leon Russell, released April 1970. Eric plays on 'Prince of Peace'.
Leon Russell and the Shelter People, released June 1971. Eric plays on 'Beware of Darkness'; 'Alcatraz'.

Otis Spann
Eric plays on 'Stirs Me Up', the A-side of a single released September 1964.
Blues Now, a various artists' compilation album released July 1965, contains 'Stirs Me Up' (see above) and another Otis Spann track on which Eric plays, 'Pretty Girls Everywhere'.

Vivian Stanshall and the Sean Head Showband
Eric plays on both sides of the single 'Labio-Dental Fricative'/'Paper Round', released February 1970. (Note: A remixed version of 'Labio-Dental Fricative' appears on the May 1974 album *The History of the Bonzos* by the Bonzo Dog Band, of which Stanshall was a founder-member).

Stephen Stills
Stephen Stills, released November 1970. Eric plays on 'Go Back Home'.
Stephen Stills 2, released July 1971. Eric plays on 'Fishes and Scorpions'.

Ringo Starr
Ringo's Rotogravure, released September 1976. Eric plays on 'THIS BE CALLED A SONG'.

Old Wave, released June 1983 (in West Germany, Canada and Brazil but not in the UK or USA). Eric plays on 'EVERYBODY'S IN A HURRY BUT ME'.

Pete Townshend/Ronnie Lane
Rough Mix, released September 1977. Eric plays on 'Rough Mix'; 'Annie'; 'April Fool'; 'Till the Rivers All Run Dry'.

Doris Troy
Eric plays on 'Get Back', the B-side of a single released August 1970 (the A-side being 'Jacob's Ladder').
Doris Troy, released September 1970. Eric's contribution unspecified, and difficult to recall personally, but he played on about five of the following thirteen tracks: 'Ain't That Cute'; 'Special Care'; 'Give Me Back My Dynamite'; 'You Tore Me Up Inside'; 'Games People Play'; 'Gonna Get My Baby Back'; 'I've Got to Be Strong'. 'Hurry'; 'So Far'; 'Exactly Like You'; 'You Give Me Joy Joy'; 'Don't Call Me No More'; 'Jacob's Ladder'*.

Martha Veléz
Fiends and Angels, released June 1969. Eric plays on 'I'm Gonna Leave You'; 'It Takes a Lot to Laugh, It Takes a Train to Cry'.

Roger Waters
The Pros and Cons of Hitch-Hiking, released April 1984. Eric plays on all tracks. '4.30am (Apparently They Were Travelling Abroad)'; '4.33am (Running Shoes)'; '4.37am (Arabs With Knives and West German Skies)'; '4.39am (For the First Time Today – Part 2)'; '4.41am (Sexual Revolution)'; '4.47am (The Remains of Our Love)'. '4.50am (Go Fishing)'; '4.56am (For the First Time Today – Part 1)'; '4.58am (Dunromin, Duncarin, Dunlivin)'; '5.01am (The Pros and Cons of Hitch-Hiking)'; '5.06am (Every Stranger's Eyes)'; '5.11am (The Moment of Clarity)'.

Bobby Whitlock
Raw Velvet, released December 1972. Eric plays on 'Hello LA, Bye Bye Birmingham'; 'The Dreams of a Hobo'.

Francis Vincent [Frank] Zappa
Lumpy Gravy, released October 1968. Eric is credited as a member of The Chorus on this album although he cannot recall any sessions. The LP contains just two, lengthy, tracks: 'Lumpy Gravy Part One'; 'Lumpy Gravy Part Two'.

---

* Eric is known not to have played on this.

VARIOUS ARTISTS' ALBUMS

The Concert for Bangla Desh, released January 1972. Eric plays on 'Wah-Wah'; 'My Sweet Lord'; 'Awaiting On You All'; 'That's the Way God Planned It'; 'It Don't Come Easy'; 'Beware of Darkness'; 'While My Guitar Gently Weeps'; 'Jumping Jack Flash/Youngblood/ Jumping Jack Flash'; 'Something'; 'Bangla Desh'.

Music from Free Creek, released May 1973. Eric plays on 'Road Song'; 'Getting Back to Molly'; 'No One Knows'.

Tommy (Original Soundtrack Recording), released July 1975. Eric plays on 'Eyesight for the Blind'; 'Sally Simpson'.

White Mansions – A Tale from the American Civil War 1861–1865, released May 1978. Eric receives a general credit on the album sleeve but remembers playing on 'White Trash'.

The Secret Policeman's Other Ball – The Music, released March 1982. Eric plays on ''Cause We Ended As Lovers'; 'Further On Up the Road'; 'Crossroads'; 'I Shall Be Released'.

Water (Original Soundtrack Recording), released May 1985. Eric plays on 'FREEDOM'.

INDEX

Page numbers in *italic* refer to the illustrations

Alcoholics Anonymous (AA), 147, 152, 154, 198-202, 203
All Things Must Pass, 80, 158
Allman, Duane, 242, 244, 246
Allman Brothers, 252
L'Angelo Misterioso, 156
Animals, 130
Another Ticket, 250, 252
Apple Records, 66, 80
Armani, Giorgio, 192
ARMS (Action Research into Multiple Schlerosis), *253*, 259, *273*
Asher, Jane, 158
Atlantic Records, 72, 95

Baba, Meher, 89
Backless, 249
Baez, Joan, 12
Baker, Ginger, 47-66, *55*, *64*, 67-70, *69*, 71, 72-5, 214, 235-6, *240-1*
Balding, Toby, 108-10
The Band, 175, 226, 244, 248
Barberstown Castle Hotel, County Kildare, 141, 194
Barrett, Syd, 89
Basie, Count, 2, 21
Beatles, 9, 10, 18, 43, 53, 66, 67, 79, 80, 89, 157-8, 160, 164, 168, 183, 222
Beck, Jeff, 16, 22, 183, 236, *253*, 259, *273*
Bee Gees, 61, 120, 138
Behind the Sun, 219, 259, 260-1, 268, 271-2
Berry, Chuck, 10, 18, 217, 219

Big Roll Band, 46
Bilk, Acker, 62
Bishop, Stephen, 192, 219
Blind Faith, 70, 71-6, 80, 84, 117, 156, 203-4, 239, *240-1*, 262
Bloomfield, Mike, 22, 60
Blue Flames, 46
Blue Horizon Records, 224
Blues Incorporated, 46, 62
Blues Project, 58
Bluesbreakers, 20-2, *23*, 44, 47, 238
Bluesbreakers, 234-5, 248
Booker T and the MGs, 252, 255
Boyd, Jenny, 167, 174, 183, 222
Boyd, Paula, 90, 91, 138, 158, 161, 162
Boyer, Charles Scott, 246
Bramlett, Bonnie, 70, 75, 80, *81*, 232, 239, 262
Bramlett, Delaney, 70, 75, 80, *81*, 232, 239, 242, 262
Brooker, Gary, 130-2, 137, 202, 204-6, 207, 216-17, 250, 252-4
Brooks, Elkie, 230
Broonzy, Big Bill, 9, 18, 32, 39
Brown, James, 58, 59
Brown, Pete, 62, 66
Bruce, Jack, 21, 47-66, *55*, *64*, 67-70, *69*, 72, 183, 214, 235-6
Buffalo Springfield, 67
Butterfield, Paul, 60

Café Au Go-Go, New York, 59
Caine, Michael, 270
Cale, J.J., 242

Capaldi, Jim, 94
Carroll, Nigel, 133, 136, 138-41, 145, 146, 182, 186-7, 191, 195, 207, 258
Casey Jones and the Engineers, 20
Cass and the Cassanovas, 20
Cassar, Brian, 20
Charles, Ray, 22, 235
Chas and Dave, 212-13
Chess Studios, Chicago, 236
Christianity, 100, 203-4
Church of England, 203
Clapp, Jack (Eric's grandfather), 26, 27, 28, 32, 33, 37-8, 39-40, 79, 83, 84, 173
Clapp, Rose (Eric's grandmother), 26, 27, 28-32, 29, 33, 34, 36-42, 79, 83, 88, 92, 108, 114, 116, 144, 173, 183-4, 217, 234
Clapton, Adrian, 31-3, 37, 51, 88
Clapton, Pattie, 6-8, 84, 90-2, 102, 106, 111, 115-16, 118-20, 125, 132-7, 140, 142, 145-7, 150-2, 155-90, *159*, *165*, *171*, *189*, 206-8, *209*, 214, 216, 222-3, 265, 271-2
Clapton, Reginald, 27, 28
Clapton, Sylvia, 31
Coasters, 217
Cocker, Joe, 94, 129, 230, 259, *273*
Collins, Mel, 216, 258
Collins, Phil, 124, 146, 213, 260-2, *263*, 268, 272
Coltrane, John, 269
Columbia records, 20
Compass Point studios, 252, 255
Concert for Bangladesh, 83, 86, 168
Cooder, Ry, 255
Cook's Ferry Inn, Edmonton, 212
Crawdaddy Club, 10, 39, 232
Cream, 22, 46, 48-66, *55*, *64*, 67-70, *69*, 71, 75-6, 84, 89, 117, 120, 130, 138, 156, 222, 235-8, *et passim*

Daily Mail, 175, 181
Daily Mirror, 72
Dallas, Ian, 78, 161
Daltrey, Roger, 207
de Burgh, Chris, 16
Dempster, Nigel, 175
Derek and the Dominos, 70-1, 80-2, 83, 84, 86, 89, 92, 106, 116, 161, 162, 239, 242, 246, 262
Derek and the Dominos – Live in

Concert, 245
Dickson, Lee, 219
Diddley, Bo, 10, 18, 246
Dire Straits, 223
Disraeli Gears, 61, 64, 236-8
Dixon, Willie, 236
Donegan, Lonnie, 183
Dortmund, 30
Dowd, Tom, 116, 117, 122, 248, 252, 255, 256-8
Downbeat magazine, 14
Dreja, Chris, 16
Dunn, Duck, 255, 266
Dupree, Champion Jack, 18
Dylan, Bob, 20-1, 44, 59, 83, 230-2, 248-9

E.C. Was Here, 248
Electric Flag, 60
Elliman, Yvonne, 117, 121, 245, *247*, 248
Ellington, Duke, 21
EMI Recording studios, 158
Epstein, Brian, 89, 120, 158
Eric Clapton, 80, 239-42
Eric Clapton At His Best, 245
Eric Clapton's Rolling Hotel (film), 137-8
Ertegun, Ahmet, 95
Esquire records, 19
Estes, Sleepy John, 250, 255
Everly Brothers, 228

Fairweather-Low, Andy, 259
Faithfull, Marianne, 72, 118-20
Fame, Georgie, 46, *215*
Family, 71
Farlowe, Chris, 22
Ferrari Owners' Club, 187
Flamingo Club, London, 46
Fleetwood, Mick, 167
Fleetwood Mac, 21
Flint, Hughie, 21
Flynn, Delia, 142
Forrester, Roger, 120-2, 126, 128, 129, 137-42, *143*, 144-5, 146-7, 152, 167, 172, 175-81, 182, 183, 187, 192-4, 195-8, 206, 208, 210, 223, 226, 254-5, 258, 265
461 Ocean Boulevard, 116, 118, 120, 121-2, 167, 195, 218-19, 245-6, 272
Fraboni, Myel, 174, 181

Fraboni, Rob, 174-5, 181, 182
Franklin, Aretha, 252, 255
Fresh Cream, 64, 222, 236
Friar Park, Oxfordshire, 6, 115, 158, 160, 163, 166-7, 170
Fryer, Edward (Eric's father), 27, 31

Gallagher, Rory, 94
Galuten, Albhy, 117, 245
Genesis, 124, 146, 261
Gibbs, Christopher, 78-9
Gomelsky, Giorgio, 10, 14, 15-16, 40
Goodbye, 65, 238
Gordon, Jim, 80, 162, 244
Gouldman, Graham, 15
Graham, Bill, 59
Graham Bond Organisation, 46, 47, 48-50, 53, 62
Grateful Dead, 60, 67
Grech, Rick, 71, 94, *240-1*
Guitar Player magazine, 213
Guy, Buddy, 50, 224, 234

Hampton, Lionel, 31
Hare Krishna sect, 163-4
Harlech, Lord, 78, 79, 93, 96-8, 100, 110
Harrison, George, 6-8, 66, 80, *81*, 83, 84, 86, 94, 115-16, 118, 138, 156-60, 163-7, 168, 170, 183, 188, 218, 222, 238
Hawkins, Roger, 255
Hazelden Foundation, 147-52
Head, Murray, 16
Hendrix, Jimi, 44, 59, 62, 66, 67, 82-3, 84, 89, 95, 106, 232, 238, 242, 244, 269
Herman's Hermits, 130
History of Eric Clapton, 245
Hitler, Adolf, 232
Holly, Buddy, 18, 33, 218
Hollyfield Road School, Surbiton, 33, 36-7
Hot Chocolate, 195
Howlin' Wolf, 236
Hurt, John, 6-8, 19, 122-4, 232, 270
Hurtwood Edge, Surrey, 78-9, 83, 84, 86-8, 89, 91, 92-3, 98, 99-102, 111, 114, 115, 116, 118, 122-6, 155, 157, 158, 160, 163, 167, 174-5, 183, 213

Jagger, Mick, 10, 43, 72, 79, 183

James, Cathy, 157, 161, 164
James, Elmore, 217, 246
Jan and Dean, 58
John, Elton, 94, 138
Johnny H, 195
Johns, Glyn, *215*, 249, 259
Johnson, Robert, 39, 112, 122, 235, 246
Jones, Brian, 18, 53, 89
Jones, Elvin, 47
Jones, Paul, 18
Joplin, Janis, 89, 106
Jupp, Mickey, 216
Just One Night, 250

Kenton, Stan, 31
Keys, Bobby, 80
King, Albert, 238, 255
King, B.B., 13, 224, 269
King, Freddie, *131*, 224, *227*, 228, 234, 235, 238
Kingston College of Art, 18, 33, 36-8, 39, 44
Kirk, Roland, 80
Knopfler, Mark, 223
Kooper, Al, 59
Korner, Alexis, 46, 62
Kramer, Carlo, 19

Laine, Frankie, 9
Lane, Katy, 216
Lane, Ronnie, 216, 259
The Last Waltz (film), 226, 248
Layla, and Other Assorted Love Songs, 92, 161-3, 222, 242-5, 248
Led Zeppelin, 16
Ledbetter, Huddie, 213
Lee, Albert, 132, 182, 213, 228, 250, 252, 255
Lennon, Cynthia, 158
Lennon, John, 43, 79-80, 158, 183
Lester, Richard, 157
Levy, Marcy, 248, 249, 272
Lightfoot, Terry, 62
Lippmann, Horst, 232
Little Walter, 10, 18
Lomax, Jackie, 66
Lovin' Spoonful, 67, 235

McCartney, Paul, 67, 158, 183, 213, 268
McCarty, Jim, 16

McDonald, Brian, 27-8, 167
McDonald, Cheryl, 27
McDonald, Frank, 27, 28-30
McDonald, Heather, 27
McDonald, Patricia Molly, *25*, 27-30, *29*, 32, 38, 40, 42, 88, 95, 107-8, 140, 145, 167, 183, 217
McGhee, Brownie, 9
McGuinness, Tom, 18-20
McLean, Jenny, 174-81, 183
McLean, Susie, 174
McNeny, Larry, 181-2
McVie, John, 21
Mad Dogs and Englishmen, 129
Maharishi Mahesh Yogi, 89, 164
Mann, Manfred, 18, 46, 50, 53
Markee, Dave, 132, 250, 252-4
Marley, Bob, 117, 246, 248
Marquee Club, London, 10, 13, 46
Martin, Charlotte, 61, 157
Mayall, John, 8, 13, 14, 20-2, *23*, 40, 44-6, 47, 50, 51, 53, 62, 67, 75, 76, 83, 88, 212, 224, 234, 246, 248, 270
Melody Maker, 52-3, 60, 65, *205*, 213
Metropolis Blues Quartet, 9, 10
Michael, Princess of Kent, *215*
Miles, Buddy, 80
Milligan, Spike, 33, 138
Miracles, 22
Mitchell, Guy, 9
Mlinaric, David, 78-9
Money, Zoot, 46
Money and Cigarettes, 252, 255-6, 261
Moon, Keith, *81*
Mothers of Invention, 59, 67
Murphy, Shaun, 272
Murray the K, 58-9, 64, 89
Music From Big Pink, 61, 175, 248

National Film Theatre, London, 138
National Jazz and Blues Festival, Windsor, 57
Newmark, Andy, 258
Nizami, 161
No Reason to Cry, 230, 248-9

O'Dell, Chris, 181
Oldaker, Jamie, 117, 182, 196, 245, 266
O'Leary, Alphi, 126-8, 129-30, 141, 182, 191, 198, 204
Olivier, Laurence, 138
Olympic Studios, 89

Ono, Yoko, 79-80
Ormsby-Gore, Alice, 78-9, 80, 83, 86-92, 93, 95, 96-102, 108, 111-14, 115-16, 118, 161, 163, 167, 170
Ormsby-Gore, Frank, 110-11
Otis, Johnny, 246, 255-6
Oz magazine, 61, 64

Page, Jimmy, 16, 94, 259, *273*
Palmer, Ben, 16, 18-19, 20, 53-4, 87, 138, 182, 183, 226, 270-1
Paramount Jazz Band, 62
Parker, Charlie, 106, 107, 269
Parrot Band, 217
Patterson, George, 98-9, 100-3, 105-10
Patterson, Dr Meg, 96-105, 106, 108-11, 117, 133, 202, 245, 268
Perrin, Sid, 137, 145, 183
Pickett, Wilson, 58
Pink Floyd, 89, 258
Plastic Ono Band, 79, *81*
Playboy magazine, 213
Plaza, Guildford, 51
Pleasance, Donald, 138
Ploughman, Sandra, 36
Powell, Enoch, 210-12
Presence of the Lord, 203-4
Presley, Elvis, 33
Preston, Billy, *81*, 248
Price, Jim, 80
Pridden, Bob, 89, 133
Procol Harum, 130
The Pros and Cons of Hitch-Hiking, 258
Pullen, Guy, 31, 33-6, 133, 137, 140, 183-4, 195
Puplett, Diana, 208
Pye International, 236
Pyke, Rex, 138

Radle, Carl, 80, 116, 117, 182, 183, 244, 245
Rainbow Hilton Hotel, Waikiki Beach, 196-8
Rainbow Theatre, London, 94-6, 98, *109*, 245
Rau, Fritz, 232-4
Reaction label, 64
Redding, Otis, 252, 255
Reed, Jimmy, 39
Relf, Keith, 9-10, *11*, 16, 22, 39
Rich, Buddy, 47

Richards, Keith, *135*
Ricky-Tick Clubs, 18, 50
Ripley Church of England Primary School, 32
Ripley Cricket Club, 36
RKO Theter, New York, 58
Robertson, Robbie, 226, 244, 248
Rock Against Racism, 210
Rock 'n' Roll Circus (film), 80
Rolling Stone magazine, 268
Rolling Stones, 9, 10, 18, 39, 43, 53, 72, 80, *135*
The Roosters, 18-20, 39, 53, 54, 271
Round Table (Cranleigh), 214-16
Royal Albert Hall, London, 67, *69*, 259
RSO, 120
Rush, Otis, 235, 248
Russell, Leon, 84, 129, 242
Ryder, Mitch, 58, 59

St Bede's Secondary Modern School, Send, 32, 33
Sam and Dave, 252
Samwell-Smith, Paul, 9-13, *11*, 14-18, 20, 230
Sanchez, Rev. Daniel, 182
Saville Theatre, London, 158
Scott, Ronnie, 62
Seamen, Phil, 47
Secombe, Harry, 33
Sellers, Peter, 33
Shadows, 12
Sharp, Martin, 61, 64, 230
Shaw, Robert, 138
Simon, Carly, 16
Simon and Garfunkel, 16, 58
Sims, Dick, 117, 182, 245
Sinatra, Frank, 53
Slowhand, 156, 249
Spann, Otis, 224
Speakeasy Club, London, 157
Spencer Davis Group, 13, 44-6, 71
Spinetti, Henry, 132, 250, 252
Stainton, Chris, 2, 128-9, 130, 132, 229-30, 250, 252-4, 266
Starr, Kay, 9
Starr, Maureen, 158
Starr, Ringo, 94, 158, 183
Station Hotel, Richmond, 39
Stevens, Cat, 16
Stigwood, Robert, 53, 57, 61, 64, 67, 68, 72, 75, 83, 93, 95, 100, 116, 120,

138, 162, 164, 235
Stills, Stephen, 80, 242
Stone, Sly, 82
Storyville Jazzmen, 62
Sumlin, Herbert, 234
Swallow, Roger, 214-16
Swan, Mr, 33
Sykes, Roosevelt, 18

Terry, George, 117, 245
Terry, Sonny, 9
Test, River, 206, 207
There's One In Every Crowd, *171*, 246-8
Tommy, *165*, 166
Townshend, Karen, 166
Townshend, Pete, 13-14, 56, 58-9, 88-90, 92-5, 96, 102, 103, 117, *119*, 122-4, 129, 137, 142, 164, 166-7, 170, 186, 218, 228, 262, 268-70
Traffic, 71, 74

United Hospital, Minneapolis, 141-4

Vernon, Mike, 224
Via Delta (racehorse), 208, 210
Voormann, Klaus, 79, 94

Waters, Muddy, 18, 138, 182, 223-6, 225, 250, 269, 271
Waters, Roger, 232, 258, 259, 269
Watts, Charlie, *215*, 259
Way, Darryl, 216
West Bromwich Albion Football Club, 124, 140, 187, 195, 196, 249
Wheels of Fire, 61, 238, 242
Whiskey-A-Gogo club, Newcastle-on-Tyne, 46
Whitlock, Bobby, 80, 244
The Who, 13, 58, 88, 89, 92
Williams, Don, 142
Williamson, Sonny Boy, 18, 232
Winwood, Steve, 13, 44-6, 47, 70, 71, 72-6, 94, 95, 218, *240-1*, 259
Wood, Ronnie, 94, *135*, 248, *273*
Wyman, Bill, 183, *253*, 259, *273*

Yardbirds, 8-16, *11*, 18, 22, 39-40, 44, 47, 53, 62, 66, 67, 76, 108, 121, 217, *231*, 232, 236

Zeeta Club, Putney, 46